# The 21st Century Quiz Book

# The 21st Century Quiz Book

### Compiled and introduced by
### David Self

Thorsons

With special thanks to
Mark Hall
and
Brian Slough

Thorsons
An Imprint of HarperCollins*Publishers*
77–85 Fulham Palace Road,
Hammersmith, London W6 8JB

The Thorsons website address is:
www.thorsons.com

First published (as *The 20th-century
Quiz Book)* by Thorsons 1992
This revised and updated edition
published 2001

10 9 8 7 6 5 4 3 2 1

A catalogue record for this book
is available from the British Library

ISBN 0 00 712006 0

Printed and bound in Great Britain by
Omnia Books Ltd, Glasgow

# Contents

Introduction                                                              vii

Theme Quiz (Number 1): *20th-century Speak*                                 1

General Knowledge Quizzes (Numbers 2–10)                                    3

Theme Quiz (Number 11): *What's Your Sport?*                               21

General Knowledge Quizzes (Numbers 12–20)                                  23

Theme Quiz (Number 21): *Capital Cities*                                   41

General Knowledge Quizzes (Numbers 22–30)                                  43

Theme Quiz (Number 31): *Soap Sagas*                                       61

General Knowledge Quizzes (Numbers 32–40)                                  63

Theme Quiz (Number 41): *Hits from the Shows*                              81

General Knowledge Quizzes (Numbers 42–50)                                  83

Theme Quiz (Number 51): *One Language, Two Nations*                       101

General Knowledge Quizzes (Numbers 52–60)                                 103

Theme Quiz (Number 61): *Top of the Pops*                                121

General Knowledge Quizzes (Numbers 62–70)                                 123

Theme Quiz (Number 71): *Modern Abbreviations*                           141

General Knowledge Quizzes (Numbers 72–80)                                 143

Theme Quiz (Number 81): *The New Millennium*                             161

General Knowledge Quizzes (Numbers 82–90)                                 163

Theme Quiz (Number 91): *The First World War*                            181

General Knowledge Quizzes (Numbers 92–100)                                183

Theme Quiz (Number 101): *More Modern Lingo*                             201

General Knowledge Quizzes (Numbers 102–10)                                203

Theme Quiz (Number 111): *A la Carte*                                    221

General Knowledge Quizzes (Numbers 112–20)          223

Theme Quiz (Number 121): *Famous Buildings*          241

General Knowledge Quizzes (Numbers 122–30)          243

Theme Quiz (Number 131): *More Capitals*          261

General Knowledge Quizzes (Numbers 132–40)          263

Theme Quiz (Number 141): *Who Wrote That?*          281

General Knowledge Quizzes (Numbers 142–50)          283

Theme Quiz (Number 151): *Singles*          301

General Knowledge Quizzes (Numbers 152–60)          303

Theme Quiz (Number 161): *Curtain Up!*          321

General Knowledge Quizzes (Numbers 162–70)          323

Theme Quiz (Number 171): *The Second World War*          341

General Knowledge Quizzes (Numbers 172–80)          343

Theme Quiz (Number 181): *Scoring the Century*          361

General Knowledge Quizzes (Numbers 182–90)          363

Theme Quiz (Number 191): *Brand Names*          381

General Knowledge Quizzes (Numbers 192–99)          383

Number 200: *The Third Millennium*          399

# Introduction

In 1900, millions of men and women laboured for long hours at dangerous jobs in mines, quarries and factories.

In 1900, long-distance travel was by rail or ship. The streets of our towns were crowded with trams and horse-drawn carriages.

In 1900, communication with those living any distance away had to be by letter.

In 1900, people played sport for fun, not money. Popular music was what you heard at the music hall.

But, since then, the world has changed more than in any other century. Since the beginning of the 20th century, we have conquered air travel and begun to explore space. Radio and television have made instant communication possible around the world – as have the telephone, the fax machine and the Internet. Many previously fatal diseases have been brought under control.

Today, provided you can afford such things, you can get a meal out of your freezer, cook it in a couple of minutes in your microwave and (when you've eaten it) put your plate in the dishwasher.

In 1900, America was a week away from Europe by ship, and Australia was a five-week journey. Now the peoples of all five continents are bound closely together by speedy travel and instant communication. We have become one global village.

And in this global village, new nations have come into being and ancient ones have regained their independence. We have seen the rise and fall of Communism and the spread of democracy to many countries where people previously did not have the freedom to vote.

But not everything has been for the good during this century. We have seen two devastating World Wars which have caused more suffering, misery and death than any previous wars. The century has also seen the period of fear and distrust known as the 'Cold War' – and also the invention and use of nuclear weapons. There are still millions of people who are homeless or living in poverty, and we have yet to conquer famine and many diseases (some of them new and frighteningly deadly).

This unique century (which has brought with it the concept of 'leisure') also saw one particularly strange invention: the quiz. The word itself is an old one. Originally it meant an odd or an eccentric person. Then it came to mean a practical joke. Its first use (meaning a question-and-answer game) seems to have occurred in the United States in 1891. The word gradually came into general use, on both sides of the Atlantic, in the early years of this century. The new 'popular' newspapers began to carry puzzles and 'quiz corners' – but it was not until the invention of radio (and later, television) that the activity (and the word) became as well known as they are today.

The first radio quizzes to attract large audiences in Britain were broadcast on continental stations, and one of the earliest quizzes seems to have been broadcast by Radio Luxembourg in 1934. It was called *The Symington's Soups Film Star Competition Programme*. Listeners had to collect entry forms from grocers' shops, fill in the answers while listening to the programme – and then post off the completed form. Winners won vouchers for powdered soup!

In Britain before the Second World War, all domestic broadcasting was controlled by the BBC – and the BBC was suspicious of quizzes! As early as 1926, it decided that 'the broadcasting of competitions should be carefully considered ... and under no circumstances is more than one a month to be held.'

In fact the first British radio quiz is believed to have been on the *Children's Hour* programme in November 1937, and was an inter-regional quiz called 'Regional Round'. Very soon after this, the first quiz for adults was broadcast. It was called *Transatlantic Quiz*.

Broadcast quizzes became really popular during the Second World War. On Christmas day in 1939, the BBC broadcast one live from northern France, with British soldiers answering questions put to them by a question-master in London. It very nearly had to be taken off the air when the servicemen's answers threatened to reveal their location to any enemy who might have been listening!

As the war went on, the broadcast quiz grew in popularity and, following the war, many new versions gained rapid popularity – especially with the spread of television. Some involved personalities answering questions; others involved the general public. For, while we obviously enjoy watching other people showing off their knowledge (and ignorance) on television, the quiz is also a very popular participant sport. In recent years it has become a frequent entertainment in village halls, social clubs and (especially) in pubs. In some pubs, Monday night is quiz night. So too are Tuesday, Wednesday, Thursday, Friday and Saturday!

These competitions may involve serious matches between teams arranged in leagues – or more friendly, unofficial quizzes. In either case they provide much fun and entertainment for both participants and spectators. But all such quizzes require a steady supply of questions – as do the most informal family competitions. It is to fill this need that this bumper book of 5,000 questions has been specially compiled – a considerably larger number than is found in most quiz books!

At this point, I must express my gratitude to Monica Dorrington for her considerable help in word-processing the text, and to Mark Hall and Brian Slough for many (respectively) popular music and sporting questions.

The book is intended for all those responsible for running quizzes in clubs, village halls, and pubs – and in hospitals and schools, the services and the social sections of large firms. It is also hoped that it will provide many hours of entertainment as a family 'run-your-own-quiz' guide, and as a 'keep-the-family-happy-in-the-back-of-the-car' book!

It is in fact a book of quizzes for all occasions. It can provide plenty of fun for the family, amongst friends or as a basis for school or 'public' contests, or when you just want to test your own knowledge.

The 200 quizzes in this book include many general knowledge quizzes, and also more specialized 'thematic' quizzes (Numbers 1, 11, 21, 31, etc.). You will find the answers on the page following each quiz. This means that you can refer to them easily, but you can also avoid any temptation to cheat! There is space on each page, which you can use either for filling in the answers or for keeping the scores – and if you do this lightly in pencil, you can use the book again and again.

It has often been said that an 'easy' question is one to which everyone knows the answer and a 'difficult' one is one to which *you* don't know the answer. An 'unfair' one is a question to which only one person happens to know the answer – and that's a fluke!

However, my experience adjudicating television and radio quiz shows has taught me a lot about which questions most people are *likely* to know answers to and which questions may cause more problems! With this in mind, the questions have been arranged in ascending order of difficulty in each quiz and the quizzes are also arranged in order of increasing difficulty.

There are 24 questions per quiz (plus a tie-breaker) arranged in two groups of 12 – so the quizzes are suitable for two teams (Team A and Team B) each of 3, 4 or 6 contestants.

- The questions are graded within each game – a pair of 'matched' easier ones for the first team-member, then getting progressively harder.

- The question-master can select from the 24 questions depending on the number of team-members and the degree of difficulty required.

- Phonetic pronunciations of tricky words are given; and, as well as the required answer, 'acceptable' variants are also included to eliminate argument and reinforce the question-master's authority!

- A tie-breaker question is provided for all games, to make 25 questions in all. These vary from the light-hearted to the trivial, and from the moderately difficult to *Mastermind*-finalist standard!

- The questions appear on the right-hand pages, with the solutions (and the tie-breaker) on the following (left-hand) page.

- In short, the intention is to provide quiz organizers with 200 quizzes ready for use 'straight from the book' without further sorting, checking, verifying, etc.

- All the questions relate to the events of this historic last century of the Second Millennium – but include, for example, geographical questions about places which have been in the news at some time since 1900.

A basic decision facing any quiz organizer is whether each question is 'open' to the first competitor who can offer an answer, or whether questions will be posed to contestants (or teams) in turn – or to let all the teams write down their answers (after conferring) for later checking. The advantage of the first style is that it generates much more pace and excitement. For it to function efficiently, each individual contestant (or, in the case of team quizzes, each team) should have a buzzer or light which will indicate quite clearly who was first to offer an answer. In this type of quiz, a person should be required to answer as soon as he or she buzzes, otherwise he or she merely handicaps his or her opponents.

While quizzes in which questions are posed to contestants in turn may lack pace, they do allow each contestant to participate equally rather than favouring the fastest thinkers. The most popular format, however, is the third, since it involves everyone in answering all the questions.

How you score is again up to you. You may want to award 2 points for a correct answer, 1 point for a 'half-correct' answer, 1 point for a corrected answer from the opposing team if a question is passed over, and nothing for a wrong answer. Or you may like to give a sequence of, say, six questions to one team (or person), and then to award a bonus for getting them all right.

In many quizzes an unanswered question or one answered incorrectly is often offered to the opposing team or to the other individual contestants. Because they have had longer to think and possibly because their recollection has been helped by the previous attempt, the question will normally be easier for them than it was for the first person to answer. It may therefore be decided not to award as many points for answering someone else's question, or for answering second, as for answering your own question or for answering first.

In any quiz, the quiz-master needs to be able to decide immediately whether he or she can accept a particular answer or not. For this reason, questions must be precise and unambiguous. They must be phrased carefully so as to elicit brief and concise answers which are clearly either right or wrong and not matters for debate. It is hoped that the questions in this book will satisfy these demands and will therefore be helpful in running quizzes that are not interrupted by delays, arguments or confusion! You should not therefore need an adjudicator, because the questions are deliberately straightforward, the answers short and to the point, and any alternative answers are supplied: but you may need a scorer, or at least someone to check the quiz-master's scoring!

The quiz-master should always make it clear whether he or she has accepted an answer or not. From a non-competing audience's point of view, it is also more interesting if they can see the score and not rely on the scorer's announcement at the end of each round.

A simple scoreboard can be made in the style of the old-fashioned cricket scoreboard where the score was shown by numbers hung on nails.

And finally, you can make up other kinds of rounds to go with the quizzes here. You can show slides, photographs or newspaper cuttings, for example of famous landmarks, famous people or important recent or current events; you can play brief excerpts of music (with a CD player, cassette tape or live pianist); you can invent questions about current pop groups, radio and television series, or local personalities; and you can ask questions about current events. And if you look closely at the questions in this book you will not only have the material for 200 ready-made quizzes, but also the ideas for many, many more.

Remember, a quiz is always great fun for both contestants and audience, provided it is well organized and fair!

When it comes to setting the questions for television and radio quizzes I always have to bear in mind the producer's instructions: all the questions must be of reasonable general knowledge and they must be about everyday subjects the average person might fairly be expected to know about. This seems to me to be one of the attractive features of general knowledge quizzes, whether they take place on television programmes, in village halls, pubs, schools or the home: in fair competition, they encourage us to show that we are informed about the world around us. Such information can be only for the good.

# No. 1: 20th-century Speak

To begin with, a round of questions to test whether you remember some of the words and expressions that came into our language recently! What is meant by the following:

**a1**   Acid house
*b1*   *An airhead*
**a2**   Aromatherapy
*b2*   *Body-popping*
**a3**   A Barbour
*b3*   *The brat-pack*
**a4**   A Brixton briefcase
*b4*   *Cardboard city*
**a5**   A 'cat' (on a motor car)
*b5*   *To cold call*
**a6**   A couch potato
*b6*   *Crucial*
**a7**   E-numbers
*b7*   *The F-Plan*
**a8**   A Mexican wave
*b8*   *Glasnost*
**a9**   A Scud
*b9*   *Semtex*
**a10**  The glitterati
*b10*  *The cutting edge*
**a11**  Friendly fire
*b11*  *A human shield*
**a12**  The Third Age
*b12*  *The grey economy*

# No. 1 Answers

**a1** A style of popular music (with a fast beat); also a youth cult associated with the music and (sometimes) with drug taking
*b1* *An empty-headed person; someone who talks nonsense*
**a2** A form of health or beauty therapy that uses natural oils
*b2* *A type of jerky, robot-like dancing*
**a3** A waxed, outdoor jacket
*b3* *Young Hollywood stars; any group of young, spoiled people*
**a4** A large, portable stereo radio/cassette player (a ghetto blaster)
*b4* *An area of a town or city where the homeless congregate*
**a5** A catalytic converter (filters pollutants from vehicle exhaust)
*b5* *To visit or telephone (without an invitation) in the hope of selling something*
**a6** A lazy person (who may spend a lot of time watching television)
*b6* *Very good, important, fantastic*
**a7** A code number describing a food additive
*b7* *A high fibre diet*
**a8** A cheer in a sports stadium, which 'ripples' round the crowd
*b8* *Open-ness; greater freedom of information*
**a9** A long-range missile (surface to surface)
*b9* *A (colourless, odourless plastic) explosive*
**a10** Celebrities or 'glittering stars'
*b10* *Most advanced, the 'latest'*
**a11** Fire or shooting from one's own side, during a war
*b11* *A person or group of people used to fend off a hostile attack*
**a12** Old age; the age of retirement
*b12* *Money not accounted for officially; unofficial earnings*

---

## Tie-breaker

**Q** What is head-hunting?
*A* *Seeking skilled employees or managers with a view to persuading them to change jobs – to join the organization the 'headhunter' works for*

---

# No. 2

**a1** Which vegetable is the emblem of Wales?
*b1* *Which flower is the emblem of Scotland?*
**a2** In which building did Princess Diana's funeral service take place?
*b2* *Who gave the address or sermon?*
**a3** In which English county is the holiday resort of Ilfracombe?
*b3* *In which English county is the holiday resort of Skegness?*
**a4** What would you do with a John Collins?
*b4* *What would you be drinking if you were drinking 'Earl Grey'?*
**a5** For what do the letters www stand?
*b5* *In transport, for what do the letters HGV stand?*
**a6** What colour do conventional traffic lights show, after they've shown amber alone?
*b6* *What colour do traffic lights show, after they've shown green?*
**a7** Ultramarine is a shade of what colour?
*b7* *Sienna is a shade of what colour?*
**a8** Cos, Webb's Wonderful, Winter Density are all types of what?
*b8* *Globe and Jerusalem are both types of which vegetable?*
**a9** With which group are or were Roger Daltrey, Keith Moon and Pete Townsend all associated?
*b9* *Which is home city of the rock group, U2?*
**a10** Which South African word meant 'separate development' or segregation?
*b10* *In which country is Pravda a newspaper?*
**a11** In rugby union, what colour jerseys are worn by the Welsh team?
*b11* *Which sport is played by the Washington Redskins?*
**a12** Which war was said to be 'the war to end all wars'?
*b12* *In which year was the Battle of Britain fought in the skies over Britain?*

# No. 2 Answers

**a1**   The leek
*b1*   *Thistle*
**a2**   Westminster Abbey
*b2*   *Earl Spencer (her brother)*
**a3**   Devon
*b3*   *Lincolnshire*
**a4**   Drink it (it consists of gin, lemon or lime, soda and sugar)
*b4*   *Tea*
**a5**   World Wide Web
*b5*   *Heavy goods vehicle*
**a6**   Red
*b6*   *Amber (yellow)*
**a7**   Blue
*b7*   *Brown (with some red)*
**a8**   Lettuce
*b8*   *Artichoke*
**a9**   The Who
*b9*   *Dublin, Ireland*
**a10**   Apartheid
*b10*   *Russia*
**a11**   Red
*b11*   *American football*
**a12**   World War I
*b12*   *1940*

---

## Tie-breaker

**Q**   Which were the six original members of the European Economic Community?

**A**   *France, West Germany, Italy, Belgium, Netherlands, Luxembourg*

# No. 3

**a1** With which part of the body is a chiropodist concerned?
*b1* *What do we call a doctor's 'listening instrument'?*
**a2** Apart from possibly being a Communist sailor, what is a Red Admiral?
*b2* *What is bladder wrack?*
**a3** What would you be most likely to test in a wind tunnel?
*b3* *What do we call a factory in which oil is processed?*
**a4** What does a jaywalker do?
*b4* *In Britain nowadays, what is a 'giro'?*
**a5** Of which Scottish region is Inverness the capital?
*b5* *Which Scottish loch has become especially famous for its monster?*
**a6** What is measured in 'decibels'?
*b6* *Which country launched 'Sputniks'?*
**a7** With which sport do you associate James Wattana?
*b7* *In which sport did Lennox Lewis become famous?*
**a8** What would you expect to find in a WPB?
*b8* *What do we call a container of liquid and gas which squirts out the liquid as mist?*
**a9** By which first name is President Clinton's wife known?
*b9* *Who was the child star of the film* Home Alone*?*
**a10** Which Irish pop star promoted the charity pop concert called 'Live Aid'?
*b10* *Which kind of music is especially associated with Bob Marley?*
**a11** On what date was Princess Diana killed?
*b11* *In the grounds of which stately home is she buried?*
**a12** For what does the abbreviation CBI stand?
*b12* *For what does the abbreviation FBI stand?*

# No. 3 Answers

**a1** Hands and/or feet
*b1* *Stethoscope*
**a2** A butterfly
*b2* *Seaweed*
**a3** Aircraft
*b3* *Refinery*
**a4** Crosses the road without proper regard for traffic signals
*b4* *A cheque or money order; especially for payment of social security benefit*
**a5** Highland
*b5* *Loch Ness*
**a6** Noise
*b6* *Soviet Union (Russia)*
**a7** Snooker
*b7* *Boxing (heavyweight)*
**a8** Waste paper, etc.
*b8* *Aerosol*
**a9** Hillary
*b9* *Macaulay Culkin*
**a10** Bob Geldof
*b10* *Reggae*
**a11** August 31, 1997
*b11* *Althorp (in Northamptonshire)*
**a12** Confederation of British Industry
*b12* *Federal Bureau of Investigation*

## Tie-breaker

**Q** Which profession did Ove Arup follow?
**A** *Architect (and civil engineer). He designed the Sydney Opera House, Penguin Pool at London Zoo and the Snape Maltings (near Aldeburgh in Suffolk)*

# No. 4

**a1**    Which flower is the emblem of Holland?
***b1**    The white rose is the emblem of which county?*
**a2**    Following the Labour election victory in 1997, who became Chancellor of the Exchequer?
***b2**    And who became Foreign Secretary?*
**a3**    Who became Northern Ireland Secretary?
***b3**    And who became deputy prime minister?*
**a4**    In which country is the holiday resort of Estoril?
***b4**    In which country is the holiday resort of Sorrento?*
**a5**    Mental arithmetic: When we talked about 'a gross and a half', what number did that represent?
***b5**    If you added together half a dozen and half a gross what did you get?*
**a6**    What is kept in a portfolio?
***b6**    What is the purpose of a periscope?*
**a7**    What do the letters HB stand for on a pencil?
***b7**    What is the word 'memo' short for?*
**a8**    What colour is the flag of the Republic of Ireland?
***b8**    What three colours are there on the national flag of the Netherlands?*
**a9**    Of which country was Bettino Craxi prime minister?
***b9**    And of which country has François Mitterand been president?*
**a10**    For which sport is Badminton House famous?
***b10**    For which sport is Bisley famous?*
**a11**    Back in 1961, who was the first man to travel in space?
***b11**    Which Briton made the first transatlantic flight by balloon (in 1987)?*
**a12**    In which city is the Brandenburg Gate?
***b12**    Which of the following would you not find in Egypt: the Pyramids, Cleopatra's Needle, the Sphinx?*

# No. 4 Answers

**a1** Tulip
*b1* *Yorkshire*
**a2** Gordon Brown
*b2* *Robin Cook*
**a3** Mo Mowlem
*b3* *John Prescott*
**a4** Portugal
*b4* *Italy*
**a5** 216
*b5* *78*
**a6** Papers
*b6* *To help you see above eye level (or round corners)*
**a7** Hard black
*b7* *Memorandum*
**a8** Green, white and orange
*b8* *Red, white and blue*
**a9** Italy
*b9* *France*
**a10** Horse-riding, three-day eventing, horse trials
*b10* *Shooting*
**a11** Yuri Gagarin
*b11* *Richard Branson*
**a12** (East) Berlin
*b12* *Cleopatra's Needle*

---

## Tie-breaker

**Q**  Which DH Lawrence novel was 'on trial' for obscenity in 1960?
**A**  *Lady Chatterley's Lover*

---

# No. 5

**a1** What product's quality is measured by its octane rating?
*b1 On a car, for what would you use the dipstick?*
**a2** If you're suffering from laryngitis, which part of your body is affected?
*b2 Which part of the body is primarily affected by conjunctivitis?*
**a3** Is talcum powder animal, vegetable or mineral?
*b3 What useful ingredient do broad bean plants put into their soil?*
**a4** Which country knocked England out of the soccer World Cup in 1998?
*b4 Which country won the Cup that year?*
**a5** In America, in which city is the Golden Gate Bridge?
*b5 In which city is the Brooklyn Bridge?*
**a6** How many centimetres are there in five metres?
*b6 How many metres are there in a kilometre?*
**a7** From 1959, of which English football club was Bill Shankly manager?
*b7 Who was Jayne Torvill's ice-skating partner?*
**a8** In which country is the Brecon Beacons National Park?
*b8 Which island is separated from the mainland by the Menai Straits?*
**a9** In America, what kind of drink is bourbon?
*b9 For what drink was chicory a wartime substitute?*
**a10** Which rock star is known as 'the groover from Vancouver'?
*b10 'Magic Moments', 'Catch a Falling Star' and 'Delaware' were all hits for which American star?*
**a11** By what abbreviation is the Organization of Petroleum Exporting Countries known?
*b11 Which organization is known as the PLO?*
**a12** Which cross was the symbol of the Free French during the Second World War?
*b12 In the Second World War, what were Gold, Juno and Sword?*

# No. 5 Answers

a1 Petrol
*b1 To measure the engine oil*
a2 Throat
*b2 The eye*
a3 Mineral (magnesium silicate)
*b3 Nitrogen*
a4 Argentina
*b4 France*
a5 San Francisco
*b5 New York*
a6 500
*b6 1,000*
a7 Liverpool
*b7 (Christopher) Dean*
a8 Wales
*b8 Anglesey*
a9 Type of whisky (made from corn or rye, not barley)
*b9 Coffee*
a10 Bryan Adams
*b10 Perry Como*
a11 OPEC
*b11 Palestine Liberation Organization*
a12 Cross of Lorraine
*b12 The British Invasion beaches in Normandy*

## Tie-breaker

Q   What is or was the profession of Lindsay Anderson?
A   *Film director*

10

# No. 6

**a1** What does the 'wonder drug' viagra cure?
*b1* *With which mammal is the disease rabies usually associated?*
**a2** Colloquially speaking, what do we mean when we talk about a cat and dog life?
*b2* *What is a fool's paradise?*
**a3** In which English county is the holiday resort of St Ives?
*b3* *In which English county is the holiday resort of Margate?*
**a4** Which sport introduced 'pinch-hitters' in the 1990s?
*b4* *Which sport has 'drop outs' and 'conversions'?*
**a5** If an artist was using burnt umber, what colour would he be using?
*b5* *Which is the colour of jealousy?*
**a6** What name did we give to the polluted precipitation that kills plants and forests and erodes buildings and statues?
*b6* *What is the usual name for the trapping of the sun's rays in the lower atmosphere, due to pollutants in the atmosphere?*
**a7** What is sometimes called a 'rubberneck-wagon'?
*b7* *What does an Australian mean when he talks about a sheila?*
**a8** In 1906, what food was first manufactured by William Kellogg?
*b8* *According to some people, which part of the edible frog is a delicacy?*
**a9** Every autumn, there are illuminations along which holiday resort's Golden Mile?
*b9* *On the second Sunday in November, where in London is the nation's Remembrance Day service held?*
**a10** For what are the letters ARP an abbreviation?
*b10* *For what do the initials WRVS stand?*
**a11** Until 1960, which coin was a quarter of one penny?
*b11* *Which new denomination of coin was introduced in 1998?*
**a12** Nicknamed 'the Boss', he had a major hit with the album 'Born in the USA'. Who was this pop or rock star?
*b12* *Which blind pop star led the campaign to turn Martin Luther King's birthday into an American national holiday?*

# No. 6 Answers

**a1** Impotence
*b1* *Dogs*
**a2** A life of quarrelling
*b2* *A state of happiness, or success which may change at any moment; an insecure situation*
**a3** Cornwall
*b3* *Kent*
**a4** Cricket
*b4* *Rugby Union*
**a5** (Dark) brown
*b5* *Green or yellow*
**a6** Acid rain
*b6* *Greenhouse effect*
**a7** Tourist coach, bus; sightseeing-bus
*b7* *A girl, woman*
**a8** Corn flakes
*b8* *The legs*
**a9** Blackpool
*b9* *At the Cenotaph in Whitehall*
**a10** Air Raid Precautions
*b10* *Women's Royal Voluntary Service*
**a11** Farthing
*b11* *£2*
**a12** Bruce Springsteen
*b12* *Stevie Wonder*

## Tie-breaker

**Q** Which British male tennis star won Wimbledon in 1934, 1935 and 1936?
**A** *Fred Perry*

# No. 7

**a1** Which Northern Ireland political party has been led by David Trimble?

*b1 And which party has been led by Gerry Adams?*

**a2** Which motor manufacturing company was started by Lord Nuffield?

*b2 Cars: what colour were all the early Model 'T' Fords?*

**a3** By what abbreviation is the American space agency known?

*b3 What do the initials NATO stand for?*

**a4** Who was leader of the Conservative party immediately before William Hague?

*b4 Which business tycoon built up the Virgin group of companies?*

**a5** In which sport was Rocky Marciano a champion?

*b5 Which sport did Giant Haystacks become well known?*

**a6** What is the county town of Cumbria?

*b6 What is the county town of Hampshire?*

**a7** In which month does the Lord Mayor's Show take place in London?

*b7 What do we call the annual ceremony on the River Thames when all the new-born cygnets are marked?*

**a8** Who first said, 'Never in the field of human conflict was so much owed by so many to so few'?

*b8 Which British prime minister told the nation, 'I have to say, no such undertaking has been received'?*

**a9** Of which chemical element is the symbol C?

*b9 Of which chemical element is the symbol the letter N?*

**a10** 'Bye, Bye Love' and 'Wake Up Little Suzie' were hits for which pop duo?

*b10 Robert Zimmerman (who wrote and sang the pop ballad 'Blowin' in the Wind') was better known by what name?*

**a11** Which is the smallest of the following: hundredweight, stone, ton?

*b11 Which is the smallest of the following: furlong, foot and chain?*

**a12** Who first reached the South Pole in December 1911?

*b12 Apart from Sherpa Tenzing, who reached the summit of Mount Everest, in 1953?*

# No. 7 Answers

a1   Ulster Unionist (accept: Unionists, UUP)
*b1   Sinn Fein*
a2   Morris (he was born William Richard Morris)
*b2   Black*
a3   NASA (National Aeronautics and Space Administration)
*b3   North Atlantic Treaty Organization*
a4   John Major
*b4   Richard Branson*
a5   Boxing
*b5   Wrestling*
a6   Carlisle
*b6   Winchester*
a7   November
*b7   Swan-upping*
a8   Sir Winston Churchill
*b8   Neville Chamberlain*
a9   Carbon
*b9   Nitrogen*
a10  The Everly Brothers
*b10  Bob Dylan*
a11  Stone
*b11  Foot*
a12  Roald Amundsen
*b12  (Sir Edmund) Hillary (Sir John Hunt was expedition leader: he did not reach the summit)*

---

## Tie-breaker

**Q**   Which Belfast musician issued albums titled 'Astral Weeks' and 'Moondance'?
*A*   *Van Morrison*

---

# No. 8

**a1**   Colloquially speaking, what do we mean when we talk about a wet blanket?

*b1*   *What is a golden handshake?*

**a2**   In which country is the holiday resort of Torremolinos?

*b2*   *In which country is the Algarve?*

**a3**   Which British breed of cat is famous for not having a tail?

*b3*   *In which part of England were coypus (say: coy-pews) found in the wild?*

**a4**   For what are the letters TSB an abbreviation?

*b4*   *For what do the initials PAYE stand?*

**a5**   From which European country does paella come?

*b5*   *From which country does the food lasagne originate?*

**a6**   What is a juggernaut?

*b6*   *Usually, what kind of transport is a 'funicular'?*

**a7**   Which sport is most often associated with Brands Hatch?

*b7*   *Which sport is played at the Riverside Stadium?*

**a8**   'Let It Be' was the last album released by which pop group?

*b8*   *Which young pop guitarist died in 1970, having had a hit with 'Hey Joe'?*

**a9**   Which university city stands on the river Isis?

*b9*   *Which university is situated at Canterbury?*

**a10**   Who led the unsuccessful British expedition to the South Pole in 1901-1904?

*b10*   *To which high position was Karol Wojtyla (say: voy-ti-wa) elected in 1978?*

**a11**   Which metal is extracted from bauxite?

*b11*   *What is the everyday name for sodium carbonate?*

**a12**   In which city is Tiananman Square?

*b12*   *Which country has been ruled by King Hussein?*

# No. 8 Answers

**a1** A depressing person, a person who always fears the worst
*b1* *A leaving present*
**a2** Spain
*b2* *Portugal*
**a3** Manx
*b3* *East Anglia*
**a4** Trustee Savings Bank
*b4* *Pay As You Earn*
**a5** Spain
*b5* *Italy*
**a6** Heavy lorry
*b6* *(Mountain) railway*
**a7** Motor racing
*b7* *Soccer*
**a8** The Beatles (1970)
*b8* *Jimi Hendrix*
**a9** Oxford
*b9* *Kent*
**a10** Captain (Robert F) Scott
*b10* *Pope*
**a11** Aluminium
*b11* *Washing soda*
**a12** Beijing (accept: Peking)
*b12* *Jordan*

## Tie-breaker

**Q** Who is or was Francis Bacon?
**A** *(Irish) painter*

# No. 9

**a1** As what did Ian McCaskill become famous?
*b1* *And for what did Terence Conran become famous?*
**a2** What was the bunny hug?
*b2* *What kind of transport is a 'whirlybird'?*
**a3** Can you name a drink which usually contains the stimulant, caffeine?
*b3* *On a menu, what is meant by 'petits pois'? (say: pu-tee pwa)*
**a4** What is meant by 'perestroika'?
*b4* *Which politician was nicknamed 'The Iron Lady'?*
**a5** What is sarin?
*b5* *And which gas was named after its inventors, Corson and Stoughton?*
**a6** In which sport did Billie Jean King become famous?
*b6* *In which sport did Mike Gatting captain England?*
**a7** How many angles has a decagon?
*b7* *How many sides has a heptagon?*
**a8** In the 1920's, who or what was a flapper?
*b8* *In which country would you be most likely to meet a geisha girl?*
**a9** For what do the initials BMA stand?
*b9* *For what do the initials PhD stand?*
**a10** From which London railway station would you leave if you were travelling to Cardiff?
*b10* *In which town or city would you be if you were driving along the Royal Mile?*
**a11** What is an alloy?
*b11* *What is bitumen?*
**a12** Digital watches use changing numbers to show the time. What do we call a watch that uses hands and a dial?
*b12* *On the top row of a typewriter, which four letters follow 'Q W E R T Y'?*

# No. 9 Answers

a1   Television weatherman
*b1   Furniture (or furniture shops) or running/designing restaurants*
a2   A dance
*b2   Helicopter*
a3   Tea or coffee (some colas)
*b3   Peas*
a4   Restructuring
*b4   Margaret Thatcher*
a5   A lethal nerve gas (accept: gas used in war)
*b5   CS gas*
a6   Tennis
*b6   Cricket*
a7   Ten
*b7   Seven*
a8   Bold young lady
*b8   Japan*
a9   British Medical Association
*b9   Doctor of Philosophy*
a10  Paddington
*b10  Edinburgh*
a11  A mixture of two (or more) metals
*b11  An oil or 'pitch' (accept: tar)*
a12  Analogue
*b12  U I O P*

---

## Tie-breaker

Q   Writers Virginia Woolf, Lytton Strachey, Clive Bell and Duncan Grant all lived in the same district of London and were known by the name of the district. What was the group's name?

A   *The Bloomsbury Group*

---

# No. 10

**a1**  What are Connex South Eastern, Thameslink and GNER?

*b1*  *And what are Anglian, Northumbrian and Severn Trent?*

**a2**  Colloquially speaking, what do we mean when we talk about a rough diamond?

*b2*  *What is meant by 'gob-smacked'?*

**a3**  What is 'fromage frais'? (say: fro-marge fray)

*b3*  *From what is macaroni chiefly made?*

**a4**  In which country is the holiday resort of Tangier?

*b4*  *If you were having a holiday on the island of Rhodes, in which country would you be?*

**a5**  In sport, what is the LTA?

*b5*  *Which body frames the rules by which horse-racing is organized?*

**a6**  With which city do you associate the comedian Billy Connelly?

*b6*  *What invention by Percy Shaw in 1934 has been a great help to motorists?*

**a7**  As what did Sir Stanley Spencer achieve fame?

*b7*  *Which painter had a 'blue period'?*

**a8**  Who became leader of the Soviet Union in 1985?

*b8*  *In which country was Adolf Hitler born?*

**a9**  For what did the initials BAOR stand?

*b9*  *On VE Day 1945, what did VE mean?*

**a10**  Of which university are Corpus Christi, Queens and Emmanuel all colleges?

*b10*  *Charing Cross and Guy's are both medical schools of which university?*

**a11**  Which film featured Bill Haley's hit song, 'Rock Around the Clock'?

*b11*  *Whose album, called 'True Blue' topped the charts in 28 countries in 1986?*

**a12**  What is the chemical formula for carbon dioxide?

*b12*  *Which scientist first formulated the important equation, $E = mc^2$?*

# No. 10 Answers

**a1** (Privatized) railway companies
*b1* *(Privatized) water companies*
**a2** A good-hearted person who has rough manners
*b2* *You are astounded, rendered speechless or incoherent*
**a3** Low-fat curd cheese; dessert based on sweetened cheese (accept: quark)
*b3* *Flour, flour paste (accept: pasta)*
**a4** Morocco
*b4* *Greece*
**a5** Lawn Tennis Association
*b5* *Jockey Club*
**a6** Glasgow
*b6* *Cat's eyes*
**a7** Artist/painter
*b7* *Picasso*
**a8** Mikhail Gorbachev
*b8* *Austria*
**a9** British Army of the Rhine
*b9* *Victory in Europe*
**a10** Cambridge
*b10* *London*
**a11** *Blackboard Jungle*
*b11* *Madonna*
**a12** $CO_2$
*b12* *Einstein*

## Tie-breaker

**Q** Which London Underground line was extended to serve the Millennium Dome?
**A** *Jubilee Line*

# No. 11: What's Your Sport?

In which sport has each of the following men and women become famous?

**a1** Michael Chang
*b1 Ken Doherty*
**a2** Fred Couples
*b2 Michelle Smith*
**a3** Sachin Tendulkar
*b3 Will Greenwood*
**a4** Henry Paul
*b4 Eamonn Darcy*
**a5** Herbie Hide
*b5 David Coulthard*
**a6** Adrian Maguire
*b6 Colin Montgomerie*
**a7** Chris Perry
*b7 Jan Ullrich*
**a8** Colin McRae
*b8 Alison Curbishley*
**a9** Jennifer Capriati
*b9 Ed Giddins*
**a10** Catherina Mckiernan
*b10 Todd Martin*
**a11** Mika Hakkinen
*b11 Simon Parke*
**a12** Kelly Morgan
*b12 Jane Sixsmith*

# No. 11 Answers

a1   Tennis
*b1   Snooker*
a2   Golf
*b2   Swimming*
a3   Cricket
*b3   Rugby union*
a4   Rugby league
*b4   Golf*
a5   Boxing
*b5   Motor racing*
a6   Horse racing
*b6   Golf*
a7   Soccer
*b7   Cycling*
a8   Rally driving
*b8   Athletics*
a9   Tennis
*b9   Cricket*
a10   Marathon Running
*b10   Tennis*
a11   Motor racing
*b11   Squash*
a12   Badminton
*b12   Hockey*

## Tie-breaker

Q   Which country led the boycott of the 1980 Summer Olympics?
A   *United States of America (the games were held in Moscow)*

# No. 12

**a1**   What would you do with 'winkle-pickers'?
*b1*   *What is the Red Duster?*
**a2**   When British Rail was denationalized, which company became responsible for the track and signals?
*b2*   *What is the name of the rail service between London and Paris?*
**a3**   What is claustrophobia?
*b3*   *What is meant by the medical term, obesity?*
**a4**   In boxing, at what 'weight' do you fight, if you weigh just under eight stone?
*b4*   *With which famous steeplechase do you primarily associate 'Red Rum'?*
**a5**   In the world of pop, who was the drummer (replaced by Ringo Starr) who was part of the original Beatles line-up?
*b5*   *Which group was formed in 1955 to back the singer Buddy Holly?*
**a6**   By what abbreviation is the Oxford Committee for Famine Relief known?
*b6*   *By what abbreviation were the Navy, Army and Air Force Institutes known?*
**a7**   By which Christian name is the Queen's second son known?
*b7*   *Which member of the Royal Family was born in Greece?*
**a8**   In which art has Joan Sutherland achieved fame?
*b8*   *Who composed the music for* Phantom of the Opera*?*
**a9**   How is asbestos obtained?
*b9*   *In what do we find the sugary substance called lactose?*
**a10**   Which acid is used in car batteries and is used to make fertilizers and explosives?
*b10*   *Of which chemical element is the symbol the letters Cu?*
**a11**   Which film, set in Sheffield, made male strippers popular?
*b11*   *Buzz Lightyear was a 'star' of which 1995 film?*
**a12**   In which European capital were there student riots in 1968?
*b12*   *Which modern school subject is named after the Latin word meaning 'to know' or 'knowledge'?*

# No. 12 Answers

a1  Wear them: they are shoes with pointed toes
*b1  A flag (The Red Ensign; flown on British merchant ships)*
a2  Railtrack
*b2  Eurostar*
a3  Fear of closed spaces, fear of being shut in
*b3  Fatness, being over-weight*
a4  Flyweight
*b4  Grand National*
a5  Pete Best
*b5  The Crickets*
a6  OXFAM
*b6  NAAFI*
a7  Andrew
*b7  Prince Philip, Duke of Edinburgh*
a8  Opera (singing)
*b8  Andrew Lloyd Webber*
a9  It is mined from the earth
*b9  Milk*
a10  Sulphuric
*b10  Copper*
a11  *The Full Monty*
*b11  Toy Story*
a12  Paris
*b12  Science*

## Tie-breaker

Q  For what product did 'Roses grow on you' become an advertising slogan in the sixties?
A  *Cadbury's Roses Chocolates*

# No. 13

**a1**  What would you usually do with a knickerbocker glory?
*b1*  *What is the Turkey Trot?*
**a2**  Which Caribbean island became a home for Princess Margaret and Mick Jagger?
*b2*  *Who is the lawyer Cherie Booth's husband?*
**a3**  Which pop singer starred in the films *The Young Ones* and *Summer Holiday*?
*b3*  *Whose home was a mansion called 'Graceland' in Memphis?*
**a4**  On which island is the holiday resort of Palma?
*b4*  *In which sea could you swim if you were on holiday on the east coast of Italy?*
**a5**  Which organization for children has as its motto, 'Lend a hand'?
*b5*  *What do we call an adult who helps run a Brownie pack?*
**a6**  What does ACAS try to do?
*b6*  *For what do the initials TUC stand?*
**a7**  Who was convicted of killing 8-month-old Matthew Eappen?
*b7*  *Which computer specialist founded the firm Microsoft?*
**a8**  Which Chinese leader became known for his 'little red books'?
*b8*  *Which peace-loving Indian leader was assassinated in 1948?*
**a9**  In Britain, how many pounds are there in a hundredweight?
*b9*  *How many acres are there in a square mile?*
**a10**  In which sport was Randolph Turpin a champion?
*b10*  *By what other name was the heavyweight boxer Mohammed Ali formerly known?*
**a11**  Which metal will flow without being heated?
*b11*  *Which of these is not an alloy: bronze, brass, pewter?*
**a12**  Which animal is a national emblem of India?
*b12*  *Which animal has been the national emblem of South Africa?*

# No. 13 Answers

**a1**    Eat it (it's an ice-cream sundae)
*b1*    *A dance*
**a2**    Mustique
*b2*    *Tony Blair*
**a3**    Cliff Richard
*b3*    *Elvis Presley's*
**a4**    Majorca
*b4*    *Adriatic*
**a5**    Brownies
*b5*    *Brown Owl (her assistants are called Tawny Owl and Snowy Owl)*
**a6**    Settle industrial disputes (strikes, etc.)
*b6*    *Trades Union Congress*
**a7**    Louise Woodward
*b7*    *Bill Gates*
**a8**    Mao Zedong (also known as: Mao Tse-Tung)
*b8*    *Mahatma Gandhi*
**a9**    112 (100 in USA)
*b9*    *640*
**a10**    Boxing (light-heavyweight)
*b10*    *Cassius Clay*
**a11**    Mercury
*b11*    *None of them; all are alloys*
**a12**    Elephant
*b12*    *Springbok*

## Tie-breaker

**Q**    Which area of southern England became Britain's twelfth national park in 1992?
**A**    *The New Forest*

# No. 14

**a1**    Which sport introduced 'referees' assistants'?
*b1*    *Which sport has 'day-night' matches?*
**a2**    What does a Spaniard mean when he says, 'adios'?
*b2*    *What does a German mean when he says, 'Danke schön'? (say: dan-ke shurn)*
**a3**    Daisy wheel and dot matrix were both types of what?
*b3*    *In computing, what is a bit?*
**a4**    Reg Smyth created which *Daily Mirror* cartoon character?
*b4*    *Of which daily paper was Sir David English editor?*
**a5**    What is induced by a narcotic?
*b5*    *What kind of drug is an amphetamine?*
**a6**    What is meadowsweet?
*b6*    *What is the Dartford Warbler?*
**a7**    In which house does the Queen speak at the State Opening of Parliament?
*b7*    *In parliament, what is a 'back bencher'?*
**a8**    Of which university are Pembroke, Nuffield and All Souls colleges?
*b8*    *Which 1960s university is situated near Norwich?*
**a9**    Which pop drummer, singer and songwriter played with the group Genesis and had a hit with 'You Can't Hurry Love'?
*b9*    *Scott McKenzie had a number one hit in 1967 with 'San Francisco'. But what was the song's subtitle?*
**a10**    For what is OM an abbreviation?
*b10*    *For what does the abbreviation C-in-C stand?*
**a11**    What is ecology?
*b11*    *What do you study if you're a vulcanologist?*
**a12**    What is the fewest number of coins you can use to pay 91p exactly?
*b12*    *What is the fewest number of coins you can use to pay 35p exactly?*

# No. 14 Answers

a1    Soccer
*b1*    *Cricket*
a2    Good bye, farewell
*b2*    *Thank you very much*
a3    (Computer) printers
*b3*    *A digit, the smallest unit of information*
a4    Andy Capp
*b4*    *Daily Mail*
a5    Sleep, drowsiness
*b5*    *Pep pill; stimulant; induces 'well-being'*
a6    A (wild) flower
*b6*    *Bird*
a7    House of Lords
*b7*    *An ordinary MP; one without office*
a8    Oxford
*b8*    *University of East Anglia*
a9    Phil Collins
*b9*    *'Be Sure to Wear Some Flowers in Your Hair'*
a10    Order of Merit
*b10*    *Commander-in-Chief*
a11    The study of the environment (the relationship of plants and animals to their environment)
*b11*    *Volcanoes*
a12    Four (50p, 20p, 20p, 1p)
*b12*    *Three (20p, 10p, 5p)*

## Tie-breaker

**Q**   What colour beret is usually worn by United Nations peace-keeping troops?
**A**   *Light blue*

# No. 15

**a1**  In the world of pop, who led the 1960s all-girl group, the Supremes?

*b1*  *Johnny Rotten and Sid Vicious were members of which group?*

**a2**  What is meant by the phrase, 'à la mode'?

*b2*  *What is most likely to have a dust jacket?*

**a3**  Which game is unique to the public school, Eton?

*b3*  *Which former captain retired from the West Indies cricket team in 1974 (and was later knighted)?*

**a4**  Which people are now known as 'Inuits'?

*b4*  *Which African country was once called Abyssinia?*

**a5**  Who was dictator of the Soviet Union for 1924 to 1953?

*b5*  *Which woman became prime minister of India in 1966?*

**a6**  In London, outside which building does the Changing of the Guard take place?

*b6*  *In what general direction does the Thames flow through London?*

**a7**  Which North American city is famous for its 'Mardi Gras' carnival?

*b7*  *In which American city were there severe earthquakes in 1906 and 1989?*

**a8**  In science, what do we call a completely empty space in which there are no atoms?

*b8*  *And also in science, what do we call a substance which cannot be split into simpler substances?*

**a9**  Jerusalem, New English and Good News are all versions of which book?

*b9*  *On what would you be seeking information if you consulted 'Burke's'?*

**a10**  In geometry, how many 'faces' (or surfaces) has a square-based pyramid?

*b10*  *How many times does a tangent touch a circle?*

**a11**  By what abbreviation did we describe the Strategic Arms Limitation Talks?

*b11*  *By what abbreviation is the Australia and New Zealand Army Corps known?*

**a12**  Which planet in our solar system is nearest to the sun?

*b12*  *Of the planets in our solar system, which is the largest?*

# No. 15 Answers

**a1** Diana Ross
*b1* *The Sex Pistols*
**a2** In fashion
*b2* *Book*
**a3** Eton Wall Game and/or Eton Fives
*b3* *Sir Garry (Garfield) Sobers*
**a4** 'Eskimo' people
*b4* *Ethiopia*
**a5** Joseph Stalin
*b5* *Indira Gandhi*
**a6** Buckingham Palace
*b6* *Eastwards*
**a7** New Orleans
*b7* *San Francisco*
**a8** Vacuum
*b8* *An element*
**a9** The Bible
*b9* *Peerage*
**a10** Five
*b10* *Once*
**a11** SALT
*b11* *ANZAC*
**a12** Mercury
*b12* *Jupiter*

## Tie-breaker

**Q** On television, whose catch phrase was 'you dirty old man, you!'?

**A** *The younger Steptoe (Harold) (to his father)*

# No. 16

**a1** What work was done by a 'clippie'?

*b1* *If you used to work 'on the footplate', what would your job have been?*

**a2** According to the film and book title, how many dalmatians were there?

*b2* *Which mammal's survival would be threatened if there was a bamboo shortage?*

**a3** What does an American mean when he talks of a janitor?

*b3* *In America, what is a billfold?*

**a4** Whereabouts in your head are your adenoids?

*b4* *Whereabouts in your body is your cerebrum?*

**a5** By what name is Princess Anne's daughter known?

*b5* *By what title was Princess Diana's father known?*

**a6** What was distinctive about the daily paper, the *Daily Worker*?

*b6* *Which Jewish girl became famous for the diary she kept while hiding from Nazi soldiers in the Netherlands?*

**a7** In which sport might you obtain a Black Belt?

*b7* *Which animals raced at White City?*

**a8** What is RoSPA concerned with preventing?

*b8* *What is the CPS?*

**a9** 'It might as well rain until September' was a hit in 1962 for which highly successful female songwriter?

*b9* *Texan male vocalist Roy Orbison was better known as who?*

**a10** Which is the largest country (by land area) in Africa?

*b10* *And which is the largest country (by population) in Africa?*

**a11** In Britain, in 'old money', how much was a guinea worth?

*b11* *How much was 40p in pre-decimal British money?*

**a12** Which American spacecraft blew up, just after being launched in 1986?

*b12* *Who was the first man to set foot on the Moon?*

# No. 16 Answers

**a1** Bus conductress
*b1* *Engine driver (or fireman)*
**a2** 101
*b2* *Panda*
**a3** Caretaker or porter
*b3* *Wallet*
**a4** Between back of nose and throat
*b4* *Brain*
**a5** Zara
*b5* *Earl Spencer (formerly Lord Althorp)*
**a6** It was a Communist paper
*b6* *Anne Frank*
**a7** Judo
*b7* *Greyhounds*
**a8** Accidents (Royal Society for the Prevention of Accidents)
*b8* *Crown Prosecution Service*
**a9** Carole King
*b9* *The Big 'O'*
**a10** Sudan
*b10* *Nigeria*
**a11** 21/- (21 shillings); £1-1/- (one pound, one shilling)
*b11* *8/- (eight shillings)*
**a12** Challenger
*b12* *Neil Armstrong*

## Tie-breaker

**Q** Which two countries are separated by the Shatt-al-Arab waterway?
**A** *Iran and Iraq*

32

# No. 17

**a1** In which industry can you win an Oscar?
*b1* *What job would you have if you used a joy-stick in your work?*
**a2** Of which country did Boris Yeltsin become president?
*b2* *And in which African country was Sani Abacha a dictator?*
**a3** In which American city did Al Capone head a gang controlling gambling, liquor and vice?
*b3* *Before capture, in which country had the train robber, Ronald Biggs, been living?*
**a4** Does a convex lens curve inwards or outwards towards its centre?
*b4* *In magnetism, do 'like' poles attract or repel?*
**a5** On an account sheet, what is meant by the letters DR?
*b5* *In the world of finance, for what is MLR an abbreviation?*
**a6** Of which country was Pierre Trudeau prime minister?
*b6* *Of which country was Sir Robert Menzies a statesman and premier?*
**a7** What was the symbol of the German Nazi Party?
*b7* *For what are the names Belsen, Buchenwald and Dachau remembered?*
**a8** Which champion jockey went to prison in 1987?
*b8* *The Brazilian soccer star, Edson Arantes do Nascimento, is better known by what nickname (of only four letters!)?*
**a9** 'Make Me Smile (Come Up and See Me)' was a seventies hit for whom?
*b9* *Who sang the title song from the James Bond film, Moonraker?*
**a10** Of which American state is Montgomery the capital?
*b10* *Of which American state is Salt Lake City the capital?*
**a11** In chemistry, what is the opposite of an alkali?
*b11* *Which scale measures the strength of acids and alkalis?*
**a12** Which country lies immediately to the west of Afghanistan?
*b12* *And which country lies to the west of Iran?*

# No. 17 Answers

**a1** Film industry
*b1* *Pilot or aviator*
**a2** Russia
*b2* *Nigeria*
**a3** Chicago
*b3* *Brazil*
**a4** Outwards
*b4* *Repel*
**a5** Debit (or debt)
*b5* *Minimum lending rate*
**a6** Canada
*b6* *Australia*
**a7** Swastika
*b7* *Nazi concentration camps*
**a8** Lester Piggott
*b8* *Pelé (say: pell-ay)*
**a9** Steve Harley and the Cockney Rebel
*b9* *Shirley Bassey*
**a10** Alabama
*b10* *Utah*
**a11** Acid
*b11* *The pH scale*
**a12** Iran
*b12* *Iraq*

## Tie-breaker

**Q** Can you name one of the British landing ships destroyed at Bluff Cove during the Falklands War?
*A* *Sir Tristram; Sir Galahad*

# No. 18

**a1** For what are the letters SWALK an abbreviation?
*b1* *What kind of electricity is meant by the initials DC?*
**a2** For what do the initials HMSO stand?
*b2* *What is an ICBM?*
**a3** In the world of medicine, for what do the initials SRN stand?
*b3* *What international organization is known by the initials, WHO?*
**a4** In which city is the Longchamps race course?
*b4* *In athletics, what is the shortest track race?*
**a5** In America, what is a faucet?
*b5* *In America, what is meant by going 'down town'?*
**a6** What is the minimum school leaving age?
*b6* *What is the youngest age you can vote?*
**a7** What is Margaret Thatcher's middle name?
*b7* *Of which political party was Clement Atlee once the leader?*
**a8** Until 1970, which British fish was traditionally a royal fish?
*b8* *With which city do we associate the liver bird?*
**a9** Mental arithmetic: What is .25 of 300?
*b9* *What is the fraction ⅔ expressed as a percentage?*
**a10** Which supergroup had hits with 'Let It Be' and 'Strawberry Fields Forever'?
*b10* *Which pop group had a hit with 'Take a Chance on Me'?*
**a11** What climatological phenomenon could raise sea levels?
*b11* *What is the Fahrenheit equivalent of 100° Centigrade?*
**a12** In Africa, which country is immediately south of Egypt?
*b12* *And which country lies to the south of Namibia and Botswana?*

# No. 18 Answers

**a1** Sealed/signed with a loving kiss
*b1* *Direct Current*
**a2** Her Majesty's Stationery Office
*b2* *(Inter-Continental Ballistic) Missile*
**a3** State Registered Nurse
*b3* *World Health Organization*
**a4** Paris
*b4* *100 metres*
**a5** Tap
*b5* *Going to a city centre, business centre*
**a6** 16
*b6* *18*
**a7** Hilda
*b7* *Labour*
**a8** Sturgeon
*b8* *Liverpool*
**a9** 75
*b9* *66²/₃ or 66.6 recurring %*
**a10** The Beatles
*b10* *ABBA*
**a11** Global warming
*b11* *212°*
**a12** Sudan
*b12* *South Africa*

## Tie-breaker

**Q** In 1978, which two statesmen shared the Nobel Peace Prize
for their efforts to bring peace to the Middle East?
**A** *President Sadat of Egypt, prime minister Begin of Israel*

# No. 19

**a1** For what did Mary Quant become famous in the sixties?
*b1* *And as what did the American Billy Graham become famous?*
**a2** At which school was Billy Bunter a pupil?
*b2* *In one of John Wyndham's books, what are the huge plants called that dominate the world?*
**a3** In which city is there a modern development called the Barbican?
*b3* *For what maximum period is a British parliament elected?*
**a4** Of which African country is Asmara the capital?
*b4* *Managua is the capital of ... where?*
**a5** From 1988 to 1992, who was vice-president of the United States of America?
*b5* *Who was the American black leader who won the Nobel Peace Prize in 1964?*
**a6** If you add together half a score and half a century, what do you get?
*b6* *What is the least number of coins you can use to pay 24p exactly?*
**a7** In the world of cinema, what is the job of the producer?
*b7* *And what is the role of the director?*
**a8** Which seventies group had a hit with 'Blockbuster'?
*b8* *Who sang 'I'm the Leader of the Gang (I am!)'?*
**a9** By what three initial letters do we call the chemical substance in our bodies which determines what we look like?
*b9* *For which organization are the initials WWF an abbreviation?*
**a10** By what name do we normally call Light Amplification by Stimulated Emission of Radiation?
*b10* *Which theory was published in 1905 by Einstein?*
**a11** Which American black athelete won four gold medals in the 1936 Berlin Olympics?
*b11* *Which American golfer won the nickname, 'Golden Bear'?*
**a12** Which woman became prime minister of Pakistan in 1988?
*b12* *Who was the woman prime minister of Israel from 1969 to 1974?*

# No. 19 Answers

**a1** Fashion, design
*b1* *Preaching Christianity; evangelizing*
**a2** Greyfriars
*b2* *Triffids*
**a3** London
*b3* *5 years*
**a4** Eritrea
*b4* *Nicaragua*
**a5** Dan Quayle
*b5* *Martin Luther King*
*a6* 60
*b6* *Three (20p, 2p, 2p)*
**a7** He is the film's business organizer; he raises the money, hires the cast and director
*b7* *He rehearses and directs the actors and cameras*
**a8** The Sweet
*b8* *Gary Glitter*
**a9** DNA
*b9* *World Wide Fund for Nature*
**a10** Laser
*b10* *Theory of Relativity*
**a11** Jesse Owens
*b11* *Jack Nicklaus*
**a12** Benazir Bhutto
*b12* *Golda Meir (say: may-ear)*

---

## Tie-Breaker

**Q** Which profession did Denys Lasdun and Edwin Lutyens both follow?
*A* *Architect*

# No. 20

**a1**    What does a Frenchman mean when he says, 'Service compris? (say: ser-vis kom-pree)

*b2*    *What does a Frenchman mean when he says, 'Comment allez-vous?' (say: kom-mon tallay voo)*

**a2**    Which famous London department store has been owned by Mohammed Fayed?

*b2*    *By what first name was his son known?*

**a3**    On what date each year do the United States celebrate their independence?

*b3*    *By what name is Mardi Gras generally known in this country?*

**a4**    Which house became the Queen Mother's home when she left Buckingham Palace?

*b4*    *Who is the president of the Save the Children Fund?*

**a5**    What is euphemism?

*b5*    *What does a mnemonic help you to do?*

**a6**    During the Second World War, what was a V2?

*b6*    *In the Second World War, who or what was a boffin?*

**a7**    Of what institution has Eddie George been governor?

*b7*    *And, also in the world of finance, what is the ECB?*

**a8**    If you drove north from Belgium, which country would you visit next?

*b8*    *If you drove west from Switzerland, which country would you enter next?*

**a9**    Which pop star created a character called Ziggy Stardust?

*b9*    *Which solo singer had a number one with 'How Can I be Sure'?*

**a10**    In which sport does the French Oaks occur?

*b10*    *In which sport was there a 'Brown Bomber'?*

**a11**    Which is larger, an American or British billion?

*b11*    *Which was the smallest of the following: florin, half-crown and crown?*

**a12**    What did Major White and Alexei Leonov both do in 1965?

*b12*    *Who was the first woman in space?*

# No. 20 Answers

**a1**    Service included
*b1*    *How are you? (How do you do?)*
**a2**    Harrods
*b2*    *Dodi*
**a3**    July 4th
*b3*    *Shrove Tuesday (accept: Pancake Day)*
**a4**    Clarence House
*b4*    *The Princess Royal (Princess Anne)*
**a5**    A polite or 'nice' way of saying something rude or unpleasant
*b5*    *Remember something*
**a6**    A missile/rocket
*b6*    *(Backroom) (research) scientist*
**a7**    Bank of England
*b7*    *European Central Bank*
**a8**    Holland
*b8*    *France*
**a9**    David Bowie
*b9*    *David Cassidy*
**a10**    Horse racing
*b10*    *Boxing (Joe Louis)*
**a11**    British (a million million) (American is only a thousand million)
*b11*    *Florin*
**a12**    Walked in space
*b12*    *Valentina Tereshkova*

---

## Tie-Breaker

**Q**    Albert Campion was the fictional detective invented by which woman crime writer?
*A*    *Margery Allingham*

---

# No. 21: Capital Cities

The following countries and their capitals have all been in the news during the 20th century. Of which country is each of the following the capital city?

**a1** Nicosia
*b1 Valletta*
**a2** Addis Ababa
*b2 Tehran*
**a3** Tirana
*b3 Freetown*
**a4** Ankara
*b4 Katmandu*
**a5** Riyadh
*b5 Phnom Penh*
**a6** Rabat
*b6 Port au Prince*

And what is the capital city of these countries?

**a7** Cuba
*b7 Indonesia*
**a8** Sudan
*b8 Uganda*
**a9** Peru
*b9 Vietnam*
**a10** Jordan
*b10 Lebanon*
**a11** Syria
*b11 Thailand*
**a12** Chile
*b12 Uruguay*

# No. 21 Answers

**a1** Cyprus
*b1* *Malta*
**a2** Ethiopia
*b2* *Iran*
**a3** Albania
*b3* *Sierra Leone*
**a4** Turkey
*b4* *Nepal*
**a5** Saudi Arabia
*b5* *Cambodia*
**a6** Morocco
*b6* *Haiti*
**a7** Havana
*b7* *Jakarta*
**a8** Khartoum
*b8* *Kampala*
**a9** Lima
*b9* *Hanoi*
**a10** Amman
*b10* *Beirut*
**a11** Damascus
*b11* *Bangkok*
**a12** Santiago
*b12* *Montevideo*

## Tie-breaker

**Q** Into which capital city did the Soviet Union airlift troops on Christmas Eve, 1979?
*A* *Kabul (Afghanistan)*

# No. 22

**a1**  With which country do you associate a Wiener Schnitzel?

*b1*  *In which kind of restaurant would you be most likely to eat a poppadom?*

**a2**  In which game do you play with 'a yellow dot' ball?

*b2*  *Which game, in an abbreviated form, switches from a red to white ball?*

**a3**  Where in your body is there an anvil, hammer and a stirrup?

*b3*  *What is a greenstick fracture?*

**a4**  Which male pop star featured in the films *Purple Rain* and *Under a Cherry Moon*?

*b4*  *Brian Jones, Mick Taylor and Ron Wood were all members of the same pop group – but not at the same time. Which group?*

**a5**  In 1963, Lester Pearson became prime minister of which country?

*b5*  *Of which country was Eamon de Valera a statesman?*

**a6**  In which novel is Winston Smith overcome by Big Brother?

*b6*  *Which international telecommunications company is known as C and W?*

**a7**  Which artist draws the 'Peanuts' cartoon strips?

*b7*  *In which children's comic can you read about Dennis the Menace and Lord Snooty?*

**a8**  In which city are Greenwich Village and Times Square?

*b8*  *Which city is generally said to be the centre of the American car industry?*

**a9**  In maths, the denary system is based on the number ten. On which number is the binary system based?

*b9*  *What is the square root of 121?*

**a10**  In the Second World War, who was the Italian Fascist leader?

*b10*  *Who commanded the Free French forces during the last war?*

**a11**  Celsius, Réaumur and Fahrenheit are all what?

*b11*  *On a map, what places are joined by isotherms?*

**a12**  Who said, 'My fellow Americans, ask not what your country can do for you, but what you can do for your country'?

*b12*  *Whose law was this: 'Work expands so as to fill the time available for its completion'?*

# No. 22 Answers

**a1** Austria
*b1* *Indian*
**a2** Squash
*b2* *Cricket*
**a3** Ear
*b3* *A partly broken (or bent) bone (especially in children)*
**a4** Prince (Prince Rogers Nelson; the artist formerly known as Prince)
*b4* *The Rolling Stones*
**a5** Canada
*b5* *Eire, Republic of Ireland*
**a6** *1984*
*b6* *Cable and Wireless*
**a7** Charles Schulz
*b7* The Beano
**a8** New York
*b8* *Detroit*
**a9** 2
*b9* *11*
**a10** Mussolini (Benito)
*b10* *General de Gaulle*
**a11** Temperature scales
*b11* *Places with the same temperature*
**a12** John F Kennedy
*b12* *(C Northcote) Parkinson*

---

## Tie-breaker

**Q** By the name of which London suburb are these films known: *Whisky Galore, Passport to Pimlico* and *The Lavender Hill Mob*?

**A** *Ealing (The Ealing Comedies)*

---

# No. 23

**a1**  In what type of needlework would you use a templet?

*b1*  *If you are ironing clothes, which require the greatest heat: wool, linen or nylon?*

**a2**  From which London railway station would you normally leave if you were travelling to Liverpool?

*b2*  *From which London station would you leave if you were travelling to Newcastle upon Tyne?*

**a3**  What does a journalist mean when he says he's got a 'scoop'?

*b3*  *In the sixties, which group of people had the slogan, 'Make love, not war'?*

**a4**  What is the unit of currency in Switzerland?

*b4*  *Which monetary system has been said to have an unacceptable face?*

**a5**  In the children's books, which bear did Michael Bond write about?

*b5*  *Who owned the teddy bear called Winnie-the-Pooh?*

**a6**  In America, what is a derby? (say: durby)

*b6*  *In America, what is or was a rustler?*

**a7**  Which political party is called Plaid Cymru?

*b7*  *In the eighties, of which political party was Dr David Owen a leading figure?*

**a8**  In America, what was 'Prohibition' (from 1920 to 1933)?

*b8*  *In America, whom did Senator McCarthy seek in his 'witch hunts'?*

**a9**  Hausa and Yoruba are languages spoken in which part of Africa?

*b9*  *And what is the commonest language in East Africa?*

**a10**  What was the home country of the long-distance runner, Emil Zatopek?

*b10*  *From which country did the young gymnast Nadia Comeneci come?*

**a11**  In which country was the explorer Sir Edmund Hilary born?

*b11*  *What was the name of Sir Ernest Shackleton's ship (which was crushed in Antarctic ice)?*

**a12**  On which Caribbean island did steel bands originate?

*b12*  *Germany has a large number of immigrant 'guest workers'. From which country principally do they come?*

# No. 23 Answers

**a1** Patchwork
*b1* *Linen*
**a2** Euston
*b2* *King's Cross*
**a3** He's got a story no other journalist has
*b3* *Hippies/flower people/flower children*
**a4** (Swiss) Franc
*b4* *Capitalism*
**a5** Paddington
*b5* *Christopher Robin (Milne)*
**a6** (Bowler) hat
*b6* *Cattle thief*
**a7** Welsh Nationalists
*b7* *Social Democrat*
**a8** A ban on the manufacture and sale of alcoholic drinks
*b8* *Communists*
**a9** West Africa
*b9* *Swahili*
**a10** Czechoslovakia
*b10* *Romania*
**a11** New Zealand
*b11* *'Endurance'*
**a12** Trinidad
*b12* *Turkey*

## Tie-breaker

**Q** Which cricketer scored a world record 501 not out against Durham in 1994?
**A** *Brian Lara*

# No. 24

**a1**  Which football team is known as The Gunners?
*b1*  *Which team plays at home at Stamford Bridge?*
**a2**  What happens if you inhale chloroform?
*b2*  *In which of your organs is there a drum?*
**a3**  Of which country is Aer Lingus the national airline?
*b3*  *Of which country is Sabena the national airline?*
**a4**  Which television comedian was famous for his blood donor show or sketch?
*b4*  *Which comedian was known as 'Big Hearted Arthur'?*
**a5**  At the end of a game of snooker, which ball must be potted immediately before the black?
*b5*  *What is the usual number of pins in a game of skittles?*
**a6**  Which pink spotty TV character held the Christmas number one chart spot in 1993?
*b6*  *Which rap artist had a number one with 'Gangster's Paradise'?*
**a7**  Before decimalization in Britain, how many old pennies were there in a half-crown?
*b7*  *What fraction of a metre is a centimetre?*
**a8**  For what sort of work are civil engineers responsible?
*b8*  *And for what are structural engineers responsible?*
**a9**  What is the official language of Uruguay?
*b9*  *What is the language of Monaco?*
**a10**  Of which country did Brian Mulroney become prime minister in 1984?
*b10*  *Of which country was Robert Muldoon prime minister from 1975 to 1984?*
**a11**  Of which American state is Little Rock the capital?
*b11*  *Of which American state is Denver the capital?*
**a12**  Of which country was Angola formerly a colony?
*b12*  *Luxor and Aswan are towns on which river?*

# No. 24 Answers

**a1** Arsenal
*b1* *Chelsea*
**a2** You become insensitive (accept: become unconscious)
*b2* *Ear*
**a3** Ireland (Eire)
*b3* *Belgium*
**a4** Tony Hancock
*b4* *Arthur Askey*
**a5** Pink
*b5* *9*
**a6** Mr Blobby
*b6* *Coolio*
**a7** 30
*b7* *One hundredth*
**a8** Constructing roads, tunnels, bridges, dams, railways, etc.
*b8* *Construction of steel and concrete buildings and bridges*
**a9** Spanish
*b9* *French*
**a10** Canada
*b10* *New Zealand*
**a11** Arkansas
*b11* *Colorado*
**a12** Portugal
*b12* *Nile*

## Tie-breaker

**Q** Which rock group issued albums called 'Meaty, Beaty, Big and Bouncy', 'Tommy' and 'A Quick One'?
**A** *The Who*

# No. 25

**a1** Which television star has been famous for the phrase, 'Didn't he do well'?

*b1* *With which comedian do you associate the catch phrase, 'Nikky, nokky, noo!'?*

**a2** Who was the longest serving British prime minister this century?

*b2* *What was Margaret Thatcher's first cabinet post?*

**a3** Which American state is nicknamed 'The Last Frontier'?

*b3* *Of which state is Nashville the capital?*

**a4** What is the official language of Malta?

*b4* *In which country is Maori a native language?*

**a5** For which comic strip did the Belgian artist Hergé (say: eyre-jay) become famous?

*b5* *In cartoons, which animal has often been used to represent Russia?*

**a6** In which country was the tennis player Martina Navratilova born?

*b6* *In which sport did Gareth Edwards captain Wales?*

**a7** Which part of the United Kingdom became a separate state in 1921?

*b7* *The 1957 Treaty of Rome founded ... what?*

**a8** Where is the M8 motorway?

*b8* *In which English county is the M2?*

**a9** Which brothers went 'Boom, Boom, Boom' in 1995?

*b9* *In 1998 which group took Fleetwood Mac's 'Dreams' back into the chart?*

**a10** Who created the detective, Hercule Poirot?

*b10* *Who wrote the children's book* Charlie and the Chocolate Factory?

**a11** Chittagong is an important city in which county?

*b11* *By what name is the Chinese city of Beijing (say: bay-jing) also known in the west?*

**a12** Which politician became famous for the phrases, 'You've never had it so good' and 'The wind of change'?

*b12* *Which member of the Royal Family once said, 'It's the biggest waste of water in the country by far. You spend half a pint and flush two gallons'?*

# No. 25 Answers

**a1**    Bruce Forsyth
*b1*    *Ken Dodd*
**a2**    Margaret Thatcher
*b2*    *Secretary of State for Education*
**a3**    Alaska
*b3*    *Tennessee*
**a4**    Maltese or English
*b4*    *New Zealand*
**a5**    Tintin
*b5*    *A bear*
**a6**    Czechoslovakia
*b6*    *Rugby union*
**a7**    Irish Free State, Eire
*b7*    *The European Economic Community (Common Market)*
**a8**    Scotland (Edinburgh to Glasgow)
*b8*    *Kent*
**a9**    Outhere Brothers
*b9*    *The Corrs*
**a10**    Agatha Christie
*b10*    *Roald Dahl*
**a11**    Bangladesh
*b11*    *Peking*
**a12**    Harold Macmillan
*b12*    *Duke of Edinburgh*

---

## Tie-breaker

**Q**    Soft, flexible watches, strange bony figures, surreal shapes – in which Spanish painter's work would you find all these?

**A**    *Salvador Dali*

# No. 26

**a1**  On American television, what is an 'anchor'?
*b1*  *Who or what was a bobby-soxer?*
**a2**  In which city is there a railway station called Waverley?
*b2*  *In which English city is there a railway station called Lime Street?*
**a3**  What job would you probably have if you were a member of the NUT?
*b3*  *Which profession is governed by the Law Society?*
**a4**  In London, what have the Palace, the Phoenix and the Piccadilly in common?
*b4*  *What did the Clean Air Act in 1956 more or less do away with in London?*
**a5**  For what are Tarot cards now used?
*b5*  *What number plays a vital part in the game of Pontoon?*
**a6**  Of which American state is Atlanta the capital?
*b6*  *Of which American state is Denver the capital?*
**a7**  In 1928, which important drug was discovered by Professor Alexander Fleming?
*b7*  *Which doctor performed the first human heart transplant operation?*
**a8**  Who plays the father in the film, *Kramer versus Kramer*?
*b8*  *Who directed the 1941 film* Citizen Kane?
**a9**  Of which country is Benfica a famous football team?
*b9*  *Name the two famous Glasgow soccer clubs.*
**a10**  Who wrote the novels, *The War of the Worlds* and *Kipps*?
*b10*  *Who wrote the novel* Women in Love?
**a11**  With which country do you associate Jomo Kenyatta?
*b11*  *What was the title of the former 'King' of Iran?*
**a12**  For which kind of music did Ella Fitzgerald become famous?
*b12*  *'Bird' and 'Yardbird' were nicknames of which jazz musician?*

# No. 26 Answers

**a1** Compère, presenter (especially of a news programme)
*b1* *Teenage fan (of pop music or of a film star)*
**a2** Edinburgh
*b2* *Liverpool*
**a3** Teacher (National Union of Teachers)
*b3* *Solicitors*
**a4** All are theatres
*b4* *Coal fires in central London, and (consequently) smog*
**a5** Fortune-telling
*b5* *21*
**a6** Georgia
*b6* *Colorado*
**a7** Penicillin
*b7* *Dr Christiaan Barnard*
**a8** Dustin Hoffman
*b8* *Orson Welles*
**a9** Portugal
*b9* *Celtic and Rangers*
**a10** H G Wells
*b10* *D H Lawrence*
**a11** Kenya
*b11* *Shah (of Persia)*
**a12** Jazz (singer), especially 'scat singing'
*b12* *Charlie Parker*

---

## Tie-breaker

**Q** Which Argentinean cruiser was sunk by the British submarine 'Conqueror' during the Falklands War?
**A** *'General Belgrano'*

# No. 27

**a1**  Which royal prince served in the navy during the Falklands War?

*b1*  *Which member of the Royal Family was educated at Cheam, Gordonstoun and Geelong Grammar schools?*

**a2**  What is 'Alitalia'?

*b2*  *Of which country is El Al the national airline?*

**a3**  Which language is spoken in Austria?

*b3*  *What is the main language spoken in Argentina?*

**a4**  What kind of music is performed by Fairport Convention, Steeleye Span and the Dubliners?

*b4*  *Which jazz trumpeter and singer had hits with 'Hello Dolly' and 'What a Wonderful World'?*

**a5**  In which sport did Chris Evert achieve success?

*b5*  *In which Olympic event did the athlete Sally Gunnell excel?*

**a6**  Of which American state is Phoenix the capital?

*b6*  *What is the capital of the American state, Massachusetts?*

**a7**  Which film star's real name was Norma Jean Baker or Mortenson?

*b7*  *In the film* Singin' in the Rain, *which star was in fact singing in the rain?*

**a8**  On which day of the week is Maundy money distributed?

*b8*  *In Great Britain, in which month is the Winter Solstice?*

**a9**  By what name is the French government known which collaborated with the Germans in the Second World War?

*b9*  *Which Frenchman led the liberation of France in 1944?*

**a10**  Who wrote the novel *Brave New World*?

*b10*  *Who wrote the novels* Decline and Fall *and* A Handful of Dust?

**a11**  Which is the largest lake in Africa?

*b11*  *In surface area, which is the largest natural lake in England?*

**a12**  In which year did Hitler invade Czechoslovakia?

*b12*  *In which year did Argentina invade the Falkland Islands?*

# No. 27 Answers

| | |
|---|---|
| **a1** | Andrew |
| *b1* | *Prince Charles* |
| **a2** | Airline (Italian) |
| *b2* | *Israel* |
| **a3** | German |
| *b3* | *Spanish* |
| **a4** | Folk |
| *b4* | *Louis Armstrong* |
| **a5** | Tennis |
| *b5* | *Hurdles* |
| **a6** | Arizona |
| *b6* | *Boston* |
| **a7** | Marilyn Monroe |
| *b7* | *Gene Kelly* |
| **a8** | Thursday |
| *b8* | *December (approx. 21st December)* |
| **a9** | Vichy Government |
| *b9* | *General de Gaulle* |
| **a10** | Aldous Huxley |
| *b10* | *Evelyn Waugh* |
| **a11** | Lake Victoria |
| *b11* | *Lake Windermere* |
| **a12** | 1939 |
| *b12* | *1982* |

## Tie-breaker

**Q** What was the job or profession of American Frank Lloyd Wright?

*A*    *Architect*

# No. 28

**a1** Which leader was briefly deposed while on holiday in 1991?

*b1 Of where was Terence O'Neill prime minister from 1963–1969?*

**a2** Which city is served by Stansted Airport?

*b2 In which country is Shannon airport?*

**a3** In which country was the 1994 football World Cup held?

*b3 Which sport has famous clubs called Frogs, Butterflies and Foresters?*

**a4** Who directed the films *Brief Encounter, Oliver Twist* and *The Bridge on the River Kwai*?

*b4 About which monster did Roland Emmerich direct a 1998 film?*

**a5** Which opera singer had a No. 1 chart hit with 'Nessum Dorma'?

*b5 Which nationality is the singer Kiri Te Kanawa's home country?*

**a6** Who wrote the book *Murder on the Orient Express*?

*b6 Which crime writer created the private eye, Philip Marlowe?*

**a7** Which is the largest country (by population) in Asia?

*b7 Which country lies to the south of Mongolia?*

**a8** Which American town is said to be the capital of country and western music?

*b8 Which record company is said to have developed 'the sound of young America' by featuring and controlling stars such as Diana Ross, Stevie Wonder and the Temptations?*

**a9** Bengali, Urdu and Hindi are all native languages of which continent?

*b9 'Singhalese' refers to which country?*

**a10** At the start of the century, what was the school leaving age in Britain? Was it 8, 12 or 14?

*b10 In Britain, when was the school leaving age raised to 16? Was it 1944, 1963 or 1973?*

**a11** From which Asian country did Soviet troops withdraw in 1989?

*b11 In 1967, which country won the Six Day War?*

**a12** What sort of world-wide epidemic killed about 20 million people immediately after the First World War?

*b12 Which group of workers are affected by the disease silicosis?*

# No. 28 Answers

**a1**  Mikhail Gorbachev
*b1*  *Northern Ireland*
**a2**  London
*b2*  *Ireland/Irish Republic/Eire*
**a3**  USA
*b3*  *Cricket*
**a4**  David Lean
*b4*  *Godzilla*
**a5**  Luciano Pavarotti
*b5*  *New Zealand*
**a6**  Agatha Christie
*b6*  *Raymond Chandler*
**a7**  China
*b7*  *China*
**a8**  Nashville (Tennessee)
*b8*  *Tamla Motown Records*
**a9**  Asia (accept: Indian sub-continent)
*b9*  *Sri Lanka/Ceylon*
**a10**  12
*b10*  *1973*
**a11**  Afghanistan
*b11*  *Israel*
**a12**  Influenza
*b12*  *Miners (slate, coal, anthracite) (also stone cutters)*

---

## Tie-breaker

**Q**  Who wrote the short novel *Breakfast at Tiffany's*?
*A*  *Truman Capote (say: ca-po-tee)*

# No. 29

**a1**  Jim Henson died in 1990. Which puppets did he create?
*b1*  *Which singing cowboy had a horse called Trigger?*
**a2**  In which city is Wenceslas Square?
*b2*  *In which city is the Prado?*
**a3**  Which film star's real name was Marion Morrison?
*b3*  *Which American child film star became the US representative to the United Nations in 1969?*
**a4**  Which pop group included Madame Cholet and Orinoco?
*b4*  *Which pianist played 'Sidesaddle' and later 'Roulette'?*
**a5**  On which river stands the English city of Cambridge?
*b5*  *On which river does Chester stand?*
**a6**  In which year did Hitler invade Austria?
*b6*  *Which war began in 1950?*
**a7**  Who has captained the England rugby union team most often?
*b7*  *Which French motor racing driver had 35 Grand Prix victories and was known as the 'professor'?*
**a8**  Who was prime minister of Great Britain for 1970 to 1974?
*b8*  *Who was prime minister of Great Britain for 1951 to 1955?*
**a9**  In which country was there a revolutionary group called the Mau Mau?
*b9*  *Which Russian leader was assassinated in Mexico in 1940?*
**a10**  Who wrote the novels Brighton Rock and The Power and the Glory?
*b10*  *Who wrote the novel The Old Man and the Sea?*
**a11**  In 1901, who sent a radio signal from Cornwall to Newfoundland?
*b11*  *What radio detection system was invented by Sir Robert Watson-Watt during the Second World War?*
**a12**  Which Russian musician composed The Rite of Spring?
*b12*  *Which famous Italian opera composer died in 1901?*

# No. 29 Answers

**a1** The Muppets
*b1* *Roy Rogers*
**a2** Prague
*b2* *Madrid*
**a3** John Wayne
*b3* *Shirley Temple (married name: Shirley Temple Black)*
**a4** The Wombles
*b4* *Russ Conway*
**a5** Cam (accept: Granta)
*b5* *Dee*
**a6** 1938
*b6* *Korean War*
**a7** Will Carling
*b7* *Alain Prost*
**a8** Edward Heath
*b8* *Winston Churchill*
**a9** Kenya
*b9* *(Leon) Trotsky*
**a10** Graham Greene
*b10* *Ernest Hemingway*
**a11** (Guglielmo) Marconi
*b11* *Radar*
**a12** (Igor) Stravinsky
*b12* *(Giuseppe) Verdi*

## Tie-breaker

**Q** Who was the American choreographer responsible for such films as *Forty-second Street*, *Gold-diggers of 1933* and *Dames*?

**A** *Busby Berkeley*

# No. 30

**a1**  Are there 6, 7 or 8 players in a volley ball team?
*b1*  *Are there 6, 7 or 8 players in a netball team?*
**a2**  At what age can you legally buy cigarettes?
*b2*  *What is the youngest age you can drink beer or wine when having a meal in a restaurant?*
**a3**  What was a Messerschmitt?
*b3*  *What is a 'STOL' aircraft?*
**a4**  In which country is Lake Como?
*b4*  *In which country is Lake Lucerne?*
**a5**  Which year was the Festival of Britain?
*b5*  *In 1932, where was a famous Harbour Bridge opened?*
**a6**  Of a psychiatrist and a psychoanalyst, which is certain to be medically qualified?
*b6*  *In what kind of illness does a paediatrician specialize?*
**a7**  According to the song, who used to wait underneath the lantern, by the barrack gate?
*b7*  *Who wrote or sang the protest ballad of the early sixties, 'The Times They are a-Changin'?*
**a8**  Which Indian prime minister was assassinated in 1989?
*b8*  *And which Indian prime minister was assassinated in 1991?*
**a9**  Which president of Egypt nationalized the Suez Canal in 1956?
*b9*  *Who was emperor of Japan from 1926 to 1989?*
**a10**  In the cinema, who played a Mafia leader in *The Godfather* and the hero's father in the 1978 version of *Superman*?
*b10*  *Which film star was married to Lauren Bacall and won an Oscar for his role in* The African Queen*?*
**a11**  In which country has a group calling itself ETA (say: ett-a) been fighting for freedom?
*b11*  *Which organization (founded in 1961) seeks to help prisoners of conscience?*
**a12**  Who became Poet Laureate in 1984?
*b12*  *Which poet wrote* Old Possum's Book of Practical Cats*?*

# No. 30 Answers

| | |
|---|---|
| **a1** | 6 |
| *b1* | *7* |
| **a2** | 16 |
| *b2* | *16* |
| **a3** | German fighter plane (accept: bubble car) |
| *b3* | *Short take-off and landing* |
| **a4** | Italy |
| *b4* | *Switzerland* |
| **a5** | 1951 |
| *b5* | *Sydney* |
| **a6** | Psychiatrist |
| *b6* | *Children's diseases* |
| **a7** | Lilli Marlene |
| *b7* | *Bob Dylan* |
| **a8** | Mrs Indira Gandhi |
| *b8* | *Rajiv Gandhi (her son)* |
| **a9** | President (Gamal Abdel) Nasser |
| *b9* | *Hirohito* |
| **a10** | Marlon Brando |
| *b10* | *Humphrey Bogart* |
| **a11** | Spain |
| *b11* | *Amnesty International* |
| **a12** | Ted Hughes |
| *b12* | *T S Eliot* |

## Tie-breaker

**Q** Who are 'the Three Tenors'?
*A* *Luciano Pavorotti, Placido Domingo, José Carreras*

# No. 31 Soap Sagas

Television soap operas became extremely popular forms of entertainment in the second half of the century. In which soap do or did the following locations feature?

**a1**   The Rover's Return
*b1*   *The Queen Vic*
**a2**   Ramsay Street
*b2*   *Southfork*
**a3**   Tarrant
*b3*   *The Woolpack*
**a4**   'The Close'
*b4*   *Wentworth Detention Centre*

In which soap do or did the following characters appear?
**a5**   Billy Corkhill
*b5*   *Blake Carrington*
**a6**   Lou Beale
*b6*   *Ena Sharples*
**a7**   Benny Hawkins
*b7*   *Sue Ellen*
**a8**   Charlene Michell
*b8*   *Dr Gillespie*

Which character was played by these actors?
**a9**   Pat Phoenix
*b9*   *Larry Hagman*
**a10**   Ronald Allen
*b10*   *Charlton Heston*
**a11**   Joan Collins
*b11*   *Richard Chamberlain*
**a12**   Noele Gordon
*b12*   *Jason Donovan*

# No. 31 Answers

**a1** *Coronation Street*
**b1** EastEnders
**a2** *Neighbours*
**b2** Dallas
**a3** *Howards Way*
**b3** Emmerdale Farm
**a4** *Brookside*
**b4** Prisoner: Cell Block H
**a5** *Brookside*
**b5** Dynasty
**a6** *EastEnders*
**b6** Coronation Street
**a7** *Crossroads*
**b7** Dallas
**a8** *Neighbours*
**b8** Dr Kildare
**a9** Elsie Tanner (later Elsie Howard, Elsie Gregory) (in *Coronation Street*)
**b9** *JR Ewing (in* Dallas*)*
**a10** David Hunter (in *Crossroads*)
**b10** *Jason Colby (in* The Colbys*)*
**a11** Alexis Rowan (in *Dynasty*)
**b11** *Dr Kildare*
**a12** Meg Richardson (in *Crossroads*)
**b12** *Scott Robinson (in* Neighbours*)*

---

## Tie-breaker

**Q** In the early days of *Coronation Street*, which character was caretaker at the Glad Tidings Mission Hall?
**A** *Ena Sharples*

# No. 32

**a1**   In Britain, when does a person legally 'come of age'?

*b1*   *How old is an octogenarian?*

**a2**   Which cricket team plays at Sophia Gardens?

*b2*   *Which rugby team's homeground is Franklin's Gardens?*

**a3**   On television, which spaceship had the mission 'to seek out new life and new civilizations, to boldly go where no man has gone before'?

*b3*   *On television, what was the name of the rabbit in the children's series,* The Magic Roundabout?

**a4**   Who was the first person to show it was possible to transmit pictures and is known as 'the father of television'?

*b4*   *The aqualung was invented, in part, by which famous French under-sea explorer?*

**a5**   Which member of the Royal Family is second in line to the throne?

*b5*   *Can you name the Duke of York's two daughters?*

**a6**   What was the name of the aircraft in which Charles Lindbergh first flew the Atlantic?

*b6*   *In 1930, who was the first woman to fly from Britain to Australia?*

**a7**   Anchorage and Fairbanks are towns in which American state?

*b7*   *In America, New York is at the mouth of which river?*

**a8**   Martha Graham died in 1991. For which art did she become famous?

*b8*   *The actor Rex Harrison died in 1990. In which musical did he play Henry Higgins?*

**a9**   What is a futon?

*b9*   *For what would you use a kilner jar?*

**a10**   'Suddenly' was a hit for Cliff Richard and who else?

*b10*   *Which comedy pop group had a hit with the song 'Lily the Pink'?*

**a11**   For what is the Montessori Method used?

*b11*   *In medicine, of what is neurology the study?*

**a12**   If, in the Bible, you add together the number of Testaments, the number of Gospels and the number of Commandments, what is the answer?

*b12*   *If you were driving at 50 mph, at how many kilometres per hour would you be going (approximately)?*

# No. 32 Answers

**a1** 18
*b1* *80 (or in their eighties)*
**a2** Glamorgan
*b2* *Northampton*
**a3** Starship Enterprise (in *Star Trek*)
*b3* *Dylan*
**a4** John Logie Baird
*b4* *Jacques Cousteau*
**a5** Prince William (of Wales)
*b5* *Beatrice and Eugenie*
**a6** 'Spirit of St Louis'
*b6* *Amy Johnson*
**a7** Alaska
*b7* *Hudson* (accept: East River)
**a8** Dance (accept: choreography, ballet)
*b8* My Fair Lady
**a9** (Japanese) low-slung bed or mattress
*b9* *To preserve fruit or vegetables (accept: preserving)*
**a10** Olivia Newton John
*b10* *The Scaffold*
**a11** Educating children
*b11* *Nervous system (or the brain)*
**a12** 16
*b12* *80 kph*

## Tie-breaker

**Q** Which two countries exploded nuclear bombs for the first time in 1998?
**A** *India, Pakistan*

# No. 33

**a1**  Who wrote the novel *Goldfinger*?

*b1*  *Who wrote the novel* The Guns of Navarone?

**a2**  Of which country was the Ayatollah Khomeini a ruler?

*b2*  *Which leader this century was known as 'il Duce' (say: doo-chay)?*

**a3**  For which city is Leonardo da Vinci an airport?

*b3*  *For which English city is Speke the airport?*

**a4**  In psychology, what is the opposite of an extrovert?

*b4*  *Which monkey has a blood factor otherwise found only in human blood?*

**a5**  In which city will you find the Trevi Fountain?

*b5*  *In which capital city is the cathedral of Notre Dame?*

**a6**  What have these in common: Scratchwood, Keele and Frankley?

*b6*  *What do Edinburgh, Chester and Chessington all have in common?*

**a7**  Which American had a hit with 'Two Can Play That Game' in 1994?

*b7*  *Which pop group won the Eurovision Song Contest with 'Love Shine a Light'?*

**a8**  Of which American political party was President Lyndon Johnson a leading member?

*b8*  *Which general commanded the American forces in Europe at the time of D-Day?*

**a9**  Between the Wars, Babe Ruth became a star in which sport?

*b9*  *Which Conservative politician was twice Olympic 1,500-metre champion?*

**a10**  Which is the RAF equivalent of the army rank of captain?

*b10*  *What is the Army equivalent of the RAF rank of squadron leader?*

**a11**  Who was the first artistic director of Britain's National Theatre?

*b11*  *In 1935, she played Juliet. Fifty years later she starred in television's* Jewel in the Crown *series. Who was she?*

**a12**  Who was the chief star of the BBC radio programme, *Round the Horne*?

*b12*  *In which radio show did we hear about Ron and Eth Glum?*

# No. 33 Answers

**a1** Ian Fleming
*b1* *Alistair Maclean*
**a2** Iran
*b2* *(Benito) Mussolini (of Italy)*
**a3** Rome
*b3* *Liverpool*
**a4** Introvert
*b4* *Rhesus monkey*
**a5** Rome
*b5* *Paris*
**a6** All are motorway service stations
*b6* *All have zoos*
**a7** Bobby Brown
*b7* *Katrina and the Waves*
**a8** Democrat
*b8* *Dwight D Eisenhower*
**a9** Baseball
*b9* *Seb Coe*
**a10** Flight Lieutenant
*b10* *Major*
**a11** Laurence Olivier (later Lord Olivier)
*b11* *Dame Peggy Ashcroft*
**a12** Kenneth Horne
*b12* Take It From Here

## Tie-breaker

**Q** In 1918, women were given the vote – but only to those over what age?

**A** 30

# No. 34

**a1** As what did Marjorie Proops become famous?

*b1* *Which musical instrument is associated with Liberace?*

**a2** In Russia, what are the Urals?

*b2* *And in which country are the Cambrian Mountains?*

**a3** Andrew Lloyd Webber composed the music for *Joseph and the Amazing Technicolor Dreamcoat*. Who wrote the lyrics?

*b3* *Name the ukulele player who made popular the song 'I'm Leaning on a Lamppost'?*

**a4** With which two comedians did you associate the phrase, 'You can't see the join'?

*b4* *In which television show did we regularly hear the phrase, 'And now for something completely different'?*

**a5** Of which organization has Sir John Birt been director general?

*b5* *Which British television channel was launched in April 1997?*

**a6** Which Australian state lies to the north of New South Wales?

*b6* *Which Australian state is a separate island?*

**a7** Which play, first performed in 1904, features fairies and a villain called Captain Hook?

*b7* *On which play by Bernard Shaw was the musical* My Fair Lady *based?*

**a8** About which year is Stanley Kubrick's film that is sub-titled *A Space Odyssey*?

*b8* *Who directed the films* The Birds, North by Northwest *and* Psycho?

**a9** Which German scientist led the team which invented the V-2 rocket (the first true missile)?

*b9* *Who designed the Morris Minor and later the Mini car?*

**a10** What high office was held by Dr Robert Runcie?

*b10* *In 1986, who became Archbishop of Cape Town?*

**a11** Which two countries fought at the Battle of Tannenberg in 1914?

*b11* *Which of these was a sea battle in the First World War: Arras, Jutland, Verdun?*

**a12** In athletics, four field events involve jumping. Name three.

*b12* *In athletics, there are four field events which involve throwing. Name three.*

# No. 34 Answers

**a1**    Agony aunt (the original one)
*b1*    *Piano*
**a2**    Mountains
*b2*    *Wales*
**a3**    Tim Rice
*b3*    *George Formby*
**a4**    Morecambe and Wise
*b4*    Monty Python's Flying Circus
**a5**    The BBC
*b5*    *Channel 5*
**a6**    Queensland
*b6*    *Tasmania*
**a7**    *Peter Pan*
*b7*    Pygmalion
**a8**    *2001*
*b8*    *Alfred Hitchcock*
**a9**    Wernher von Braun
*b9*    *Alec Issigonis*
**a10**    Archbishop of Canterbury
*b10*    *Desmond Tutu*
**a11**    Germany and Russia
*b11*    *Jutland*
**a12**    Long jump, high jump, triple jump, pole vault
*b12*    *The hammer, the discus, the shot, the javelin*

---

## Tie-breaker

**Q**    'I Get Around', 'Good Vibrations' and 'California Girls' were popular hits for which group?

**A**    *The Beach Boys*

---

# No. 35

**a1** In which European city would you be most likely to travel by gondola?

*b1* *In which city is a street called 'Unter den Linden'?*

**a2** Which pop superstar released the albums, 'Off the Wall' and 'Thriller'?

*b2* *Reg Dwight's uncle was a professional footballer and Reg has supported Watford Football Club. By what name is he better known?*

**a3** Who is the present queen's first grandson?

*b3* *What is the name of Princess Margaret's eldest child?*

**a4** On which principal river does Dublin stand?

*b4* *On which river stands the city of Nottingham?*

**a5** Which very high office was held by Fisher of Lambeth?

*b5* *What occupations have Russell, Losey and Fellini in common?*

**a6** What is a psychosomatic illness?

*b6* *What is the medical name for the collar bone?*

**a7** In which sport do Sheffield Eagles and London Broncos compete?

*b7* *Which Swedish tennis player was Wimbledon champion from 1976 to 1980?*

**a8** Of which American political party was John F Kennedy a leader?

*b8* *What was the American president Richard Nixon's middle name?*

**a9** Which Russian science fiction writer is famous for his 'Foundation' trilogy?

*b9* *What kind of novels are written by Jean Plaidy?*

**a10** Who was the first man to fly the Channel by aeroplane?

*b10* *Which airship made a round-the-world flight in 1929?*

**a11** Which English county's industrial landscape was often painted by L S Lowry?

*b11* *Guernica is a famous painting inspired by the Spanish Civil War. Who painted it?*

**a12** Which Russian composed the musical narrative, *Peter and the Wolf*?

*b12* *Which British composer founded the Aldeburgh Festival in Suffolk?*

# No. 35 Answers

**a1** Venice
*b1* *Berlin*
**a2** Michael Jackson
*b2* *Sir Elton John*
**a3** Peter Phillips (son of the Princess Royal and Captain Mark Phillips)
*b3* *(David) Viscount Linley*
**a4** River Liffey
*b4* *Trent*
**a5** Archbishop of Canterbury
*b5* *They are all film directors*
**a6** One brought on by psychological causes
*b6* *Clavicle*
**a7** Rugby league
*b7* *Bjorn Borg*
**a8** Democrat
*b8* *Milhous*
**a9** (Isaac) Asimov
*b9* *Historical novels (accept: historical romances, romantic novels)*
**a10** (Louis) Bleriot (in 1909)
*b10* *(Graf) Zeppelin*
**a11** Lancashire
*b11* *(Pablo) Picasso*
**a12** (Sergei) Prokofiev
*b12* *Benjamin Britten (Lord Britten)*

## Tie-breaker

**Q** Who is this film star? 'I was born in Massachussets, USA; and studied acting in New York. I often, but not always, played cruel and selfish characters – as, for example, in the film *All about Eve*. In a much later film, I terrorized my screen sister and audiences – who worried about *Baby Jane*.'

**A** *Bette Davis (1908–1989)*

# No. 36

**a1** Who became prime minister of Britain in 1979?

*b1* *Of which south American country has President Alfonsin been ruler?*

**a2** In which sport or game was Cliff Thorburn a world champion?

*b2* *Which snooker player gained the nickname Hurricane?*

**a3** What have these in common: Shannon, Lundy and South East Iceland?

*b3* *What have these in common: Crosville, Ribble and Midland Red?*

**a4** Who played the female lead in the film version of *The Sound of Music*?

*b4* *Which film star is Liza Minelli's mother?*

**a5** At which American airbase did women protest in the early eighties?

*b5* *In 1993 a European economic treaty was signed in which Dutch town?*

**a6** Who was head of state in Spain before Juan Carlos became king (in 1975)?

*b6* *Over which country did the King of the Hellenes rule?*

**a7** Which campaigning organization had a ship called the 'Rainbow Warrior'?

*b7* *Which Townsend Thorensen car ferry capsized with disastrous results off Zeebrugge in 1987?*

**a8** Which English county lies south of the former county of Avon?

*b8* *Which 'new' county was created in 1974 between Lincolnshire and North Yorkshire?*

**a9** In a popular song, which musical instrument was called 'Tubby'?

*b9* *For what would a musician use a 'plectrum'?*

**a10** About which deaf and blind woman was the play (later filmed) called *The Miracle Worker*?

*b10* *Which English nurse was shot by the Germans in 1915 for helping British soldiers?*

**a11** Who was the first man to fly the Atlantic solo?

*b11* *Who were the first two men to fly the Atlantic, non-stop?*

**a12** In which year this century did hurricane-force winds devastate southern England?

*b12* *In which year did Hong Kong become part of China?*

# No. 36 Answers

**a1**   Margaret Thatcher
*b1*   *Argentina*
**a2**   Snooker
*b2*   *(Alex) Higgins*
**a3**   They're all sea areas (in the shipping forecasts)
*b3*   *All are bus companies*
**a4**   Julie Andrews
*b4*   *Judy Garland*
**a5**   Greenham Common
*b5*   *Maastricht*
**a6**   General Franco
*b6*   *Greece*
**a7**   Greenpeace
*b7*   *Herald of Free Enterprise*
**a8**   Somerset
*b8*   *Humberside*
**a9**   Tuba
*b9*   *Plucking strings of an instrument (zither, guitar etc.)*
**a10**   Helen Keller
*b10*   *Edith Cavell*
**a11**   (Charles) Lindberg (in 1917)
*b11*   *Alcock and Brown (in 1919)*
**a12**   1987
*b12*   *1997*

---

## Tie-breaker

**Q**   Which race starts at Cowes on the Isle of Wight and requires competitors to approach and return from the southwest coast of Ireland?

**A**   *Fastnet Race (yachting)*

---

# No. 37

**a1** What was the name of Mickey Mouse's wife?
*b1* *Name the cartoon cat who 'kept on walking'?*
**a2** 3½ pints of milk equals approximately how many litres?
*b2* *If you buy a kilo package of sugar, what is the weight (approximately) in pounds?*
**a3** Of which country has President Botha been ruler?
*b3* *Of which country was David Ben Gurion prime minister?*
**a4** Who composed the musicals *On the Town* and *West Side Story*?
*b4* *Which American musician composed* An American in Paris *and the opera,* Porgy and Bess?
**a5** Near which European city is Schiphol airport? (say: ship-pol)
*b5* *For which English town is Squire's Gate the airport?*
**a6** Who was the first Labour Member of Parliament?
*b6* *Which former Labour minister was imprisoned as a fascist in 1940?*
**a7** On stage, who was Chesney Allen's partner?
*b7* *In the theatre, which writer and actor was often known simply as 'Noël'?*
**a8** Whereabouts in Liverpool were there race riots in 1981?
*b8* *In 1987 Michael Ryan made the town of Hungerford into headline news. How?*
**a9** Which Roman Catholic nun became famous for her work among the poor of Calcutta?
*b9* *Who is generally said to be the greatest American architect of the century?*
**a10** Who was Pope from 1958 to 1963?
*b10* *This century, who was pope for only 33 days?*
**a11** The 1953 FA Cup Final is sometimes called 'The Matthews Final' because of the goals scored by Stanley Matthews. Which team won the final?
*b11* *With which English league football club was George Best principally associated – and most successful?*
**a12** Who wrote the novel *Kim*, first published in 1901?
*b12* *Which writer created a hero called Aslan (who was a lion)?*

# No. 37 Answers

**a1**    Minnie
*b1*    *Felix*
**a2**    2
*b2*    *2.2 lb (accept: 2¼)*
**a3**    South Africa
*b3*    *Israel*
**a4**    (Leonard) Bernstein
*b4*    *(George) Gershwin*
**a5**    Amsterdam (in the Netherlands)
*b5*    *Blackpool*
**a6**    Keir Hardie
*b6*    *Sir Oswald Mosley*
**a7**    Bud Flanagan
*b7*    *Noël Coward*
**a8**    Toxteth (Liverpool 8)
*b8*    *He shot dead 14 people (and wounded 15) for no apparent reason*
**a9**    Mother Teresa
*b9*    *Frank Lloyd Wright*
**a10**    Pope John XXIII (born Angelo Roncalli)
*b10*    *John Paul I (in 1978)*
**a11**    Blackpool
*b11*    *Manchester United*
**a12**    Rudyard Kipling
*b12*    *C S Lewis (in* The Lion, the Witch and the Wardrobe*)*

## Tie-breaker

**Q**    What nationality was the surrealist painter René Magritte?
*A*    *Belgian*

# No. 38

**a1** 'Clunk click, every trip' was a slogan intended to encourage ... what?

*b1* *Which is the 'off-side' of a car?*

**a2** Who was the star of the film *Crocodile Dundee*?

*b2* *Who were the stars of the film* Duck Soup?

**a3** In America which is the principal job of the FBI?

*b3* *Where, in Texas, were almost 100 members of a religious group all killed?*

**a4** What are: the Atheneum, the Carlton, the Reform?

*b4* *And what are: Cheltenham, Benenden and Roedean?*

**a5** In 1979, in which European country did workers win the right to join free trade unions?

*b5* *And also in 1979, Abel Muzorewa became the first black prime minister of which country?*

**a6** Who wrote the play *The Doctor's Dilemma*?

*b6* *Who wrote the plays* Blithe Spirit, Hay Fever *and* Private Lives?

**a7** Which national leader had to flee his country in 1959 to escape from the Chinese?

*b7* *Which country was ruled by the military dictator, Juan Peron?*

**a8** Which Argentinean cruiser was sunk by a British submarine during the Falklands War?

*b8* *Henry VIII's flagship was rescued from the sea bed in 1982. What was she called?*

**a9** Which British university twice refused to honour Mrs Thatcher?

*b9* *In 1986, the 'Westland Affair' saw which cabinet minister resign and stalk off along Downing Street?*

**a10** Into which sea does the River Ribble flow?

*b10* *Which is the principal river that flows into the Bristol Channel?*

**a11** Why was businessman Greville Wynne imprisoned in Moscow?

*b11* *By what first names were the Kray Brothers known?*

**a12** Which famous black South African leader was released from prison in February 1990?

*b12* *Emmeline, Christabel and Sylvia were all members of which family dedicated to women's rights?*

# No. 38 Answers

**a1**     The wearing of car seat belts
*b1*     *The driver's side*
**a2**     Paul Hogan
*b2*     *The Marx Brothers*
**a3**     Crime detection, investigation
*b3*     *Waco*
**a4**     London clubs
*b4*     *They are all girls' public schools*
**a5**     Poland
*b5*     *Rhodesia (later Zimbabwe)*
**a6**     G B Shaw
*b6*     *Noël Coward*
**a7**     Dalai Lama (of Tibet)
*b7*     *Argentina*
**a8**     General Belgrano
*b8*     *Mary Rose*
**a9**     Oxford
*b9*     *Michael Heseltine*
**a10**    Irish Sea
*b10*    *Severn*
**a11**    Spying
*b11*    *Reggie and Ronnie*
**a12**    Nelson Mandela
*b12*    *Pankhurst*

---

## Tie-breaker

**Q**    In which book will you read that: 'Whatever goes on two legs is an enemy. Whatever goes on four legs, or has wings, is a friend'?

**A**    *Animal Farm* by George Orwell

# No. 39

**a1** What is Popeye's favourite vegetable?
*b1* *What was the name of the Lone Ranger's horse?*
**a2** With which means of transport is IATA concerned?
*b2* *Of which country is KLM the national airline?*
**a3** In 1981, who became president of Britain's National Union of Mineworkers?
*b3* *'Solidarity' became a trades union movement in which country, principally?*
**a4** Whitney Houston spent 10 weeks at No. 1 in 1992–3 with which song?
*b4* *Who made up the eighties duo Wham!?*
**a5** For what did Barbara Hepworth become famous?
*b5* *As what did Artur Rubenstein achieve international fame?*
**a6** Who wrote the novel, *From Russia with Love*?
*b6* *Which writer created Inspector Maigret?*
**a7** After Harold Wilson retired in 1976, who became the British prime minister?
*b7* *Who was England's prime minister when India gained independence?*
**a8** Why did Broadwater Farm become notorious in 1985?
*b8* *November 1987 saw a tragic fire on London's underground. At which station?*
**a9** In which sport did Carl Lewis become a champion?
*b9* *Which woman tennis star won all four Grand Slam tournaments in 1988?*
**a10** Which city was once called Byzantium and Constantinople?
*b10* *In which European country is the city of Turin?*
**a11** Tumbledown Mountain is on which group of islands?
*b11* *'Uluru' is an Aborigine name for which Australian landmark?*
**a12** Arthur Miller's play, *The Crucible*, deals with witchcraft in which American town?
*b12* *Who is the central character who is murdered in the play, Murder in the Cathedral?*

# No. 39 Answers

**a1** Spinach
*b1* *Silver*
**a2** Air travel (International Air Transport Association)
*b2* *Holland*
**a3** Arthur Scargill
*b3* *Poland*
**a4** 'I Will Always Love You'
*b4* *George Michael and Andrew Ridgeley*
**a5** (Abstract) Sculpture
*b5* *Pianist*
**a6** Ian Fleming
*b6* *(Georges) Simenon*
**a7** James Callaghan
*b7* *(Clement) Atlee (in 1947)*
**a8** For riots (in which a policeman was killed) (It's a housing estate in North London)
*b8* *King's Cross*
**a9** Athletics (accept: track and field)
*b9* *Steffi Graf*
**a10** Istanbul
*b10* *Italy*
**a11** Falklands (East Falkland)
*b11* *Ayers Rock*
**a12** Salem (Massachusetts)
*b12* *Thomas à Becket, Becket of Canterbury*

---

## Tie-breaker

**Q** Which island became the focus of a 'missile crisis' in 1962?

**A** *Cuba*

---

# No. 40

**a1**  Which month of the year is the principal 'marching season' in Ulster?

*b1*  *What caused £1 billion damages in the City of London in 1993?*

**a2**  According to the First World War song, where was 'the sweetest girl I know'?

*b2*  *Which singer was called the 'Sweetheart of the Forces'?*

**a3**  From 1945, who was President of Yugoslavia?

*b3*  *Of which country was Jan (say: yan) Christiaan Smuts twice prime minister?*

**a4**  In which industry does BAFTA give awards?

*b4*  *A famous Hollywood film company uses the trade mark of a mountain peak surrounded by a circle of stars. What is the name of the company?*

**a5**  For which English county did Geoffrey Boycott play cricket?

*b5*  *The ice-skaters Torvill and Dean became famous for skating to which composer's 'Bolero'?*

**a6**  Of which English county is the Isle of Sheppey a part?

*b6*  *Which island has a law making council called the Tynwald?*

**a7**  Who wrote the play, *The Deep Blue Sea*?

*b7*  *Who wrote the long-running play,* The Mousetrap*?*

**a8**  On whom are Australians who live in the 'outback' of that country dependent for medical help?

*b8*  *What information does a pilot get from his altimeter?*

**a9**  Which two British political parties formed an alliance in 1981?

*b9*  *Which was regularly televised first, the House of Commons or the House of Lords?*

**a10**  Which major ship canal was completed in 1914?

*b10*  *Which major North American seaway or canal was opened in 1959?*

**a11**  Where does the European Court of Justice meet?

*b11*  *By what abbreviation is the International Criminal Police Commission usually known?*

**a12**  'Sonny' Ramphal was secretary-general of which organization from 1975 to 1990?

*b12*  *In which country was Dr Sakharov banished for his beliefs?*

# No. 40 Answers

**a1**   July
*b1*   *An IRA bomb*
**a2**   Tipperary
*b2*   *Vera Lynn*
**a3**   Tito
*b3*   *South Africa*
**a4**   Film and Television (British Academy of Film and Television Arts)
*b4*   *Paramount*
**a5**   Yorkshire
*b5*   *Ravel's*
**a6**   Kent
*b6*   *Isle of Man*
**a7**   Terence Rattigan
*b7*   *Agatha Christie*
**a8**   Flying doctors
*b8*   *His altitude or height, how high the plane is flying*
**a9**   Liberals, Social Democrats
*b9*   *House of Lords*
**a10**   Panama Canal
*b10*   *St Lawrence Seaway*
**a11**   The Hague (in the Netherlands) (accept: Den Haag)
*b11*   *Interpol*
**a12**   British Commonwealth
*b12*   *Soviet Union (Russia) (He was sent into 'internal exile')*

---

## Tie-breaker

**Q**   'In a while, crocodile' was an answer to what remark in a classic film and pop hit of the fifties?
**A**   *'See you later, alligator!'*

# No. 41 Hits from the Shows

In which musical does each of the following numbers occur?

**a1** 'On the Street Where You Live'
*b1* *'The Farmer and the Cowhand'*
**a2** 'We Said We Wouldn't Look Back'
*b2* *'Matchmaker, Matchmaker'*
**a3** 'Some Enchanted Evening'
*b3* *'Good Morning, Starshine'*
**a4** 'Day by Day'
*b4* *'Climb Every Mountain'*
**a5** 'I Could Be Happy With You'
*b5* *'Shall We Dance, Shall We Dance'*
**a6** 'One'
*b6* *'Flash! Bang! Wallop!'*
**a7** 'Luck be a Lady'
*b7* *'You've Got to Pick a Pocket or Two'*
**a8** 'If You Could See Her Through My Eyes'
*b8* *'There's No Business Like Show Business'*
**a9** 'Another Opening, Another Show'
*b9* *'Don't Cry for Me, Argentina'*
**a10** 'Tonight'
*b10* *'Shakin' at the High School Hop'*
**a11** 'You'll Never Walk Alone'
*b11* *'Let's Do a Deal'*
**a12** 'The Lambeth Walk'
*b12* *'Well Did You Evah'*

# No. 41 Answers

**a1** *My Fair Lady*
**b1** Oklahoma!
**a2** *Salad Days*
**b2** Fiddler on the Roof
**a3** *South Pacific*
**b3** Hair
**a4** *Godspell*
**b4** The Sound of Music
**a5** *The Boy Friend*
**b5** The King and I
**a6** *A Chorus Line*
**b6** Half a Sixpence
**a7** *Guys and Dolls*
**b7** Oliver!
**a8** *Cabaret*
**b8** Annie Get Your Gun
**a9** *Kiss Me Kate*
**b9** Evita
**a10** *West Side Story*
**b10** Grease
**a11** *Carousel*
**b11** Charlie Girl
**a12** *Me and My Girl*
**b12** High Society

---

## Tie-breaker

**Q**  Who composed the musicals *Brigadoon*, *The Day Before Spring* and *Paint Your Wagon*?

**A**  *Frederick Loewe*

---

# No. 42

**a1** Which All-England Judo champion won an Olympic Silver medal in 1980 and was World Champion in 1981?

***b1*** *In which sport did Evonne Cawley become famous?*

**a2** In the 1942 film *A Yank at Oxford*, who played the Yank?

***b2*** *Norma Jean Baker became a film star and starred in* The Seven Year Itch, Bus Stop *and* Some Like It Hot. *What was her screen name?*

**a3** Which nationwide university awarded its first degree in 1973?

***b3*** *What motoring safety device became compulsory in 1983?*

**a4** What is, or was, the Luftwaffe?

***b4*** *Which is the world's oldest air force?*

**a5** Who gave her name to the 1993 Camillagate scandal?

***b5*** *Whom did Princess Margaret marry in 1960?*

**a6** In which town did a car bomb kill 28 people in 1998?

***b6*** *Orgreave in South Yorkshire became widely known during which industrial dispute?*

**a7** In which English county are the Seven Sisters?

***b7*** *Which English county adjoins Cornwall?*

**a8** What did Jack Teagarden, Benny Goodman and Tommy Dorsey all have in common?

***b8*** *Which Rodgers and Hammerstein musical is set in the American West?*

**a9** What is army equivalent of the RAF rank of Marshal of the Royal Air Force?

***b9*** *What is the RAF equivalent of the army rank of colonel?*

**a10** What is the religion of most people in Afghanistan?

***b10*** *Though repressed by the Communists, what is the principal religion of Albania?*

**a11** Which writer is particularly associated with Ayot St Lawrence?

***b11*** *How did T E Lawrence (known as 'Lawrence of Arabia') die?*

**a12** On stage which pop star has been Jesus in *Godspell*, Che Guevara, and Lord Byron?

***b12*** *On stage, by what names are Dr Evadne and Dame Hilda better known?*

# No. 42 Answers

**a1**  Neil Adams
*b1*  *Tennis*
**a2**  Mickey Rooney
*b2*  *Marilyn Monroe*
**a3**  Open University
*b3*  *Seat belts (in front seats)*
**a4**  German airforce
*b4*  *Britain's Royal Air Force (founded 1918)*
**a5**  Camilla Parker-Bowles
*b5*  *Antony Armstrong-Jones (later he became the Earl of Snowdon)*
**a6**  Omagh
*b6*  *Miner's strike, 1984*
**a7**  (East) Sussex
*b7*  *Devon*
**a8**  Bandleaders (Big band, swing)
*b8*  *Oklahoma!*
**a9**  Field Marshal
*b9*  *Group Captain*
**a10**  Muslim (Islam)
*b10*  *Muslim (Islam)*
**a11**  G B Shaw
*b11*  *He was killed in a motorcycle accident*
**a12**  David Essex
*b12*  *Hinge and Bracket*

---

## Tie-breaker

**Q**  The Janata Party (or People's Front) is a political organization in which country?
**A**  *India*

---

# No. 43

**a1**  What is the capital of Finland?
***b1***  *Before the re-unification of Germany, what was the capital of West Germany?*
**a2**  In which country was there a secret police force called the KGB?
***b2***  *1981 saw the abolition of which means of execution in France?*
**a3**  'Just like that' was a catch phrase of which British comedian and conjuror?
***b3***  *Who originally became famous for his remark, 'You cannot be serious'?*
**a4**  In which English county is the town of Preston?
***b4***  *In which English county is the holiday resort, Hastings?*
**a5**  What had these in common: Michael Wilding, Mike Todd, Eddie Fisher and Richard Burton?
***b5***  *Fantasia, Dumbo and Pinocchio are all famous cartoon films. Which studio made them?*
**a6**  With which dance do you associate Bill Haley?
***b6***  *What kind of dance would you be most likely to do at a Hoe-down?*
**a7**  Eugene Terre Blanche has been an extreme right-wing leader in which country?
***b7***  *Of which country was Ferdinand Marcos president until 1986?*
**a8**  Steve Cram held the world record in which event?
***b8***  *Yachting: which country held the America's Cup from 1932 till 1983?*
**a9**  In 1958, the American submarine 'Nautilus' succeeded in crossing which ocean?
***b9***  *Which famous sailor is associated with the yacht, 'Gypsy Moth'?*
**a10**  Of which country has President Kaunda been the leader?
***b10***  *Of which country was Georges Pompidou formerly prime minister?*
**a11**  Which diminutive and very young Russian gymnast was a star of the 1972 Olympics?
***b11***  *For which country did Diego Maradona play soccer?*
**a12**  As what did Tommy Dorsey achieve fame?
***b12***  *As what has Judy Blume achieved fame?*

# No. 43 Answers

**a1**  Helsinki
**b1**  *Bonn*
**a2**  Soviet Union (Russia)
**b2**  *Guillotine*
**a3**  Tommy Cooper
**b3**  *John McEnroe*
**a4**  Lancashire
**b4**  *Sussex (East)*
**a5**  All were husbands of Elizabeth Taylor
**b5**  *Walt Disney*
**a6**  Rock 'n' roll
**b6**  *Square dancing*
**a7**  South Africa
**b7**  *Philippines*
**a8**  1,500 metres
**b8**  *United States of America*
**a9**  Arctic Ocean
**b9**  *Sir Francis Chichester*
**a10**  Zambia
**b10**  *France*
**a11**  Olga Korbut
**b11**  *Argentina*
**a12**  Bandleader (swing and jazz)
**b12**  *Novelist; author of novels for teenagers*

## Tie-breaker

**Q**  Which comedy group used to sing, 'Ying-tong-iddle-i-po'?
**A**  *The Goons (The Ying Tong Song)*

# No. 44

**a1**  On which English racecourse is the Derby run?
***b1***  *What ceremony takes place on Horse Guards Parade on the Sovereign's Official Birthday?*
**a2**  What was the Black Bottom?
***b2***  *In dance, what do you do when you pirouette?*
**a3**  In the original film, who played Dr Dolittle?
***b3***  *In which film did Baloo sing about the bare necessities of life?*
**a4**  By what name are 'Las Malvinas' islands known in Britain?
***b4***  *Las Palmas and Santa Cruz de Tenerife are the two main groups of which islands?*
**a5**  In 1937, which airship burst into flames when mooring near New York?
***b5***  *Which two countries jointly developed the aircraft Concorde?*
**a6**  Which prime minister was assassinated by her own body-guard in 1984?
***b6***  *Yasser Arafat became a leader of which people?*
**a7**  Hyde Park and Regent's Park both saw bomb explosions on the same day in 1982. Which organization was responsible?
***b7***  *Where, in Britain, did a Trident airliner crash in June 1972, killing 118 people?*
**a8**  Who was prime minister of Great Britain at the time of Edward VIII's abdication?
***b8***  *Of which British political party was Arthur Balfour a leader?*
**a9**  'Economical with the truth' became a diplomatic expression for ... what?
***b9***  *Former MI5 officer Peter Wright wrote a book which was headline news in 1987. What was its title?*
**a10**  What tragedy at Bhopal in India killed at least 2,000 people in 1984?
***b10***  *In which Indian city is the Sikh holy shrine, the Golden Temple?*
**a11**  In which radio show did we hear the catch phrase, 'Give him the money, Barney!'?
***b11***  *Which entertainer was associated with the phrase, 'Here's to the next time'?*
**a12**  In which art did Bertolt Brecht become famous?
***b12***  *As what did Philip Larkin (1922–85) achieve fame?*

# No. 44 Answers

**a1** Epsom
*b1* *Trooping of the Colour*
**a2** A dance (type of foxtrot)
*b2* *Turn/spin round on one leg*
**a3** Rex Harrison
*b3* The Jungle Book
**a4** The Falkland Islands
*b4* *Canary Islands*
**a5** The Hindenburg
*b5* *Britain and France*
**a6** Mrs Indira Gandhi (India)
*b6* *The Palestinians*
**a7** IRA
*b7* *Near Heathrow (accept: near Staines)*
**a8** Stanley Baldwin
*b8* *Conservative*
**a9** Lying, evading saying the truth
*b9* *Spycatcher*
**a10** Leak from a chemical factory, a gas leak
*b10* *Amritsar*
**a11** *Have a Go*
*b11* *Henry Hall*
**a12** Theatre
*b12* *Poet*

---

## Tie-breaker

**Q**  Which is the world's longest road tunnel?
*A*  *St Gotthard Road Tunnel (southern Alps, in Switzerland)*

---

# No. 45

**a1**   Which disc jockey used the catch phrase, 'How's about that then, guys and gals'?

*b1*   *Which DJ's catchphase is 'Not arff'?*

**a2**   Which minister had an affair with Sarah Keays?

*b2*   *From which cabinet post was Norman Lamont sacked in 1993?*

**a3**   Which brothers starred in the film, *A Night at the Opera*?

*b3*   *Who was the star of the first successful talking feature film?*

**a4**   Until abolished in 1986, what was the GLC?

*b4*   *In which metropolitan area are Tameside, Trafford and Wigan?*

**a5**   In which country is the sea-port of Antwerp?

*b5*   *Which sea-port do sailors nickname 'Pompey'?*

**a6**   How did Chris Bonington become well-known in the sixties and seventies?

*b6*   *In which art has Peter O'Toole achieved fame?*

**a7**   Of which island is Honolulu the capital?

*b7*   *Which capital city is on Honshu island?*

**a8**   After the assassination of her husband, Cory Aquino became a political leader of which country?

*b8*   *Joshua Nkomo unsuccessfully aimed to become leader of which African nation when it became independent?*

**a9**   Which cricketer had a highest score of 452 not out – and made a duck in his last Test innings as captain of Australia?

*b9*   *In swimming, who won seven gold medals at the Munich Olympics in 1972?*

**a10**   Of which country was Jack Lynch the prime minister?

*b10*   *Of which country was Sir Keith Holyoake prime minister?*

**a11**   In which year was the first motorway opened in Britain: 1951, 1959 or 1963?

*b11*   *In which year did commercial television begin in Britain: 1947, 1953 or 1955?*

**a12**   Who wrote the novel, *The Hobbit*?

*b12*   *Under which pen-name did Eric Blair write?*

# No. 45 Answers

**a1**  Jimmy Savile
*b1*  *Alan Freeman*
**a2**  Cecil Parkinson
*b2*  *Chancellor of the Exchequer*
**a3**  Marx Brothers
*b3*  *Al Jolson*
**a4**  Greater London Council
*b4*  *(Greater) Manchester*
**a5**  Belgium
*b5*  *Portsmouth*
**a6**  As a mountaineer
*b6*  *Acting*
**a7**  Hawaii
*b7*  *Tokyo*
**a8**  Philippines
*b8*  *Zimbabwe (formerly Rhodesia)*
**a9**  Donald Bradman
*b9*  *Mark Spitz*
**a10**  Eire; Ireland
*b10*  *New Zealand*
**a11**  1959
*b11*  *1955*
**a12**  J R R Tolkien
*b12*  *George Orwell*

## Tie-breaker

**Q**  Who is this film director? 'When I was a boy, I borrowed my father's ciné camera to film toy trains. By the age of 21, I was directing television series – including *Columbo*. I've made a "purplish" story about racial conflict, and "lost" an ark.'

**A**  *Steven Spielberg*

# No. 46

**a1** Which television presenter was famous for saying, 'Hello, good evening and welcome'?

*b1* *Which comedian committed suicide in a Sydney hotel in 1968?*

**a2** Of which country is the island of Zealand a part?

*b2* *To which country does the island of Corfu belong?*

**a3** For which art did Maria Callas become famous?

*b3* *Born Peggy Hookham, she became a famous ballerina, partnering Rudolf Nureyev. What was her stage name?*

**a4** Which important bridge, east of London, was opened in 1991?

*b4* *Roughly, in which direction from the Midlands does the M6 go?*

**a5** Who was King of Great Britain from 1901 to 1910?

*b5* *And who was King from 1910 to 1936?*

**a6** Which continent has the longest coastline: Africa or Europe?

*b6* *Which is the largest country in South America?*

**a7** Which film star made famous the expression, 'Come up and see me sometime'?

*b7* *Which star appeared in the films* The Graduate *and (in drag) in* Tootsie?

**a8** Which great house in Derbyshire is sometimes called 'The Palace of the Peak'?

*b8* *In which county is Wookey Hole?*

**a9** Who composed the music for *West Side Story*?

*b9* *Who composed the music for the musical* Starlight Express?

**a10** What was the name of the original trophy in soccer's World Cup?

*b10* *In 1990 England lost in the semi-finals of the World Cup on penalties. Who were they playing?*

**a11** Which American president became famous for his election slogan, 'Read my lips: no new taxes'?

*b11* *Which president had a sign on his desk saying, 'The buck stops here'?*

**a12** 'Papa Doc' and 'Baby Doc' were both hated dictators in which country?

*b12* *Enver Hoxha (say: hodja) was head of state of which country?*

# No. 46 Answers

**a1** David Frost
*b1* *Tony Hancock*
**a2** Denmark
*b2* *Greece*
**a3** Opera (singing)
*b3* *Margot Fonteyn*
**a4** The Queen Elizabeth II Bridge (or Dartford Bridge)
*b4* *Northwards*
**a5** Edward VII
*b5* *George V*
**a6** Europe
*b6* *Brazil*
**a7** Mae West
*b7* *Dustin Hoffman*
**a8** Chatsworth House
*b8* *Somerset*
**a9** Leonard Bernstein
*b9* *Andrew Lloyd Webber*
**a10** Jules Rimet Trophy
*b10* *Germany*
**a11** George Bush
*b11* *Harry S Truman*
**a12** Haiti
*b12* *Albania*

## Tie-breaker

**Q** Robert Bolt's play *A Man for All Seasons* is about Sir Thomas More and which English King?
**A** *King Henry VIII*

# No. 47

**a1**  What is the capital of Norway?
*b1*  *Name the capital of Denmark.*
**a2**  Which of the Marx brothers had a cigar and moustache?
*b2*  *Which director of suspense movies always made a brief appearance in each of his films?*
**a3**  Who led the winning side in the Spanish Civil War?
*b3*  *Who invaded Cuba in 1956 and later turned the country into a Communist state?*
**a4**  Which former deputy chairman of the British Conservative party has also been a very successful novelist?
*b4*  *The Moon's a Balloon was the autobiography of which debonair actor?*
**a5**  President Theodore Roosevelt's distant cousin also became president of the United States. What was his name?
*b5*  *Who was President Franklin D Roosevelt's wife?*
**a6**  Soccer: Who won the World Cup in 1966?
*b6*  *And who was the English goalkeeper in that match?*
**a7**  Which Polish political movement was led by Lech Walesa? (say: wa-len-sa)
*b7*  *In which country were there rebels known as the 'Contras'?*
**a8**  Name one of the three Baltic states which were independent between 1920 and 1940 and again from 1991?
*b8*  *Can you name a European country which came into being at the end of the First World War?*
**a9**  Thelonius Monk became famous as what sort of musician?
*b9*  *Which English composer became famous for many film scores and for his suite called 'Façade'?*
**a10**  Kenneth Clark became famous for a major cultural television series. What was it called?
*b10*  *On BBC television, who played Smiley in Smiley's People?*
**a11**  With which country did Tanganyika form Tanzania?
*b11*  *By what name (beginning with 'B') is the former African country of Bechuanaland now known?*
**a12**  Which male dancer starred in *L'Après-midi d'un faun*?
*b12*  *Which female dancer founded the Royal Ballet (originally the Sadler's Wells Ballet)?*

# No. 47 Answers

**a1**    Oslo
*b1*    *Copenhagen*
**a2**    Groucho
*b2*    *Alfred Hitchcock*
**a3**    General Franco
*b3*    *Fidel Castro*
**a4**    Jeffrey Archer
*b4*    *David Niven*
**a5**    Franklin D Roosevelt
*b5*    *Eleanor*
**a6**    England
*b6*    *Gordon Banks*
**a7**    Solidarity
*b7*    *Nicaragua*
**a8**    Estonia, Latvia, Lithuania
*b8*    *Yugoslavia, Czechoslovakia*
**a9**    Jazz (pianist)
*b9*    *William Walton*
**a10**    *Civilisation*
*b10*    *Alec Guinness*
**a11**    Zanzibar
*b11*    *Botswana*
**a12**    Nijinsky
*b12*    *(Dame) Ninette de Valois*

## Tie-breaker

**Q**    Along which frontier were SWAPO forces active in the seventies?

**A**    *Angola–Namibia*

# No. 48

**a1** Who hosted television's *Strike It Lucky*?
*b1* *Who returned to present* The Generation Game *in 1991?*
**a2** By what name has East Pakistan been known since 1971?
*b2* *What was the former name of Sri Lanka?*
**a3** With whom do we associate the phrase, 'Here's looking at you, kid'?
*b3* *Which television detective is associated with the catch phrase, 'Who loves you, baby'?*
**a4** In which mountain range is the Eiger?
*b4* *What do we call the range of hills which forms the border between England and Scotland?*
**a5** At which stadium in Belgium was there a football tragedy in 1985?
*b5* *In 1991 which country hosted the first women's football World Cup: a) China, b) Italy, c) Brazil?*
**a6** On television, on which sport did Kent Walton commentate?
*b6* *And on which sport did Dan Maskell commentate?*
**a7** Which American leader is famous for a speech which included the words, 'I have a dream'?
*b7* *Whose election campaign slogan was 'I like Ike'?*
**a8** In the world of cinema, what is a 'spaghetti' western?
*b8* *About what activity was the film* Pumping Iron?
**a9** Menachem Begin was prime minister of which country?
*b9* *General Jaruzelski was formerly leader of which country?*
**a10** Who composed many popular musicals and the song, 'Keep the Home Fires Burning'?
*b10* *Who wrote the music which goes with the words, 'Land of Hope and Glory'?*
**a11** In which English city is the Jorvik Viking Centre?
*b11* *What was discovered at Sutton Hoo in Suffolk in 1939?*
**a12** Beside being a Conservative, to which other political party did Winston Churchill belong during his life?
*b12* *Which Labour minister inaugurated the National Health Service?*

# No. 48 Answers

**a1** Michael Barrymore
*b1* *Bruce Forsyth*
**a2** Bangladesh
*b2* *Ceylon*
**a3** Humphrey Bogart
*b3* *Kojak (Telly Savalas)*
**a4** Alps
*b4* *The Cheviots*
**a5** Heysel Stadium, Brussels
*b5* *China*
**a6** Wrestling commentaries
*b6* *Tennis*
**a7** Martin Luther King
*b7* *Dwight D Eisenhower (USA, 1952)*
**a8** A western or cowboy film made outside America (possibly in Italy or Spain)
*b8* *Body-building*
**a9** Israel
*b9* *Poland*
**a10** Ivor Novello
*b10* *Elgar (Sir Edward)*
**a11** York
*b11* *The remains of an Anglo-Saxon ship*
**a12** Liberal
*b12* *Aneurin Bevan*

## Tie-breaker

**Q** Which British architect designed the Stansted Airport?
*A* *Norman Foster*

# No. 49

**a1**  Which television show has featured the Gotcha Oscar and the Gung Tank?

*b1*  *On television, what was Arthur Daley's supposed main job?*

**a2**  In which ocean is the so-called Bermuda Triangle?

*b2*  *What kind of vessel is a U-Boat?*

**a3**  Who played Lawrence in the film, *Lawrence of Arabia*?

*b3*  *In which film did Orson Welles play Harry Lime?*

**a4**  In which country is the Nullarbor Plain?

*b4*  *In which country would you find the veldt?*

**a5**  Pipe, steel, wind and brass are all types of ... what?

*b5*  *C60, C90 and C120 are all types of ... what?*

**a6**  Yuri Andropov became president of which country in 1982?

*b6*  *Who became chancellor of West Germany in 1982?*

**a7**  Which English cathedral was set on fire by a bolt of lightning in 1984?

*b7*  *Which English cathedral was rebuilt after the Second World War as a sign of reconciliation with Germany?*

**a8**  Which Democrat did Ronald Reagan defeat to become president in 1980?

*b8*  *Which American president resigned because of the Watergate scandal in 1974?*

**a9**  In 1997 Linford Christie ran his final race for Britain. Was he 37, 35 or 32?

*b9*  *19 wickets were taken by one bowler in a 1956 cricket test match. Who was he?*

**a10**  'The Gang of Four' formed the new Social Democrat party in 1981. To which party did they formerly belong?

*b10*  *Which Welsh statesman started an old age pension scheme and became prime minister in 1916?*

**a11**  Who was the lead singer with Madness?

*b11*  *Which eighties band was fronted by Paul King?*

**a12**  Who led the Indian National Congress party for 20 years prior to Indian independence?

*b12*  *Who was the King's viceroy (or representative) in India at the time of independence?*

# No. 49 Answers

**a1**   *Noel's Houseparty*
**b1**   *Second-hand car dealer*
**a2**   (North) Atlantic
**b2**   *Submarine (in German: Unter-see Boot, or under-sea boat)*
**a3**   Peter O'Toole
**b3**   The Third Man
**a4**   Australia
**b4**   *South Africa*
**a5**   Bands
**b5**   *Cassette tapes*
**a6**   Soviet Union
**b6**   *Helmut Kohl*
**a7**   York Minster
**b7**   *Coventry*
**a8**   Jimmy Carter
**b8**   *Richard Nixon*
**a9**   37
**b9**   *(Jim) Laker*
**a10**   Labour
**b10**   *Lloyd George*
**a11**   Suggs
**b11**   *King!*
**a12**   Mahatma Gandhi
**b12**   *Louis Mountbatten (later: Earl Mountbatten of Burma)*

---

## Tie-breaker

**Q**   Which poet wrote about the Old Vicarage, Granchester?
**A**   *Rupert Brooke*

---

**a1** What is the official national anthem of the USA?

*b1* *Which singer is particularly associated with the song, 'Ol' Man River'?*

**a2** If G is the postcode for Glasgow, which city is indicated by the initial letter M?

*b2* *And by the letter B?*

**a3** Which town has the code IP?

*b3* *And which has the code PL?*

**a4** Who was Richard Burton's co-star in the film *Cleopatra*?

*b4* *Who co-stars with Meryl Streep in the film,* The French Lieutenant's Woman?

**a5** Mysore, Hyderabad and Madras are all parts of which country?

*b5* *The Polish port of Gdansk (say: gu-dansk) was formerly known by what name in Britain?*

**a6** Dr Garrett Fitzgerald was prime minister of which country?

*b6* *Of which country was Dr Kurt Waldheim president?*

**a7** Daniel Kaminski played Walter Mitty and Hans Andersen on screen. What was his 'stage' name?

*b7* *She was a musical comedy star, starred in* Wake Up and Dream *and later played Mrs Dale on BBC Radio. Who was she?*

**a8** In 1985, there was a tragic fire at an English football ground. Which ground?

*b8* *For which World Cup team did Eusebio play?*

**a9** Who was the drummer in the group The Who?

*b9* *Who developed a chain of shops specializing in fabrics and dresses which became known around the world?*

**a10** Can you name a country (besides Britain) which joined the Common Market in 1973?

*b10* *In which year was Winston Churchill first elected to parliament?*

**a11** Who wrote the novel, *Catcher in the Rye*?

*b11* *Who wrote the novel,* To Kill a Mocking Bird?

**a12** In which radio programme did we hear the catch phrase: 'And the next object is...'?

*b12* *In which radio programme did we hear the catch phrase: 'After you Claude; No, after you, Cecil!'*

# No. 50 Answers

**a1** 'The Star Spangled Banner'
*b1* *Paul Robeson*
**a2** Manchester
*b2* *Birmingham*
**a3** Ipswich
*b3* *Plymouth*
**a4** Elizabeth Taylor
*b4* *Jeremy Irons*
**a5** India
*b5* *Danzig*
**a6** Ireland (Eire)
*b6* *Austria*
**a7** Danny Kaye
*b7* *Jessie Matthews*
**a8** Bradford
*b8* *Portugal*
**a9** Keith Moon
*b9* *Laura Ashley*
**a10** Denmark; Irish Republic
*b10* *1900*
**a11** J D Salinger
*b11* *Harper Lee*
**a12** *Twenty Questions*
*b12* ITMA

---

## Tie-breaker

**Q** In London, which underground line was once known as the 'Tuppenny Tube'?

**A** *Central Line (Central Railway)*

---

# No. 51: One Language, Two Nations

It has often been said that America and Britain are two nations separated by a common language – because, of course, words mean different things in the two countries.
What is the British equivalent of the following?

**a1** Apartment
*b1* Bill
**a2** Cuffs
*b2* Diaper
**a3** Collect call
*b3* Caravan
**a4** Rubber
*b4* A game of checkers
**a5** Back-up lights (on a car)
*b5* Odometer
**a6** Barette
*b6* Comforter

And what is the American equivalent of these British words?

**a7** Wallet
*b7* (Policeman's) truncheon
**a8** Tap
*b8* Spanner
**a9** Post code
*b9* Pelmet
**a10** Lay-by
*b10* Goose pimples
**a11** Estate car
*b11* Caretaker
**a12** Courgettes
*b12* Aubergine

# No. 51 Answers

| | |
|---|---|
| **a1** | Flat |
| **b1** | *Banknote* |
| **a2** | Turn-ups |
| **b2** | *Nappy* |
| **a3** | Reverse charge call |
| **b3** | *Trailer* |
| **a4** | Contraceptive, condom |
| **b4** | *A game of draughts* |
| **a5** | Reversing lights |
| **b5** | *Mileometer* |
| **a6** | Hair slide |
| **b6** | *Eiderdown (accept: duvet)* |
| **a7** | Billfold |
| **b7** | *Night stick* |
| **a8** | Faucet |
| **b8** | *Monkey wrench* |
| **a9** | Zip code |
| **b9** | *Valence* |
| **a10** | Pull-off |
| **b10** | *Goose bumps* |
| **a11** | Station wagon |
| **b11** | *Janitor* |
| **a12** | Zucchini |
| **b12** | *Eggplant* |

## Tie-breaker

**Q** What was the purpose of 'Callanetics'?
**A** *To build up muscles, to develop muscle tone (through exercise)*

# No. 52

**a1**   In which trade did Lovejoy operate?

**b1**   *Who is the chief presenter of* The Antiques Roadshow?

**a2**   In which domestic product are you likely to find enzymes?

**b2**   *Besides tomatoes and meat, from what is tinned ravioli principally made?*

**a3**   Which south London exhibition centre burned down in 1936?

**b3**   *Whereabouts in London are the Crown Jewels now kept?*

**a4**   Which instrument did the jazz musicians Art Tatum and Earl Hines both play?

**b4**   *Which instrument did the jazz musician Dizzy Gillespie play?*

**a5**   Which radio sports commentator later became his country's leader?

**b5**   *Of which American state was Ronald Reagan once governor?*

**a6**   In which film did Bing Crosby first sing, 'White Christmas'?

**b6**   *Who was the Swedish star of the films* Queen Christina *and* Anna Karenina?

**a7**   Basrah is a port in which country?

**b7**   *In which country is the port of Aqaba?*

**a8**   Mrs Bandaranaike was prime minister of which island?

**b8**   *Before becoming involved in politics, what was Rajiv Gandhi's profession?*

**a9**   'Who shot J R?' To which television series did that question apply?

**b9**   *Which television private eye was played by Tom Selleck?*

**a10**   In which sport do the Kansas City Wizards play Chicago Fire?

**b10**   *Is volleyball played in 47, 89 or 157 affiliated countries?*

**a11**   In which two cities or towns does the European parliament meet?

**b11**   *Which European 'Act' allows the free movement of money, goods and people within the EC?*

**a12**   Which female novelist wrote *The Pursuit of Love* and *Love in a Cold Climate*?

**b12**   *Which Russian author wrote* The Gulag Archipelago?

# No. 52 Answers

**a1** Antiques
*b1* *Michael Aspel*
**a2** Detergent
*b2* *Semolina* (or wheat)
**a3** Crystal Palace
*b3* *Tower of London*
**a4** Piano
*b4* *Trumpet*
**a5** Ronald Reagan
*b5* *California*
**a6** *Holiday Inn*
*b6* *Greta Garbo*
**a7** Iraq
*b7* *Jordan*
**a8** Sri Lanka (formerly Ceylon)
*b8* *Airline pilot*
**a9** *Dallas*
*b9* Magnum
**a10** Soccer
*b10* *157*
**a11** Strasbourg (France) and Luxembourg
**a12** Nancy Mitford
*b12* *Alexander Solzhenitsyn*

## Tie-breaker

**Q** *The Seventh Seal, Wild Strawberries* and *Smiles of a Summer Night* were all made by which Swedish film director?
**A** *Ingmar Bergman*

# No. 53

**a1** What sort of animals were Chi-Chi and An-An?
*b1* *What are tigons and ligers?*
**a2** Romanies and Diddikois are both names for which people?
*b2* *From which country do 'Hispanic' people originate?*
**a3** In Greece, what kind of food is moussaka?
*b3* *And what kind of drink is Retsina?*
**a4** Which couple became famous for their dancing in the films *Top Hat* and *Swing Time*?
*b4* *In the film,* The Wizard of Oz, *who sang 'Over the Rainbow'?*
**a5** Which part of a car's engine mixes petrol and air in the right proportions?
*b5* *Which device in a car's engine drives the water pump and the alternator?*
**a6** Which of the Queen's cousins was killed by the IRA in 1979?
*b6* *Roddy Llewellyn was a close friend of which royal princess?*
**a7** On board ship, what is the purpose of a gyroscope?
*b7* *Which means of transport went into public use in 1965 (between the English mainland and the Isle of Wight)?*
**a8** Bavaria and Saxony are both states within which country?
*b8* *In which country is the original Legoland theme park?*
**a9** Which famous production trio was the background team behind many popular music hits in the late eighties?
*b9* *What was the first name and surname of Art Garfunkel's partner in a folk-rock duo in the sixties and seventies?*
**a10** Who founded the Vietnamese communist party and became president of North Vietnam?
*b10* *Who became president of Nationalist China on the island of Taiwan in 1949?*
**a11** At which English football ground was there a major disaster in 1989, involving Liverpool fans?
*b11* *In which country were the finals of the 1982 soccer World Cup?*
**a12** In Government, what is the job of the 'legislature'?
*b12* *And what do we call the part of the Government that puts the laws into effect?*

# No. 53 Answers

**a1** (Giant) pandas
*b1* *Hybrid tigers/lions, cross-bred lions and tigers*
**a2** Travelling people (gypsies)
*b2* *Spain or Portugal*
**a3** Baked aubergines and minced meat
*b3* *Wine (flavoured with pine resin)*
**a4** Fred Astaire and Ginger Rogers
*b4* *Judy Garland*
**a5** Carburettor
*b5* *Fan belt*
**a6** Earl Mountbatten (of Burma)
*b6* *Princess Margaret*
**a7** Either to improve the ship's stability (it counteracts the ship's movement) or to help the process of navigation (gyroscopic compass)
*b7* *Hovercraft*
**a8** Germany
*b8* *Denmark*
**a9** Stock, Aitken and Waterman
*b9* *Paul Simon*
**a10** Ho Chi Minh
*b10* *Chiang Kai-Shek (Also known as: Jiang Jieshi)*
**a11** Hillsborough (Sheffield Wednesday ground)
*b11* *Spain*
**a12** The passing of new laws
*b12* *The executive (accept: the Cabinet or civil servants or Whitehall)*

---

## Tie-breaker

**Q** Was Britain's first black mayor (John Archer, in Battersea) elected in 1913, 1963 or 1973?
**A** *1913*

---

# No. 54

**a1** On television, who became famous for his Madhouse?

*b1* *In which television hotel did a waiter come from 'Bar-th-elona'?*

**a2** In which Italian cathedral is there a shroud thought by some to show the face of Christ?

*b2* *What was the popular name of the special vehicle in which Pope John Paul II often toured the cities he visited?*

**a3** Which sport was revolutionized by Kerry Packer?

*b3* *Robin Cousins was a 1980 Olympic star in which sport?*

**a4** As what did the Italian Tito Gobbi become famous?

*b4* *In which profession did the Frenchman François Truffaut achieve fame?*

**a5** The invasion of which country in 1990 brought about the Gulf War?

*b5* *Which general commanded American forces in the Gulf War?*

**a6** What form of transport was the Sinclair C5?

*b6* *With which industry is the name Pilkington associated?*

**a7** In which capital city was the 1916 Easter Rising?

*b7* *Which European country conquered Ethiopia in 1936?*

**a8** In France, to what do the initials TGV refer?

*b8* *Before nationalization, which railway company ran the Cornish Riviera Express?*

**a9** What was the Alexander Kielland?

*b9* *Off what country's coast did the oil tanker Amoco Cadiz go aground and break up in 1978?*

**a10** Which young star became a teen idol with his film *Rebel without a Cause*, released after his death in a car crash?

*b10* *What film role has been played by (among others) Sean Connery, George Lazenby and Roger Moore?*

**a11** In 1960, who became president of Ghana?

*b11* *Of which country was Julius Nyerere the first president?*

**a12** Which system of medicine was plants and minerals in very small quantities, and treats 'like with like'?

*b12* *What name is given to the medical condition in which old people suffer from a dangerous loss of body heat?*

# No. 54 Answers

**a1**   Russ Abbot
*b1*   *Fawlty Towers*
**a2**   Turin
*b2*   *Pope-mobile*
**a3**   Cricket
*b3*   *Ice-skating*
**a4**   Singer, opera singer
*b4*   *Film direction*
**a5**   Kuwait
*b5*   *General Schwarzkopf*
**a6**   Electric tricycle (very small)
*b6*   *Glass-making*
**a7**   Dublin
*b7*   *Italy*
**a8**   High-speed trains (*Trains Grande Vitesse*)
*b8*   *Great Western (GWR)*
**a9**   A (North Sea) oil platform (used as a 'hotel' for oil workers)
*b9*   *France (Brittany)*
**a10**   James Dean
*b10*   *James Bond (007)*
**a11**   (Kwame) Nkrumah
*b11*   *Tanganyika and/or Tanzania (he was president of both)*
**a12**   Homoeopathic medicine
*b12*   *Hypothermia*

---

## Tie-breaker

**Q**   'Highway 61 Revisited' and 'Blood on the Tracks' were both albums released by which popular singer?
**A**   Bob Dylan

# No. 55

**a1**  What was the Holocaust?

*b1*  *On which Japanese city was the second atomic bomb dropped?*

**a2**  Which ventriloquist do you associate with the dummy Archie Andrews?

*b2*  *And which dummy do you associate with Ray Alan?*

**a3**  Who became Duke of Windsor in 1936?

*b3*  *Who was our present Queen's father?*

**a4**  In which London embassy was there a six-day siege in 1980?

*b4*  *In which building did Prince Charles marry Lady Diana Spencer?*

**a5**  Before invading the Falklands, which other British island was invaded by the Argentineans in 1982?

*b5*  *In 1963, which island was volcanically created off Iceland?*

**a6**  Mary-Lou Retton (USA) became a wealthy woman. What was her sport?

*b6*  *Jason Robinson has played two sports professionally. For which is he better known?*

**a7**  By what name did the illegal use of private knowledge on the Stock Exchange come to be known?

*b7*  *Which country produces three-quarters of the world's gold?*

**a8**  In 1979, the Queen's art adviser was named as a Russian spy. What was his name?

*b8*  *A Turkish gunman shot a religious leader in May 1981. Who was the victim?*

**a9**  Who was the American president during the First World War?

*b9*  *Which American president represented his country at the Yalta conference (at the end of the Second World War)?*

**a10**  A father and daughter appeared together in the film *On Golden Pond*. What was their surname?

*b10*  *The uncovering of which political scandal is described in the film,* All the President's Men*?*

**a11**  In 1952, which was the first jet airliner to enter passenger service?

*b11*  *Exactly what type of fuel do jet aircraft engines use?*

**a12**  Shahpur Bakhtiar was appointed prime minister of Iran under which regime?

*b12*  *In which country did the Khmer Rouge exercise power?*

# No. 55 Answers

**a1** The systematic destruction of Jewish people by the Nazis in the Second World War
***b1*** *Nagasaki*
**a2** Peter Brough
***b2*** *Lord Charles*
**a3** Edward VIII
***b3*** *George VI*
**a4** Iranian
***b4*** *St Paul's Cathedral*
**a5** South Georgia
***b5*** *Surtsey*
**a6** Gymnastics
***b6*** *Rugby league*
**a7** Insider trading (accept: insider dealing)
***b7*** *South Africa*
**a8** Sir Anthony Blunt
***b8*** *Pope John Paul II*
**a9** Woodrow Wilson
***b9*** *(Franklin D) Roosevelt*
**a10** Fonda (Henry and Jane)
***b10*** *Watergate*
**a11** The Comet (the de Haviland Comet)
***b11*** *Kerosene (a type of paraffin)*
**a12** Under the last Shah of Persia/Iran
***b12*** *Cambodia (Kampuchea)*

---

## Tie-breaker

**Q** From which musical do the songs 'What's the Use of Wond'rin?' and 'June Is Bustin' Out All Over' come?

**A** *Carousel*

---

# No. 56

**a1**  Which comedian had the catch phrase, 'Shut that door'?
*b1*  *Whose catch phrase was 'I'm free'?*
**a2**  Which poisonous metal is used in sheets or tiles to make waterproof roofs?
*b2*  *Which rare, radioactive metal is used to provide energy in nuclear reactors?*
**a3**  For what was Sir Cecil Beaton principally famous?
*b3*  *For what was Sir Thomas Beecham famous?*
**a4**  According to the film title, which was the 'Longest Day'?
*b4*  *About which battle is the film, A Bridge Too Far?*
**a5**  In judo, what colour belt denotes a beginner?
*b5*  *Which Eastern martial art is called by a word which means, literally, 'open hands'?*
**a6**  Which television series was named after American mobile army surgical hospitals?
*b6*  *On television, who played Sergeant Bilko?*
**a7**  Which saint did Mrs Thatcher quote on first entering Downing Street as prime minister?
*b7*  *Which Tory MP was killed by a car bomb when driving out of the House of Commons car park?*
**a8**  Which city in the world has the largest population?
*b8*  *The USA invaded which British colony in 1983?*
**a9**  Of which Caribbean island was Marcus Garvey a political leader?
*b9*  *Who became prime minister of Zimbabwe in 1980?*
**a10**  What sort of picture is a hologram?
*b10*  *What are polygraphs sometimes used to reveal?*
**a11**  Two Jumbo jets collided on the ground in 1977 to create the worst tragedy in aviation history. On which holiday islands did it occur?
*b11*  *Also in 1977, Archbishop Luwum was killed in mysterious circumstances. In which country?*
**a12**  Who wrote the novel, *Lolita*?
*b12*  *Who wrote the novels* Tropic of Cancer *and* Tropic of Capricorn?

# No. 56 Answers

**a1**  Larry Grayson
*b1*  *John Inman (as Mr Humphries in* Are You Being Served?)
**a2**  Lead
*b2*  *Uranium*
**a3**  Photography (of glamorous people), also stage and film design
*b3*  *Conductor; music*
**a4**  D-Day (June 6th 1944)
*b4*  *Arnhem*
**a5**  White
*b5*  *Karate*
**a6**  M*A*S*H
*b6*  *Phil Silvers*
**a7**  St Francis ('Where there is discord may we bring harmony ...')
*b7*  *Airey Neave*
**a8**  Mexico City
*b8*  *Grenada*
**a9**  Jamaica
*b9*  *Robert Mugabe (say: mu-gah-bay)*
**a10**  A three-dimensional one (accept: one that is projected)
*b10*  *Whether someone is lying*
**a11**  Canary Islands
*b11*  *Uganda*
**a12**  Vladimir Nabokov
*b12*  *Henry Miller*

---

## Tie-breaker

**Q**  Which is the largest library in the world?
*A*  *The library of Congress, Washington DC*

# No. 57

**a1** Tortillas are part of the staple diet of which country?
*b1* *What is sold in the pâtisserie?*
**a2** In a film title, which rabbit was 'framed'?
*b2* *What were Jespa, Gopa and Little Elsa?*
**a3** Name the two men who star in the film *Butch Cassidy and the Sundance Kid.*
*b3* *His real name was William Pratt, but by what name did he become famous for playing Frankenstein?*
**a4** In 1923, who married Lady Elizabeth Bowes-Lyon?
*b4* *Which royal prince was born in April 1964?*
**a5** Johan Cruyff (say: yo-han kroyff) played soccer for which country?
*b5* *Ajax is the name of a football team – in which Dutch city?*
**a6** Between which two countries is the tiny principality of Liechtenstein?
*b6* *On the borders of which two countries are the Golan Heights?*
**a7** Which actor played the television detective, Ironside?
*b7* *Which actor played the television detective, Columbo?*
**a8** Which republic's parliament consists of the Senate and the Dail? (say: doyle)
*b8* *To what did the Ecology Party change its name in the mid eighties?*
**a9** Were the first old age pensions in Britain paid out in 1909, 1919 or 1945?
*b9* *In which year did adoption become legal in Britain? Was it 1901, 1926 or 1947?*
**a10** Where does the International Court of Justice sit?
*b10* *Where does the European Court of Justice sit?*
**a11** For what particular reason did the artist Tom Keating become well known?
*b11* *Who gave orders for Graham Sutherland's controversial portrait of Winston Churchill to be destroyed?*
**a12** The black African leader Albert John Luthuli is famous for his autobiography. What is it called?
*b12* *Which French left-wing thinker and author wrote a work called* Being and Nothingness?

# No. 57 Answers

**a1**   Mexico
*b1*   *Cakes*
**a2**   Roger (*Who Framed Roger Rabbit?*)
*b2*   *Lion cubs (in* Born Free *by Joy Adamson)*
**a3**   Paul Newman and Robert Redford
*b3*   *Boris Karloff*
**a4**   The Duke of York, later King George VI
*b4*   *Edward*
**a5**   Holland (the Netherlands)
*b5*   *Amsterdam*
**a6**   Switzerland and Austria
*b6*   *Israel and Syria*
**a7**   Raymond Burr
*b7*   *Peter Falk*
**a8**   Irish
*b8*   *The Green Party*
**a9**   1909
*b9*   *1926*
**a10**   The Hague (in the Netherlands)
*b10*   *Luxembourg*
**a11**   Forging or copying old masters
*b11*   *Lady Churchill*
**a12**   *Let My People Go*
*b12*   *Jean-Paul Sartre*

---

## Tie-breaker

**Q**   Which English artist is known for both a painting and a film called *A Bigger Splash*?

**A**   *David Hockney*

---

# No. 58

**a1** In the English legal system, what is another name for a JP (or justice of the peace)?

*b1 In law, what is a 'hung jury'?*

**a2** In 1998 Andy Ripley almost made the Cambridge boat race crew, aged 50. In which sport did he play for England?

*b2 In which sport did Niki Lauda compete?*

**a3** Which metal is a good conductor of heat and electricity and is used to make pipes for plumbing and wiring?

*b3 Which light, strong metal is used to make drink cans, kitchen foil and aircraft?*

**a4** Which political party was led by President Jimmy Carter?

*b4 Which American political party did Ronald Reagan lead?*

**a5** For which television role was Jack Warner best known?

*b5 Which television comedian often wore a fez?*

**a6** If you flew in a straight line from Tunisia to Egypt, which one intervening country would you cross?

*b6 Which country lies immediately south of Belgium?*

**a7** Where did a nuclear disaster occur in April 1986?

*b7 What tragedy occurred at Skopje in 1963?*

**a8** In which film did Robert Shaw play Captain Quint?

*b8 Who was the star of the films* The Gold Rush, Modern Times *and* The Great Dictator*?*

**a9** From 1978, who was the most important leader of China?

*b9 Who was the Indian prime minister Indira Gandhi's father?*

**a10** In which year was Korea divided into North and South Korea? Was it 1905, 1945 or 1951?

*b10 Until 1949, which European country governed Indonesia?*

**a11** Who was the first musician to be made a life peer?

*b11 By what name was the jazz pianist William Basie more usually known?*

**a12** In which Middle East country did Ba'ath Socialist party hold power?

*b12 In which central American republic were Sandinista rebels active in the late seventies and eighties?*

# No. 58 Answers

**a1** Magistrate
*b1* *One where the members cannot agree on a verdict*
**a2** Rugby Union
*b2* *Motor-racing*
**a3** Copper
*b3* *Aluminium*
**a4** Democrats
*b4* *Republican*
**a5** Dixon of Dock Green (PC George Dixon)
*b5* *Tommy Cooper*
**a6** Libya
*b6* *France*
**a7** Chernobyl (in the Ukraine)
*b7* *Earthquake*
**a8** Jaws
*b8* *Charlie Chaplin*
**a9** Deng Xiaoping (also spelled in other ways: e.g. Teng Hsiao-p'ing)
*b9* *Jawaharlal Nehru (India's first prime minister)*
**a10** 1945
*b10* *The Netherlands (Holland)*
**a11** Benjamin Britten
*b11* *'Count' Basie*
**a12** Iraq and/or Syria
*b12* *Nicaragua*

## Tie-breaker

**Q** Who first said, 'Because it was there' (when asked why he climbed a certain mountain)?

**A** *Sir Edmund Hilary, on having climbed Everest*

# No. 59

**a1** Which part of a hi-fi or home stereo system relies on lasers?

*b1* *Which part of a car's engine sends sparks to the plugs in the right order?*

**a2** In *Goldfinger*, what was the name of the villain with the dangerous hat?

*b2* *Which was the Beatles' first film?*

**a3** In Rugby Union internationals, what colour shirts does the England team wear?

*b3* *In Rugby Union internationals, what colour are Scotland's shirts?*

**a4** 'Cosa nostra' (meaning 'our cause') is another name for which secret society?

*b4* *Besides Italy, in which country has the Mafia been widely active this century?*

**a5** Until independence which European power controlled the Lebanon?

*b5* *Until independence in 1961, under which country's protection was Kuwait?*

**a6** In which year did Britain have three kings?

*b6* *Which king was married to Princess Mary of Teck?*

**a7** Which radio programme was invented by Roy Plomley and introduced by him until his death 44 years later?

*b7* *Who was the star of the radio show, ITMA?*

**a8** 'Colonel' Tom Parker was manager of which famous pop star who died in 1977?

*b8* *Mark David Chapman shot dead which pop star in 1980?*

**a9** Of which country was Bangladesh formerly a part?

*b9* *Kowloon is part of which country or colony?*

**a10** 'The Earl of Avon' was the title taken by which former prime minister?

*b10* *Former leader of the Liberal party Jeremy Thorpe was in court in 1979. On what charge?*

**a11** In 1969, which colonel seized power in Libya?

*b11* *Of which revolutionary group was Pol Pot the leader?*

**a12** In which country did Steve Biko die in police custody in 1977?

*b12* *Following an assassination, of which country did Mubarak become president?*

# No. 59 Answers

**a1**   A CD player
*b1*   *Distributor*
**a2**   Odd job
*b2*   *A Hard Day's Night*
**a3**   White
*b3*   *Blue*
**a4**   The Mafia
*b4*   *United States of America*
**a5**   France
*b5*   *Britain's*
**a6**   1936 (George V, Edward VIII, George VI)
*b6*   *George V*
*a7*   *Desert Island Discs*
*b7*   *Tommy Handley*
**a8**   Elvis Presley
*b8*   *John Lennon*
**a9**   Pakistan (East Pakistan) and, before that, India
*b9*   *Hong Kong*
**a10**   Sir Anthony Eden
*b10*   *(Plotting a) murder*
**a11**   Colonel Qaddafi
*b11*   *Khmer Rouge*
**a12**   South Africa
*b12*   *Egypt*

---

## Tie-breaker

**Q**   Jimmy Porter, Alison and Cliff are characters in which British play, first performed in 1956?

**A**   *Look Back in Anger*

# No. 60

**a1** Which failed television soap was set on the Costa del Sol?

*b1* *Which television series featured a London cabbie service run by women?*

**a2** In 1998 which soccer club was relegated from the Premiership, having been promoted there for the first time in 1997?

*b2* *Which club won Rugby's Tetley's Bitter Cup, for the first time, in 1998?*

**a3** By what name is London's Central Criminal Court best known?

*b3* *If criminal law deals with people accused of committing a crime, what deals with cases where no crime has been committed?*

**a4** Which war ended when President Nixon gave the order to withdraw?

*b4* *Who was shot by John Hinckley III in Washington in 1981?*

**a5** Who played Hutch in Starsky and Hutch?

*b5* *In the television series The New Avengers, who played Steed?*

**a6** In 1933, who became Chancellor of Germany?

*b6* *Josef Mengele was known as the 'Angel of Death'. With which concentration camp was the Nazi associated?*

**a7** Which bank has regularly advertised itself with a black horse?

*b7* *And which bank advertised itself as 'the listening bank'?*

**a8** Which dull-coloured metal is used to coat steel to prevent rust?

*b8* *Which strong, hard metal is used to make light bulb filaments?*

**a9** Athletes Harold Abrahams and Eric Liddell were commemorated in which film?

*b9* *Which film star visited Hanoi to show her disapproval of America's role in the Vietnam War?*

**a10** Which country or countries launched the Ariane rockets?

*b10* *Which nation put Skylab into orbit?*

**a11** Bishop Abel Muzorewa was a black leader in which country?

*b11* *Betty Williams and Mairead (say: mo'raid) Corrigan led a movement for peace – in which province?*

**a12** Which famous poet of the First World War was shot dead just one week before the end of the war?

*b12* *Which English poet was once married to the American poet, Sylvia Plath?*

# No. 60 Answers

**a1** *Eldorado*
**b1** Riders
**a2** Barnsley
**b2** *Saracens*
**a3** The Old Bailey
**b3** *Civil law*
**a4** Vietnam War
**b4** *President Reagan (also a policeman, a secret service agent and the president's press secretary)*
**a5** David Soul
**b5** *Patrick MacNee*
**a6** Adolf Hitler
**b6** *Auschwitz*
**a7** Lloyds Bank
**b7** *Midland Bank*
**a8** Zinc
**b8** *Tungsten*
**a9** *Chariots of Fire*
**b9** *Jane Fonda*
**a10** European countries, jointly
**b10** *United States of America*
**a11** Rhodesia (later Zimbabwe)
**b11** *Northern Ireland*
**a12** Wilfred Owen
**b12** *Ted Hughes*

---

## Tie-breaker

**Q** Name four European countries in which communist governments lost power in 1989.
**A** *Poland, Hungary, East Germany, Czechoslovakia*

---

# No. 61: Top of the Pops

Which pop star or group made it into the charts with these records or albums?

**a1** 'When Will I be Famous?' and 'I Owe You Nothing'
***b1*** *'Green, Green Grass of Home', 'I'll Never Fall in Love Again' and 'Delilah'*
**a2** 'Super Trooper', 'Dancing Queen' and 'Waterloo'
***b2*** *'Making Your Mind Up', 'Land of Make Believe' and 'My Camera Never Lies'*
**a3** 'Every Picture Tells a Story', 'You Wear It Well' and 'Sailing'
***b3*** *'Sacrifice', 'Rocketman' and 'Something About the Way You Look Tonight'*
**a4** 'Only the Lonely', 'It's Over' and 'Oh, Pretty Woman'
***b4*** *'Stand By Your Man', 'The Ways to Love a Man' and 'He Loves Me All the Way'*
**a5** 'Tubular Bells'
***b5*** *'Missing and Wrong'*
**a6** 'Alone Again (Naturally)', 'Clair' and 'Get Down'
***b6*** *'Dark Side of The Moon' and 'Another Brick in The Wall'*
**a7** 'Long Tall Sally', 'The Girl Can't Help It' and 'Lucille'
***b7*** *'Cry, The Little White Cloud that Cried' and 'Here Am I – Brokenhearted'*
**a8** 'Garden of Eden', 'Green Door' and 'Tower of Strength'
***b8*** *'Never Do a Tango With An Eskimo', 'Dreamboat' and 'Stairway of Love'*
**a9** 'Love is All Around' and 'Wishing I was Lucky'
***b9*** *'All Together Now' and 'Groovy Train'*
**a10** 'Midnight Train to Georgia' and 'Neither One of Us'
***b10*** *'I've Got to Get a Message to You' and 'Don't Forget to Remember'*
**a11** 'Happy To Be On An Island In The Sun' and 'When Forever Has Gone'
***b11*** *'White Cliffs of Dover' and 'We'll Meet Again'*
**a12** 'Fort Worth', 'Early Morning Rain' and 'Blue Train'
***b12*** *'Wake Up Little Susie', 'All I Have to Do is Dream' and 'Bye, Bye Love'*

# No. 61 Answers

**a1**   Bros
*b1*   *Tom Jones*
**a2**   ABBA
*b2*   *Bucks Fizz*
**a3**   Rod Stewart
*b3*   *(Sir) Elton John*
**a4**   Roy Orbison
*b4*   *Tammy Wynette*
**a5**   Mike Oldfield
*b5*   *Everything but the Girl*
**a6**   Gilbert O'Sullivan
*b6*   *Pink Floyd*
**a7**   Little Richard
*b7*   *Johnny Ray*
**a8**   Frankie Vaughan
*b8*   *Alma Cogan*
**a9**   Wet Wet Wet
*b9*   *The Farm*
**a10**   Gladys Knight and the Pips
*b10*   *The Bee Gees*
**a11**   Demis Roussos
*b11*   *Vera Lynn*
**a12**   George Hamilton IV
*b12*   *The Everly Brothers*

---

## Tie-breaker

**Q**   Born Tommy Hicks, he had a hit with 'Little White Bull' and starred in *Half A Sixpence*. Who is he?
**A**   *Tommy Steele*

---

# No. 62

**a1**  Which comedian became famous for supposedly having short, fat hairy legs?

*b1*  *With which comedian do you associate Knotty Ash?*

**a2**  Which Scottish group spent 15 weeks at the top of the chart with 'Love is All Around'?

*b2*  *Who left Take That because of 'tension'?*

**a3**  Who created the television detective Reg Wexford?

*b3*  *And which detective series originally starred the late Mark McManus in its title role?*

**a4**  In which field event was Tessa Sanderson a leading competitor?

*b4*  *And in which sport did John Conteh compete?*

**a5**  In the United States Congress, which is the name of 'the Upper House'?

*b5*  *And what is the name of the Lower House?*

**a6**  On a London Underground diagram map, what colour is the Bakerloo line?

*b6*  *On a London Underground map, what colour is the District line?*

**a7**  Who starred in the film *The Deer Hunter*?

*b7*  *In the 1978 re-make of* Superman, *who played Superman?*

**a8**  The common unit for measuring electrical power equals 1,000 watts. What is it called?

*b8*  *What name is commonly given to solid carbon dioxide used in refrigeration?*

**a9**  In which year was the Battle of the Somme?

*b9*  *In which year was the first Battle of Ypres? (say: ee-preh)*

**a10**  Who wrote the 'Pop Larkin' novels?

*b10*  *And who played Pop Larkin on television?*

**a11**  What do Europeans call the area Asians know as West Asia?

*b11*  *Which island's name is derived from 'mel', the Latin word for honey?*

**a12**  Sunnis (say: sunnies), Shiites (say: shee-ites) and Druze militia all fought in which eastern Mediterranean city?

*b12*  *Which terrorist brigade kidnapped and killed the former Italian prime minister, Aldo Moro?*

# No. 62 Answers

**a1** Ernie Wise
*b1* *Ken Dodd*
**a2** Wet Wet Wet
*b2* *Robbie Williams*
**a3** Ruth Rendell
*b3* Taggart
**a4** Javelin
*b4* *Boxing*
**a5** The Senate
*b5* *House of Representatives*
**a6** Brown
*b6* *Green (dark green)*
**a7** Robert de Niro
*b7* *Christopher Reeve*
**a8** Kilowatt
*b8* *Dry ice*
**a9** 1916
*b9* *1914*
**a10** H E Bates
*b10* *David Jason*
**a11** The Middle East
*b11* *Malta*
**a12** Beirut
*b12* *Red Brigade*

---

## Tie-breaker

**Q** The American city of New York consists of five boroughs. How many can you name?

**A** *Manhattan, the Bronx, Queens, Brooklyn, and Staten Island*

---

# No. 63

**a1**    Which famous actress stood out in the films, *One Million Years* BC and *The Biggest Bundle of Them All?*

*b1*    *Who was the young male star of the film* Saturday Night Fever*?*

**a2**    What is a dissident?

*b2*    *What is 'disinformation'?*

**a3**    Which member of the Cabinet presents the annual budget speech?

*b3*    *What title is given to the chairman or woman of the House of Commons?*

**a4**    Why did the American millionaire Howard Hughes become famous?

*b4*    *And also in the states, as what did Busby Berkeley achieve fame?*

**a5**    In which year was the Battle of Britain?

*b5*    *In which year did the Japanese bomb Pearl Harbor?*

**a6**    Who played Fletcher in *Porridge* and *Going Straight?*

*b6*    *In which series did Warren Mitchell first play Alf?*

**a7**    Between which cities did the Flying Scotsman train travel?

*b7*    *And between which cities did the Royal Scot travel?*

**a8**    Who became king of Spain in 1975?

*b8*    *In which year did Queen Elizabeth II celebrate her silver jubilee?*

**a9**    Which northern painter became famous for his 'matchstalk men'?

*b9*    *Which cartoonist created Li'l Abner?*

**a10**    Which leader died in 1978 after only 33 days in office?

*b10*    *What nationality are the Papal Guards at the Vatican?*

**a11**    In 1976, three days of unrest and rioting resulted in 100 dead in which South African township?

*b11*    *UNITA was a nationalist movement in which African country?*

**a12**    Which influential book (in which the title became a slogan) was written by E F Schumacher?

*b12*    *Which doctor wrote* The Common Sense Book of Baby and Child Care*?*

# No. 63 Answers

**a1** Raquel Welch
*b1* *John Travolta*
**a2** Someone who disagrees with the policies of his or her own country
*b2* *False information spread with the purpose of confusing others*
**a3** Chancellor of the Exchequer
*b3* *The Speaker, Mr (or Madame) Speaker*
**a4** He was a recluse; always seeking total privacy
*b4* *Choreographer; dance arranger*
**a5** 1940
*b5* *1941*
**a6** Ronnie Barker
*b6* Till Death Us Do Part
**a7** London and Edinburgh
*b7* *London and Glasgow*
**a8** King Juan Carlos
*b8* *1977*
**a9** L S Lowry
*b9* *Al Capp*
**a10** Pope John-Paul I
*b10* *Swiss*
**a11** Soweto
*b11* *Angola*
**a12** *Small Is Beautiful*
*b12* *(Benjamin) Spock*

---

## Tie-breaker

**Q** Four English counties disappeared from the map in the 1974 local government reorganization. Can you name them?

**A** *Cumberland, Huntingdonshire, Rutland, and Westmorland*

---

# No. 64

**a1**   In which city is the Shankill Road?

*b1*   *In which English city did the IRA trigger the 1974 'Pub Bombings'?*

**a2**   For playing which musical instrument did Larry Adler become famous?

*b2*   *Musician Jacqueline du Pré had to give up her career owing to illness. What was her instrument?*

**a3**   What kind of missile is a SAM?

*b3*   *For what do the military initials SAS stand?*

**a4**   London Monarchs and Scottish Claymores perform in which sport?

*b4*   *Gregor Townsend and Alan Tait were British Lions in 1997. What is their other Rugby link?*

**a5**   Which motorway links South Wales and London?

*b5*   *Which motorway crosses the Pennines from Manchester to Leeds?*

**a6**   In the Korean War which international force supported South Korea?

*b6*   *And, in the same war, which super-power supported North Korea?*

**a7**   By what nickname was the murderer Peter Sutcliffe generally known?

*b7*   *Which 'lucky' earl disappeared after the murder of his child's nanny?*

**a8**   For which Manchester club did footballer Rodney Marsh play?

*b8*   *For which country did Rodney Marsh keep wicket?*

**a9**   Where in Britain is the National Railway Museum?

*b9*   *In which city is the Ashmolean Museum?*

**a10**   Which famous fictional barrister has been played on television by Leo McKern?

*b10*   *On television, who played 'Wonder Woman'?*

**a11**   Who wrote the novel *Saturday Night and Sunday Morning*?

*b11*   *Who wrote the novel* Billy Liar?

**a12**   Giscard d'Estaing (say: ji-skar dess-tan) became president of France in 1974. What was his first name?

*b12*   *Which was the last year in which Russia was ruled by a Tsar?*

# No. 64 Answers

**a1** Belfast
*b1* *Birmingham*
**a2** Harmonica (mouth organ)
*b2* *Cello*
**a3** Surface-to-air missile
*b3* *Special Air Service*
**a4** (American-style) football
*b4* *Both are Scottish*
**a5** M4
*b5* *M62*
**a6** United Nations
*b6* *China*
**a7** The Yorkshire Ripper
*b7* *Earl of Lucan (Lord Lucan)*
**a8** Manchester City
*b8* *Australia*
**a9** York
*b9* *Oxford*
**a10** Rumpole (created by John Mortimer)
*b10* *Lynda Carter*
**a11** Alan Sillitoe
*b11* *Keith Waterhouse*
**a12** Valéry
*b12* *1917*

---

## Tie-breaker

**Q** In which country do the people live in traditional villages, pay no taxes, receive free services and mainly drive air-conditioned cars?

**A** *Brunei (offshore oil wells make it a very rich country)*

---

# No. 65

**a1**  In which country did Datsun cars originate?
*b1*  *And which is the home country of the Fiat car company?*
**a2**  On television, which famous puppet was worked by Harry Corbett?
*b2*  *In which television programme was there a snail called Brian?*
**a3**  What do members of the House of Commons mean by 'another place'?
*b3*  *Who may not visit the House of Commons when it is in session?*
**a4**  By what name is the Windscale Nuclear plant now known?
*b4*  *Why did Flixborough on Humberside hit the headlines in 1974?*
**a5**  Which singer thanked heaven for little girls and had trouble remembering it well?
*b5*  *Which song (it became famous in the Second World War) was first sung by the German Lale Anderson?*
**a6**  What was the name of the Northern Ireland parliament building?
*b6*  *In which Northern Ireland city did the events known as 'Bloody Sunday' occur (in 1972)?*
**a7**  Why did Balcombe Street, London hit the headlines in December 1975?
*b7*  *A tragic London underground train crash in 1975 killed 35. At which station?*
**a8**  As what did Ezra Pound achieve fame?
*b8*  *And as what did Sir John Barbirolli achieve fame?*
**a9**  From which country did the tennis star Ilie Nastase come?
*b9*  *Which was the home country of chess champion Bobby Fischer?*
**a10**  In which year was the African battle of El Alamein?
*b10*  *In which two years has Germany invaded Belgium?*
**a11**  In which year did the Vietnam War end?
*b11*  *In which year was the Russian October Revolution?*
**a12**  Which Irish poet wrote the poem 'The Lake Isle of Innisfree'?
*b12*  *Which poet wrote 'The Love Song of J Alfred Prufrock'?*

# No. 65 Answers

**a1** Japan
**b1** *Italy*
**a2** Sooty (or Sweep)
**b2** The Magic Roundabout
**a3** House of Lords
**b3** *The monarch*
**a4** Sellafield
**b4** *Chemical plant exploded, factory explosion (killing 28)*
**a5** Maurice Chevalier
**b5** *'Lili Marlene'*
**a6** Stormont
**b6** *Derry*
**a7** Because of a siege (IRA held two people hostage)
**b7** *Moorgate*
**a8** Poet
**b8** *Conductor (accept: cellist)*
**a9** Romania
**b9** *United States of America*
**a10** 1942
**b10** *1914, 1940*
**a11** 1975 (America withdrew in 1973)
**b11** *1917*
**a12** W B Yeats (say: yates)
**b12** *T S Eliot*

## Tie-breaker

**Q**  Who is this famous actor? 'I was born in Miami, USA. I took acting lessons at the American Negro Theatre in New York. I was in *The Blackboard Jungle*, but in my best-known film I was a New York cop, solving a murder in the heat of a small town in the south of the USA.'

**A**  *Sidney Poitier (best known film:* In the Heat of the Night*)*

# No. 66

**a1** Which soccer team would Notts Forest play in a local 'derby' match?

*b1* *Who would oppose Bristol City in their 'derby'?*

**a2** Who played the Mafia chief in the film *The Godfather*?

*b2* *Which comic actor starred in radio's* The Goon Show *and played Inspector Clouseau on screen?*

**a3** Which illegal activity has been responsible for reducing the number of elephants in Africa?

*b3* *Which virus was deliberately spread to control the number of rabbits?*

**a4** What instrument was played by the musician Pablo Casals?

*b4* *Which popular singer died on a Spanish golf course in 1977?*

**a5** In the House of Lords, who are the Lords Spiritual?

*b5* *Who presides over or 'chairs' the debates in the House of Lords?*

**a6** Who was assassinated by a Bosnian student in 1914?

*b6* *What world organization was founded at the end of the First World War?*

**a7** On BBC radio, who sends a weekly *Letter from America*?

*b7* *Who was the original quizmaster of the television series* University Challenge?

**a8** Name one of the countries which boycotted the 1980 Moscow Olympics?

*b8* *Which country's headquarters were stormed in the Olympic Village at Munich in 1972?*

**a9** After which American president were teddy bears named?

*b9* *Dwight D Eisenhower – what did the 'D' stand for?*

**a10** On a London Underground diagram map, what colour is the Northern line?

*b10* *On a London Underground diagram map, what colour is the Central line?*

**a11** Who wrote the novel *The French Lieutenant's Woman*?

*b11* *Who wrote the novel* A Clockwork Orange?

**a12** Before being sent to prison for corruption, what was John Poulson's profession?

*b12* *What took a man called Evil Knievel into the headlines?*

# No. 66 Answers

| | |
|---|---|
| **a1** | Notts County |
| **b1** | *Bristol Rovers* |
| **a2** | Marlon Brando |
| **b2** | *Peter Sellers* |
| **a3** | Poaching for ivory |
| **b3** | *Myxomatosis* |
| **a4** | Cello |
| **b4** | *Bing Crosby* |
| **a5** | The Bishops (and archbishops) |
| **b5** | *The Lord Chancellor* |
| **a6** | Archduke Ferdinand of Austria |
| **b6** | *League of Nations* |
| **a7** | Alistair Cooke |
| **b7** | *Bamber Gascoigne (Jeremy Paxman is the present quizmaster)* |
| **a8** | United States of America, West Germany, Kenya |
| **b8** | *Israel's* |
| **a9** | Theodore ('Teddy') Roosevelt |
| **b9** | *David* |
| **a10** | Black |
| **b10** | *Red* |
| **a11** | John Fowles |
| **b11** | *Anthony Burgess* |
| **a12** | Architect |
| **b12** | *His stunts; driving a car over double-decker buses* |

---

## Tie-breaker

**Q**  On whose BBC radio show did we hear the question, 'What's the recipe today?'?

**A**  *Jimmy Young's*

---

# No. 67

**a1** Which group from Denmark hit the number one spot in late 1997 with 'Barbie Girl'?

*b1* *Which was the longest-running television sci-fi series?*

**a2** First published 1938, closed in 1957. What was *Picture Post*?

*b2* *Which weekly listings magazine was published for the first time in 1923?*

**a3** Franz Beckenbauer captained which team in the 1974 soccer World Cup?

*b3* *Which speedway team is nicknamed 'The Witches'?*

**a4** A movement called 'Enosis' wanted the unification of which island with Greece?

*b4* *Which war was ended by the Treaty of Panmunjon?*

**a5** In the House of Commons, what is a Bill?

*b5* *How many 'readings' are there to a Parliamentary Bill?*

**a6** Which infamous leader committed suicide on April 30, 1945?

*b6* *Manila, Rangoon and Singapore were all captured by which country in 1942?*

**a7** On radio where would you once have met Mr Growser, Dennis and Larry the Lamb?

*b7* *On which sport was John Arlott a famous commentator?*

**a8** Which is longer, the Suez or the Panama Canal?

*b8* *Which sea lies between Iran and Saudi Arabia?*

**a9** Which entrepreneur started cheap transatlantic flights on his so-called 'Skytrain'?

*b9* *What kind of clothing was associated with the name 'Gannex'?*

**a10** Who wrote the novels *The Odessa File* and *The Day of the Jackal*?

*b10* *Who wrote the novels* Whisky Galore *and* Sinister Street*?*

**a11** Which political system believes in a classless society with state-run means of production and trade?

*b11* *What name is given to the socialist community farms found in Israel?*

**a12** In which year did Britain have a three-day week (to conserve energy supplies)?

*b12* *Which country celebrated its 'Bicentennial' in 1976?*

# No. 67 Answers

**a1** Aqua
*b1* Doctor Who *(695 episodes)*
**a2** Weekly (illustrated) news magazine
*b2* Radio Times
**a3** West Germany
*b3* *Ipswich Town*
**a4** Cyprus
*b4* *Korean War*
**a5** A proposed law, a proposed Act of Parliament
*b5* *Three*
**a6** Adolf Hitler
*b6* *Japan*
**a7** In 'Toytown'
*b7* *Cricket*
**a8** The Suez (it's twice as long)
*b8* *Persian Gulf*
**a9** Freddie Laker
*b9* *Raincoats*
**a10** Frederick Forsyth
*b10* *Compton Mackenzie*
**a11** Communism
*b11* *Kibbutzim (kibbutzim is the plural of kibbutz)*
**a12** 1973
*b12* *United States of America (1776–1976)*

---

## Tie-breaker

**Q** Which British cruiser was reduced to a blazing hulk by Argentinean Exocet missiles during the Falklands War?
**A** *HMS Sheffield*

# No. 68

**a1** Which politician had to resign for causing a salmonella scare?

*b1* *What are Lakeside, Meadowhall and Brent Cross?*

**a2** Who directed the films *ET* and *Close Encounters of the Third Kind*?

*b2* *Who directed the cinema epic,* The Ten Commandments*?*

**a3** In the Second World War, in which year did the Germans occupy Paris?

*b3* *In which year during the Second World War was Germany defeated at the Battle of Stalingrad?*

**a4** What medical term is given to the state of being very over-weight?

*b4* *Whereabouts in your body are your largest and strongest muscles?*

**a5** What is the army equivalent of the naval rank of lieutenant?

*b5* *What is the naval equivalent of the army rank of general?*

**a6** The surname 'Singh' indicates membership of which religion?

*b6* *To which city do Muslims hope to make a once-in-a-lifetime pilgrimage?*

**a7** In which television series did we see Cowley, Doyle and Bodie?

*b7* *Name the actor who played Kojak in the television series.*

**a8** From which country did Israel capture the Gaza Strip in 1967?

*b8* *And also in 1967, from which country did Israel take over the Golan Heights?*

**a9** Of which country is the Indus the principal river?

*b9* *In which country is the mouth (or delta) of the River Ganges?*

**a10** Which former Labour MP faked his own disappearance on a Miami beach?

*b10* *Which post was held in the Soviet Government for 28 years by Andrei Gromyko?*

**a11** Of which country was William Taft president early this century?

*b11* *Who was the first United States president to resign office?*

**a12** Which metal is needed to provide the fuel for most nuclear power stations?

*b12* *Which country produces the highest percentage of its electricity by nuclear power? Is it France, Britain or the United States?*

# No. 68 Answers

**a1** Edwina Currie
*b1* *(Large) shopping centres*
**a2** Steven Spielberg
*b2* *Cecil B DeMille*
**a3** 1940
*b3* *1942*
**a4** Obese, obesity
*b4* *In the buttocks*
**a5** Captain
*b5* *Admiral*
**a6** Sikhism
*b6* *Mecca*
**a7** *The Professionals*
*b7* *Telly Savalas*
**a8** Egypt
*b8* *Syria*
**a9** Pakistan
*b9* *Bangladesh*
**a10** John Stonehouse
*b10* *Foreign minister*
**a11** United States of America (1909–1913)
*b11* *President Nixon (1974)*
**a12** Uranium
*b12* *France*

## Tie-breaker

**Q** Which three female artists performed 'Love Can Build a Bridge' for Comic Relief in 1995?
**A** *Cher, Neneh Cherry, Chrissie Hinde*

# No. 69

**a1**    Were the first parking meters installed in 1951, 1958 or 1969?

*b1*    *Did the first Oxfam shop open in 1927, 1948 or 1963?*

**a2**    Which religion celebrates its new year during September or early October?

*b2*    *Which new year festival occurs between 21st January and 19th February?*

**a3**    Into which movement were young people enrolled in Nazi Germany?

*b3*    *Who were on trial at the Nuremburg Trials in 1946?*

**a4**    For what do the initials PWR stand?

*b4*    *In Northern Ireland, for what do the initials UDA stand?*

**a5**    In the world of motoring, for what do the initials GT stand?

*b5*    *In the world of motorcycle racing, for what do the initials TT stand?*

**a6**    Who played Rett Butler in the classic film *Gone with the Wind*?

*b6*    *Who composed the music for the 1945 show* Carousel?

**a7**    Which country has been ruled by King Hassan II?

*b7*    *On which island was Rauf Denktash a Turkish leader?*

**a8**    Who was the President of the USA just before Jimmy Carter?

*b8*    *On which American paper did the reporters work who uncovered the Watergate affair?*

**a9**    On television, who played Rigsby and Norman Tripper?

*b9*    *And who played Hyacinth Bucket, pronounced Bouquet?*

**a10**    This century, who composed an operatic version of *A Midsummer Night's Dream*?

*b10*    *And who composed the opera* Madam Butterfly?

**a11**    In which continent is Papua New Guinea?

*b11*    *In which continent is Greenland?*

**a12**    Who wrote the novel *Cry, the Beloved Country*?

*b12*    *Who wrote the novels* Anglo-Saxon Attitudes, The Old Men at the Zoo *and* Hemlock and After?

# No. 69 Answers

**a1**  1958
*b1*  *1948*
**a2**  Jewish
*b2*  *Chinese*
**a3**  The Hitler Youth Movement
*b3*  *Nazi leaders*
**a4**  Pressurized Water Reactor (type of nuclear reactor)
*b4*  *Ulster Defence Association*
**a5**  Grand Touring
*b5*  *Tourist Trophy*
**a6**  Clark Gable
*b6*  *Richard Rodgers*
**a7**  Morocco
*b7*  *Cyprus*
**a8**  Gerald Ford
*b8*  *Washington Post*
**a9**  Leonard Rossiter
*b9*  *Patricia Routledge*
**a10**  Benjamin Britten
*b10*  *Puccini*
**a11**  Oceania (accept: Australasia)
*b11*  *The Arctic*
**a12**  Alan Paton
*b12*  *Angus Wilson*

---

## Tie-breaker

**Q**  What are the 'Six Counties' of Northern Ireland?
**A**  *Antrim, Armagh, Down, Fermanagh, Londonderry, Tyrone*

---

138

# No. 70

**a1** In Northern Ireland, who are or were known as the 'Provos'?

*b1* In Northern Ireland, what change happened to some court-room procedures in 1973?

**a2** Who created the detective Inspector Morse?

*b2* And who created Adam Dalgleish?

**a3** On television, who plays Arthur Daley?

*b3* In Coronation Street, which character was played by Doris Speed?

**a4** When is United Nations Day each year?

*b4* What famous event takes place at Munich in October?

**a5** Nine hands were shown clasped on a special British coin. Which coin?

*b5* What colour is the standard European Community passport?

**a6** What is the naval equivalent of the army rank of colonel?

*b6* What is the army equivalent of the naval rank of Admiral of the Fleet?

**a7** In which year did the *Titanic* sink?

*b7* In which year did the violence of the present troubles in Northern Ireland begin?

**a8** In Britain, which tax replaced purchase tax in 1973?

*b8* Which east European pact was formed to oppose NATO?

**a9** Name a country in which you would find the Inuit people.

*b9* In which country was a 'terra cotta' army of 6,000 life-size models of soldiers uncovered in 1975?

**a10** In which London square were there anti-Vietnam War demonstrations in 1968?

*b10* Which was Britain's biggest ever robbery?

**a11** Which planet has two tiny moons called Phobos and Deimos?

*b11* And which planet has twenty moons, the biggest of which is called Titan?

**a12** Who wrote the 12-volume sequence of novels titled *A Dance to the Music of Time*?

*b12* Who wrote the novels To the Lighthouse *and* The Waves?

# No. 70 Answers

**a1**   Members of the 'Provisional' IRA (Irish Republican Army)
*b1*   *Trial without jury was introduced*
**a2**   Colin Morris
*b2*   *P D James*
**a3**   George Cole
*b3*   *Annie Walker*
**a4**   October 24
*b4*   *Beer festival (Oktoberfest)*
**a5**   50p piece (to celebrate membership of the Common Market)
*b5*   *Red*
**a6**   Captain
*b6*   *Field Marshal*
**a7**   1912
*b7*   *1969*
**a8**   VAT (Value Added Tax)
*b8*   *Warsaw Pact*
**a9**   Greenland; Arctic North America (Canada, Alaska)
*b9*   *China*
**a10**   Grosvenor Square
*b10*   *The Brinks Matt robbery (£26 million stolen at Heathrow Airport 1983)*
**a11**   Mars
*b11*   *Saturn*
**a12**   Anthony Powell
*b12*   *Virginia Woolf*

---

## Tie-breaker

**Q**   Which three countries make up the continent of North America?

**A**   *Canada, United States, Mexico*

---

# No. 71: Modern Abbreviations

The following abbreviations have all come into use in recent years.
What do they each stand for or mean?

**a1**   K
*b1*   *PC*
**a2**   PIN
*b2*   *VCR*
**a3**   BMX
*b3*   *DBS*
**a4**   DTP
*b4*   *FTSE or Footsie*
**a5**   AIDS
*b5*   *CFC*
**a6**   CD-ROM
*b6*   *DAT*
**a7**   BSE
*b7*   *HIV*
**a8**   NIMBY
*b8*   *PEP*
**a9**   EPOS
*b9*   *ATM*
**a10**   EMS
*b10*   *TESSA*
**a11**   WYSIWYG
*b11*   *ERM*
**a12**   ME
*b12*   *RSI*

# No. 71 Answers

**a1**   1,000

*b1*   *Personal computer*

**a2**   Personal identification number (used with cash machines, etc.)

*b2*   *Video cassette recorder*

**a3**   Bicycle moto-cross; cycle racing on dirt tracks

*b3*   *Direct broadcasting by satellite*

**a4**   Desk-top publishing; using a computer to produce books, newsletters, etc.

*b4*   *Financial Times Stock Exchange 100 share index (shares of the 100 largest companies in Britain)*

**a5**   Acquired immune deficiency syndrome

*b5*   *Chlorofluorocarbon (gas used in aerosols, refrigerators, etc.)*

**a6**   Compact disc with 'read-only' memory

*b6*   *Digital audio tape*

**a7**   Bovine spongiform encephalopathy, 'mad cow disease'

*b7*   *Human immunodeficiency virus, virus which can cause AIDS*

**a8**   'Not in my backyard'; person objecting to building scheme, etc. in his or her locality

*b8*   *Personal Equity Plan*

**a9**   Electronic point of sale; shop till system that reads bar-codes

*b9*   *Automated teller machine; 'hole-in-the-wall' cash machine*

**a10**  European Monetary System

*b10*  *Tax exempt special savings account (UK tax free savings account)*

**a11**  'What you see is what you get'; when computer screens show exactly what will be printed (and nothing else)

*b11*  *Exchange-rate mechanism (within the European Community)*

**a12**  A long-lasting illness; myalgic encephalomyelitis; sometimes cruelly called 'yuppy flu'

*b12*  *Repetitive strain injury; pains caused by extended use of computers*

---

## Tie-breaker

**Q**   What is the OAU?

*A*   *Organization for African Unity*

# No. 72

**a1**  Which European country is sometimes called the 'Land of the Midnight Sun'?

*b1*  *Two fifths of which European country was once covered by the sea, lakes or marsh?*

**a2**  In the 1919 pop music hit, what shouldn't you do 'on the way'?

*b2*  *And another popular song in the same year, what were you forever blowing?*

**a3**  What is the usual name for a motorcycle which has an engine capacity of less than 50cc?

*b3*  *And what does an octane rating indicate?*

**a4**  With whom was Yoko Ono arrested on drugs charges in 1968?

*b4*  *Of which secretive organization was Stella Rimington the boss?*

**a5**  Of which long-running television programme was Leonard Sachs the chairman?

*b5*  *On which quiz show did contestants have the choice of taking the money or opening the box?*

**a6**  In France, what is the Baccalaureate? (say: back-a-lor-re-att)

*b6*  *Which examinations in England and Wales were replaced by the GCSE in 1988?*

**a7**  Where in the Netherlands is the seat of government?

*b7*  *Which is the capital city of the Netherlands?*

**a8**  In which film did Humphrey Bogart say, 'Here's lookin' at you, kid'?

*b8*  *And which actress in the same film had the line, 'Play it, Sam. Play As Time Goes By'?*

**a9**  Which poet's verse autobiography is titled Summoned by Bells?

*b9*  *Which First World War poet wrote the poems 'Anthem for Doomed Youth' and 'Exposure'?*

**a10**  Members of which British political party were banned from broadcasting from 1988?

*b10*  *In which country did the Frelimo movement fight?*

**a11**  Which infamous Biblical character is also the title of an opera by Richard Strauss?

*b11*  *Who wrote the score for the musical, A Little Night Music?*

**a12**  In J M Barrie's play The Admirable Crichton (say: Cry-ton), what was Crichton's job?

*b12*  *Which London theatre was managed by Miss Lilian Baylis?*

# No. 72 Answers

**a1** Norway
*b1* *The Netherlands*
**a2** Dilly-dally ('Don't dilly-dally on the way')
*b2* *Bubbles ('I'm forever blowing bubbles')*
**a3** Moped
*b3* *The power and/or quality of petrol*
**a4** John Lennon
*b4* *MI5*
**a5** *The Good Old Days*
*b5* Take Your Pick
**a6** School examination (taken at 17-plus)
*b6* *GCE 'O' (ordinary) level and CSE*
**a7** The Hague
*b7* *Amsterdam*
**a8** *Casablanca*
*b8* *Ingrid Bergman*
**a9** Sir John Betjeman's
*b9* *Wilfred Owen*
**a10** Sinn Fein
*b10* *Mozambique*
**a11** Salomé
*b11* *Stephen Sondheim*
**a12** Butler
*b12* *Old Vic*

---

## Tie-breaker

**Q** Four film stars (Mary Pickford, Douglas Fairbanks, Charlie Chaplin and D W Griffith) formed their own film company in 1919. What was it called?

**A** *United Artists*

---

# No. 73

**a1**    What was the name of the first artificial satellite?

*b1    Which satellite carried the first television pictures across the Atlantic in 1962 (and was also the name of a pop record)?*

**a2**    Which soccer supremo played for England at every level and then managed them?

*b2    Which cricket supremo wrote the novel Testkill: Ray Illingworth or Ted Dexter?*

**a3**    Which two countries generally have the 49th Parallel as their boundary?

*b3    In which province do the majority of French-speaking Canadians live?*

**a4**    Can you name a keyboard musical instrument besides the piano?

*b4    The saxophone will be found in which section of the orchestra?*

**a5**    Which United Nations organization agency is concerned with education, science and culture?

*b5    And which UN organization helps children in trouble?*

**a6**    In which Eastern country was there a revolution in 1949?

*b6    Which rebellion occurred in China at the start of the century?*

**a7**    Who sailed a yacht called 'Morning Cloud'?

*b7    Which politician, on stopping free milk supplies in schools, became known as the Milk Snatcher?*

**a8**    Can you name a principal export of Finland?

*b8    And what is the main export of Iceland?*

**a9**    Who played Hudson in the television series *Upstairs, Downstairs*?

*b9    In a television soap opera, which famous character was played by Jean Alexander?*

**a10**    In 1900, which British playwright died in disgrace in Paris?

*b10    Who wrote a book called Kim, first published in 1901?*

**a11**    Which music hall artist sang the song 'I'm One of the Ruins Cromwell Knocked About a Bit'?

*b11    Which music hall star sang 'Roamin' in the Gloamin'?*

**a12**    A new form of public transport was seen in London's streets for the first time in 1903. What was it?

*b12    Which motoring organization was founded in 1905 to protect and help motorists?*

# No. 73 Answers

**a1**   Sputnik 1
*b1*   *Telstar*
**a2**   Terry Venables
*b2*   *Ted Dexter*
**a3**   United States of America and Canada
*b3*   *Quebec*
**a4**   Organ, harmonium, accordion, harpsichord, clavichord, synthesizer, virginal, spinet
*b4*   *Woodwind (although made of brass, it has a reed)*
**a5**   UNESCO (United Nations Education, Scientific and Cultural Organization)
*b5*   *UNICEF (United Nations International Children's Emergency Fund)*
**a6**   China
*b6*   *Boxer Rebellion*
**a7**   Edward Heath
*b7*   *Margaret Thatcher*
**a8**   Paper, paper products, wood
*b8*   *Fish*
**a9**   Gordon Jackson
*b9*   *Hilda Ogden (in* Coronation Street*)*
**a10**  Oscar Wilde
*b10*  *Rudyard Kipling*
**a11**  Marie Lloyd
*b11*  *Harry Lauder*
**a12**  Electric trams
*b12*  *AA (Automobile Association)*

---

# Tie-breaker

**Q**   Up to 1991, how long was the world's longest traffic jam? Was it 7 miles, 21 miles or 109 miles?
**A**   *109 miles (towards Paris from Lyon, in 1980)*

# No. 74

**a1** Which TV star often said, 'He's done a whoopsie'?

*b1* *Which radio and TV star used to start his shows by shouting 'Wakey Wakey'?*

**a2** In which town or city is the administrative headquarters of West Sussex?

*b2* *And in which town or city is the administrative headquarters of West Yorkshire?*

**a3** What were the *Lusitania* and *Mauretania*?

*b3* *To which empire did the Battleship Potemkin belong?*

**a4** In which film did the two main characters describe their jobs by saying, 'We rob banks'?

*b4* *In which film did Dustin Hoffman say, 'Mrs Robinson, you're trying to seduce me, aren't you?'?*

**a5** In America, what is Mount St Helens?

*b5* *In Holland, what is a 'polder'?*

**a6** Which murderer was captured at sea in 1910, thanks to the use of radio?

*b6* *Who were the Romanovs who were put to death in a cellar in 1918?*

**a7** Complete the title of this Bob Marley hit: 'No Woman ...'

*b7* *Reggae group Inner Circle had a hit with what?*

**a8** Which is the richest country in the Middle East?

*b8* *Is Saudi Arabia a republic, a kingdom or a dependency?*

**a9** Who composed the music 'On Hearing the First Cuckoo in Spring'?

*b9* *Which Russian composed many ballet scores including* The Firebird *and* Petrushka?

**a10** For what has Seamus Heaney become famous?

*b10* *What was the profession of Mrs Lillie Langtry?*

**a11** Why was Piper Alpha in the news in July 1998?

*b11* *In which year did the first high speed train run through the Channel Tunnels?*

**a12** In which year did women (over 30) vote for the first time in Britain? Was it 1911, 1918 or 1922?

*b12* *Who was the first British woman MP to take her seat?*

# No. 74 Answers

**a1** Michael Crawford (Frank Spencer) in *Some Mothers Do 'Ave 'Em*
**b1** *Billy Cotton*
**a2** Chichester
**b2** *Wakefield*
**a3** Ocean liners (Cunard liners)
**b3** *Russian*
**a4** *Bonnie and Clyde*
**b4** The Graduate
**a5** A volcano (active in 1980)
**b5** *Area of drained land, area reclaimed from the sea*
**a6** Dr Crippen
**b6** *The Russian tsar and his family*
**a7** '... No Cry'
**b7** *'Sweat'*
**a8** Saudi Arabia
**b8** *Kingdom*
**a9** (Frederick) Delius
**b9** *(Igor) Stravinsky*
**a10** His poetry; as a poet
**b10** *Actress*
**a11** (Worst ever) North Sea oil rig explosion (accept: oil rig disaster)
**b11** *1993*
**a12** 1918
**b12** *Nancy Astor (Lady Astor)*

---

## Tie-breaker

**Q** Which Russian scientist became known for his studies of how dogs learned to expect food whenever a bell was rung?

**A** *(Ivan) Pavlov*

---

# No. 75

**a1**  For which sport is Indianapolis especially famous?
*b1*  *In which sport is the Curtis Cup awarded?*
**a2**  Whose was the ragtime band in the popular hit of 1911?
*b2*  *And in a 1908 hit, which moon was invited to 'shine on'?*
**a3**  What is the official language of Brazil?
*b3*  *What is the official language of Nicaragua?*
**a4**  What type of food are vermicelli, macaroni and spaghetti?
*b4*  *Which is the best source of protein: peanuts, eggs or rice?*
**a5**  The comic actor Buster Keaton played an engine driver in which classic silent film?
*b5*  *What was the name of the 'crazy cops' created by the film producer, Mack Sennett?*
**a6**  In 1914, which country was likely to be split by the 'Home Rule' question?
*b6*  *How did the suffragette Emily Davison die?*
**a7**  Which author wrote the 'Forsyte Saga'?
*b7*  *Who wrote the novel* Anna of the Five Towns?
**a8**  Which country, principally, contains the homeland of the Kurdish people?
*b8*  *By what name was the country Myanmar formerly known?*
**a9**  Which is the most crowded nation or state (that is, which is most densely populated)?
*b9*  *And which is the most densely populated island in Europe?*
**a10**  Which wealthy diamond mine owner gave his name to a country in southern Africa?
*b10*  *Which infamous Russian monk was murdered by supporters of the Czar?*
**a11**  Which part of England receives its programmes from the Winter Hill transmitter?
*b11*  *Emley Moor television transmitter covers which part of England?*
**a12**  What did the archaeologist Howard Carter discover in 1922?
*b12*  *Which explorer is credited with saying, 'I am just going outside and may be some time'?*

# No. 75 Answers

**a1** Motor racing
*b1* *(Woman's) golf*
**a2** Alexander ('Alexander's Ragtime Band')
*b2* *Harvest moon ('Shine on Harvest Moon')*
**a3** Portuguese
*b3* *Spanish*
**a4** Pasta
*b4* *Peanuts*
**a5** *The General* (1927)
*b5* *Keystone Cops*
**a6** Ireland
*b6* *She threw herself under the king's horse in the Derby (1913)*
**a7** James Galsworthy
*b7* *Arnold Bennett*
**a8** Iraq
*b8* *Burma*
**a9** Singapore
*b9* *Malta*
**a10** Cecil Rhodes (Rhodesia)
*b10* *Rasputin*
**a11** Lancashire; northwest England
*b11* *Yorkshire*
**a12** Tomb of Egyptian boy-king, Tutan Khamun
*b12* *Captain Oates*

---

# Tie-breaker

**Q** Who is this actor? 'I made my first stage appearance in 1856 and often acted with Ellen Terry. I was one of the last great actor-managers and the first actor to be knighted and I died in 1905.'

**A** *Sir Henry Irving*

# No. 76

**a1** A pop tune of 1902 asked someone: 'Won't you please come home'. Who was he?

*b1* *In 1912 the singer Eugene Stratton had a hit song about a lily. It was called 'Lily of ...' what or where?*

**a2** By what name is the Spanish holiday coast north of Barcelona generally known?

*b2* *And by what name is the southern coast of Spain (around Malaga) generally known?*

**a3** Which is the principal city of the Metropolitan county of Tyne and Wear?

*b3* *Which is the principal city in Scotland's Tayside region?*

**a4** In which film did Vivien Leigh say, 'Tomorrow is another day'?

*b4* *To whom did Mae West say 'Why don't you come up sometime 'n see me?' (in* She Done Him Wrong*)?*

**a5** In the world of motoring, what is 'bhp'?

*b5* *And what is 'kph'?*

**a6** What is absolute alcohol?

*b6* *What is ultrasonic sound?*

**a7** 1982 saw a new television channel start in Britain. What was it?

*b7* *What is Sianel Pedwar Cymru?*

**a8** What is the principal export of Kenya?

*b8* *What is the principal export of Zambia?*

**a9** Which church was formed in 1972 by the amalgamation of the Congregational and Presbyterian churches in England?

*b9* *Members of which religious movement can be identified by their custom of wearing their hair in dreadlocks?*

**a10** In which eastern European country was a rebellion put down by Soviet troops in 1956?

*b10* *Which country did Arab states fight in the 1973 Yom Kippur War?*

**a11** Which novelist wrote *The Portrait of a Lady*?

*b11* *Which author said (on reading his premature obituary) 'Reports of my death are greatly exaggerated'?*

**a12** Whose last outpost, in 1917, was the Winter Palace?

*b12* *At Christmas 1989, in which country was a Communist dictator overthrown?*

# No. 76 Answers

**a1**   Bill Bailey
*b1*   *'Lily of Laguna'*
**a2**   Costa Brava
*b2*   *Costa del Sol*
**a3**   Newcastle upon Tyne
*b3*   *Dundee*
**a4**   *Gone With the Wind*
*b4*   *Cary Grant*
**a5**   Brake horse power
*b5*   *Kilometres per hour*
**a6**   Alcohol free of any water
*b6*   *Sound that is too high for the human ear to hear*
**a7**   Channel 4
*b7*   *The (fourth) Welsh television channel (literally: Channel 4 Wales)*
**a8**   Coffee and/or tea (Also animal hides)
*b8*   *Copper*
**a9**   United Reformed Church
*b9*   *Rastafarians*
**a10**  Hungary
*b10*  *Israel*
**a11**  Henry James
*b11*  *Mark Twain*
**a12**  The Russian Tsar's (Tsar Nicholas II's)
*b12*  *Romania (President Ceausescu) (say: chow-cheskew)*

## Tie-breaker

**Q**   In 1935 the British government asked the scientist Robert Watson-Watt to invent an anti-aircraft 'death ray'. He said it was impossible. What did he invent instead?

**A**   *Radar (first radar system for detecting enemy planes)*

# No. 77

**a1**  With which political party do you associate William Whitelaw?

*b1*  *And with which party do you associate Jo Grimmond?*

**a2**  Which early rock musician was known as 'Chuck'?

*b2*  *With which group did the pop musician Sting perform for a period?*

**a3**  Which town is the administrative headquarters of the Isle of Wight?

*b3*  *In which city are the administrative headquarters of Hampshire?*

**a4**  What was the name of the bear on *The Muppet Show*?

*b4*  *On television's* Muppet Show, *which animals were famous for space travel?*

**a5**  Who wrote the play *French Without Tears*?

*b5*  *In 1901 a play called* Three Sisters *was first performed in Moscow. Who is it by?*

**a6**  Which Polish-born French scientist was the first woman to win a Nobel prize (for discoveries about radio-activity)?

*b6*  *Which scientist first split the atom by artificial means?*

**a7**  As what did Henri de Toulouse-Lautrec (who died in 1901) achieve fame?

*b7*  *Which American artist became famous for his paintings of Campbell's soup cans and Marilyn Monroe?*

**a8**  What is the official language in Nigeria?

*b8*  *What is the official language in the African country, Congo?*

**a9**  Who wrote the novel *The Moon and Sixpence*?

*b9*  *Which author (who died in 1905) wrote* Around the World in 80 Days?

**a10**  Before independence, which European country ruled Libya?

*b10*  *And which European country ruled Tunisia?*

**a11**  Which modern poet was also a librarian in Hull?

*b11*  *Which Merseyside poet was also a member of the pop group, The Scaffold?*

**a12**  What is a pulsar?

*b12*  *And what is a quasar? (The first was discovered in 1963)*

# No. 77 Answers

**a1**  Conservatives
*b1*  *Liberal*
**a2**  (Charles) 'Chuck' Berry
*b2*  *The Police*
**a3**  Newport
*b3*  *Winchester*
**a4**  Fozzie
*b4*  *Pigs (as in 'Pigs in Space')*
**a5**  Terence Rattigan
*b5*  *(Anton) Chekhov*
**a6**  Madame Marie Curie
*b6*  *(Professor Ernest) Rutherford*
**a7**  Artist, painter of scenes at the Moulin Rouge
*b7*  *Andy Warhol*
**a8**  English
*b8*  *French*
**a9**  Somerset Maugham
*b9*  *Jules Verne*
**a10**  Italy
*b10*  *France*
**a11**  Philip Larkin
*b11*  *Roger McGough*
**a12**  A star which sends out a series of bleeps; very dense stars; a type of neutron star (discovered in 1967)
*b12*  *A 'quasi-stellar radio source'; a very distant source of radio waves (they may be 'black holes' at the centres of distant galaxies)*

---

## Tie-breaker

**Q**  What four colours are generally used in colour printing?
**A**  *Yellow, magenta, cyan (blue), and black*

---

# No. 78

**a1**  Of what common device or implement was there a type called a Brownie?

**b1**  *What device was first marketed in 1901 by a man called King Camp Gillette?*

**a2**  On television, who travelled by Tardis?

**b2**  *What was the name of the short, fat, dumpy robot in the film Star Wars?*

**a3**  How many watts make a kilowatt?

**b3**  *How many watts make a megawatt?*

In which cities would you find these sporting venues?

**a4**  Welford Road

**b4**  *The Stoop*

**a5**  Elland Road

**b5**  *Anfield*

**a6**  The Parks

**b6**  *Fenners*

**a7**  Name two of the Goons

**b7**  *Who was the smallest of the comedy team, the Goodies?*

**a8**  Beatrix became queen of which country in 1980?

**b8**  *Which monarch died in January 1901?*

**a9**  Long, medium and short waves are used in ... what?

**b9**  *For what purpose were ultra-high frequency (or UHF) radio waves originally used?*

**a10**  Who wrote the children's 'Peter Rabbit' books?

**b10**  *Which author wrote The Call of the Wild and White Fang?*

**a11**  As what did Augusta Rodin achieve fame?

**b11**  *As what did Sarah Bernhardt achieve fame?*

**a12**  In 1917, which party did Lenin lead to power in Russia?

**b12**  *Which political party was founded by the Italian Benito Mussolini in 1919?*

# No. 78 Answers

**a1**  Camera
***b1***  *Safety razor*
**a2**  Dr Who
***b2***  *R2D2*
**a3**  1,000
***b3***  *1,000,000 (one million)*
**a4**  Leicester
***b4***  *London*
**a5**  Leeds
***b5***  *Liverpool*
**a6**  Oxford
***b6***  *Cambridge*
**a7**  Spike Milligan, Harry Secombe, Peter Sellers (Michael Bentine, briefly)
***b7***  *Bill Oddie*
**a8**  The Netherlands
***b8***  *Queen Victoria*
**a9**  Radio transmission
***b9***  *Television transmission*
**a10**  Beatrix Potter
***b10***  *Jack London*
**a11**  As a sculptor
***b11***  *Actress*
**a12**  Bolshevik
***b12***  *Fascist*

---

## Tie-breaker

**Q**  What was made illegal in Britain in October 1915, in the hope of cutting down the consumption of alcohol?

**A**  *'Treating' or the buying of 'rounds' in public houses (punishment for those caught was £100 fine or six months in jail)*

# No. 79

**a1**  In personal adverts, what is GSOH?
*b1*  *And what is meant by WLTM?*
**a2**  Which fictional detective had to be brought back to 'life' in 1905?
*b2*  *Which county is visited by tourists interested in the novels of Thomas Hardy?*
**a3**  What is an ocarina?
*b3*  *And what is an oculist?*
**a4**  Which war ended in 1902?
*b4*  *In which year was the so-called 'Winter of Discontent'?*
**a5**  Which organization links the police forces of 146 countries?
*b5*  *What is OPEC?*
**a6**  Which besieged South African town, commanded by Colonel Baden Powell, was relieved in 1900?
*b6*  *Which South African town was relieved after a 118-day siege earlier in 1900?*
**a7**  Until 1905, which country ruled Norway?
*b7*  *Which Scandinavian country became independent of Russian rule in 1917?*
**a8**  In the film *I'm No Angel*, which actress said, 'Beulah, peel me a grape'?
*b8*  *In which film did Greta Garbo say 'I want to be alone' (to John Barrymore)?*
**a9**  Which is the principal city on New Zealand's southern island?
*b9*  *Which is the largest city in New Zealand?*
**a10**  As what did the American Ogden Nash achieve fame?
*b10*  *As what did the Italian Enrico Caruso achieve fame?*
**a11**  Which Irish nationalist (famous for his diaries) was hanged for treason in 1916?
*b11*  *In Irish history, which party was supported by Sir Edward Carsun?*
**a12**  Which Welsh poet wrote: 'The Hunchback in the Park', 'After the Funeral' and 'Poem in October'?
*b12*  *Who wrote the poems 'Bagpipe Music' and 'Prayer Before Birth'?*

# No. 79 Answers

**a1**   Good Sense of Humour
*b1*   *Would Like To Meet*
**a2**   Sherlock Holmes
*b2*   *Dorset*
**a3**   Musical instrument (played by blowing)
*b3*   *Specialist in eye diseases*
**a4**   Boer War
*b4*   *1978–9*
**a5**   Interpol (International Criminal Police Organization)
*b5*   *Organization of Petroleum Exporting Countries*
**a6**   Mafeking
*b6*   *Ladysmith*
**a7**   Sweden
*b7*   *Finland*
**a8**   Mae West
*b8*   Grand Hotel
**a9**   Christchurch
*b9*   *Auckland*
**a10**   Poet
*b10*   *As a singer (tenor)*
**a11**   (Sir Roger) Casement
*b11*   *Ulster Unionists*
**a12**   Dylan Thomas
*b12*   *Louis MacNeice*

---

## Tie-breaker

**Q**   In 1903, the king and queen of which middle European country were shot in a bedroom cupboard?
**A**   *Serbia (King Alexander and Queen Draga)*

# No. 80

**a1** On television, which comic character regularly asked, 'Permission to speak, sir?'?

*b1 In Dallas, who played J R Ewing?*

**a2** Cagliari is the capital of which Mediterranean island?

*b2 And Palermo is the capital of which other Mediterranean island?*

**a3** In the thirties and forties, as what did Ambrose achieve fame?

*b3 Which chain of shops was run by Joseph Sieff?*

**a4** Which three Scandinavian countries have ruling royal families?

*b4 How did Princess Grace of Monaco die (in 1982)?*

**a5** Which English major led Arabs into Damascus to free it from the Turks?

*b5 In which country did Mahatma Gandhi first campaign?*

**a6** Why is Knock (say: nok) in Ireland, visited by many people each year?

*b6 Which police force is based at New Scotland Yard?*

**a7** Which theory was proposed by Albert Einstein in 1905?

*b7 For what medical research and practice did Patrick Steptoe become famous?*

**a8** Which war was fought from August 1990 to April 1991?

*b8 The invasion of which country started that war?*

**a9** What is a Scud?

*b9 And what are Harriers, Jaguars and Tornados?*

**a10** 'Me Tarzan ... You Jane' was spoken to Maureen O'Sullivan by which actor in the film *Tarzan the Ape Man*?

*b10 In which film did Anthony Perkins have the line, 'Mother – what's the phrase – isn't quite herself today'?*

**a11** Of which church organization has Terry Waite been a member?

*b11 Which emperor had the title 'Lion of Judah'?*

**a12** Who was re-elected prime minister of Britain in 1900?

*b12 Sir Henry Campbell-Bannerman became prime minister in 1906. Which party did he lead?*

# No. 80 Answers

**a1** Lance-Corporal Jones (Clive Dunn) in *Dad's Army*
*b1* *Larry Hagman*
**a2** Sardinia
*b2* *Sicily*
**a3** Bandleader
*b3* *Marks and Spencer*
**a4** Norway, Sweden, Denmark
*b4* *In a car crash*
**a5** T E Lawrence, Lawrence of Arabia
*b5* *South Africa*
**a6** It's a religious shrine; a Catholic place of pilgrimage
*b6* *Metropolitan Police*
**a7** Theory of (special) relativity
*b7* *Test-tube babies; fertilization of the egg in a test tube*
**a8** Gulf War
*b8* *Kuwait*
**a9** A missile (Soviet surface-to-surface missile)
*b9* *Fighter aircraft ('strike' aircraft)*
**a10** Johnny Weissmuller (in fact he said, 'Tarzan ... Jane', pointing first to himself and then to her)
*b10* Psycho
**a11** Church Army
*b11* *Haile Selassie of Ethiopia/Abyssinia*
**a12** Lord Salisbury
*b12* *Liberal*

## Tie-breaker

**Q** The film *The Old California* was famous for being the first film to be made in which town?

**A** *Hollywood (in 1910)*

# No. 81: The New Millennium

Which year in this century will be:

**a1** Queen Elizabeth II's Golden Jubilee?
*b1* *The centenary of Queen Victoria's death?*
**a2** The centenary of powered flight by aircraft?
*b2* *The centenary of the first colour cinema film?*
**a3** The centenary of the Battle of the Somm?
*b3* *The centenary of the retreat at Dunkirk?*
**a4** The centenary of the electric washing machine?
*b4* *The centenary of the first jukebox?*
**a5** The golden jubilee of manned flight in space?
*b5* *The golden jubilee of heart transplant surgery?*
**a6** The centenary of the founding of the BBC?
*b6* *The golden jubilee of ITV?*
**a7** The 500th anniversary of the death of Henry VIII?
*b7* *The 500th anniversary of Queen Elizabeth I's accession?*
**a8** The 500th anniversary of the Battle of Flodden?
*b8* *The 500th anniversary of the Spanish Armada?*
**a9** The 500th anniversary of the union of England and Wales?
*b9* *The 500th anniversary of the birth of Shakespeare?*
**a10** The bicentenary of the Battle of Trafalgar?
*b10* *The bicentenary of the Battle of Waterloo?*
**a11** The bicentenary of the Indian Mutiny?
*b11* *The bicentenary of the Abolition of Slavery (in British law)?*
**a12** The 250th anniversary of the Independence of the USA?
*b12* *The 300th anniversary of the union of England and Scotland?*

# No. 81 Answers

| | |
|---|---|
| **a1** | 2002 |
| *b1* | *2001* |
| **a2** | 2003 |
| *b2* | *2008* |
| **a3** | 2016 |
| *b3* | *2040* |
| **a4** | 2004 |
| *b4* | *2005* |
| **a5** | 2011 |
| *b5* | *2017* |
| **a6** | 2022 |
| *b6* | *2005* |
| **a7** | 2047 |
| *b7* | *2058* |
| **a8** | 2013 |
| *b8* | *2088* |
| **a9** | 2036 |
| *b9* | *2064* |
| **a10** | 2005 |
| *b10* | *2015* |
| **a11** | 2057 |
| *b11* | *2034* |
| **a12** | 2032 |
| *b12* | *2007* |

## Tie-breaker

**Q** Which year will be the first millennial anniversary of the Battle of Hastings?

**A** *2066*

# No. 82

**a1**  In the films, who played Rocky?
*b1*  *Whose catch phrase was 'Rock on, Tommy'?*
**a2**  If something is porous, what can pass through it?
*b2*  *And if something is translucent, what can pass through it?*
**a3**  In which sport did Bill Beaumont captain England?
*b3*  *In which sport did David Gower captain England?*
**a4**  What is the cost of eight items, each costing £2.10?
*b4*  *And what is the cost of 32 items, each costing 30p?*
**a5**  In computing, what is 'Spam'?
*b5*  *What is or was Hale-Bopp?*
**a6**  What is the tangent of a circle?
*b6*  *What is a cyberpet?*
**a7**  Which mountain range separates Argentina and Chile?
*b7*  *Which river separates the two historic towns of Buda and Pest?*
**a8**  In which famous house did Queen Victoria die?
*b8*  *At Windsor, in which chapel are members of the Royal Family buried?*
**a9**  Milan is the capital of which Italian region?
*b9*  *And Florence is the capital of which Italian region?*
**a10**  In which industry did the firm Saatchi and Saatchi operate?
*b10*  *What did the 1923 Matrimonial Act allow women to do to men for the first time?*
**a11**  Which crime writer created a detective called Commander Adam Dalgleish?
*b11*  *And which writer created Chief Inspector Reg Wexford?*
**a12**  In physics, what do we call the external agency which can change the state of rest or motion of a body?
*b12*  *Which of the following substances will not combine with oxygen: gold, mercury, carbon sulphur, hydrogen?*

# No. 82 Answers

**a1**  Sylvester Stallone
*b1*  *(Bobby) Ball (to Tommy Cannon)*
**a2**  Liquids or gas
*b2*  *Light*
**a3**  Rugby union
*b3*  *Cricket*
**a4**  £16.80
*b4*  *£9.60*
**a5**  Electronic 'junk mail', (unwanted e-mails)
*b5*  *A comet (appeared in 1997)*
**a6**  A line which touches it once and only once
*b6*  *Electronic toy that imitates the behaviour of a real pet*
**a7**  Andes
*b7*  *Danube*
**a8**  Osborne House, Isle of Wight
*b8*  *St George's*
**a9**  Lombardy
*b9*  *Tuscany*
**a10**  Advertising
*b10*  *Divorce them (for adultery)*
**a11**  P D James
*b11*  *Ruth Rendell*
**a12**  Force
*b12*  *Gold*

## Tie-breaker

**Q**  Until 1954, which three countries made up French Indo-China?
**A**  *Vietnam, Laos, Cambodia (Kampuchea)*

# No. 83

**a1** If you describe something as a rip-off, what would you mean?

*b1* *If you buy a hatchback, can you say precisely what you would be acquiring?*

**a2** If we say someone 'rabbits on' about something, what do we mean?

*b2* *What do we mean if we say that a building is listed?*

**a3** If you buy something that is zero-rated, which tax does not apply to it?

*b3* *Can you explain what a 'Catch-22' situation is?*

**a4** In the area of house purchasing, what does 'gazumping' mean?

*b4* *In the area of foreign policy, what is 'the domino theory'?*

**a5** On which river is the former West German capital of Bonn?

*b5* *On which river is the historic French town of Rouen?*

**a6** Which is the smallest country in the Common Market?

*b6* *Which was the largest republic within the USSR?*

**a7** Which European country's stamps and coins bear its old Latin name, Helvetia?

*b7* *On which country's coins can be found the slogan, 'Liberty, Equality, Brotherhood' (or 'Fraternity')*

**a8** In which television series were Doris, Bruno and Miss Sherwood regular characters?

*b8* *In which television series did we meet Donna, Ray and Cliff?*

**a9** What name do we give to the resistance encountered when one solid body moves while in contact with another?

*b9* *What do we call the force with which a celestial body, such as the earth or moon attracts an object?*

**a10** What colour are copper sulphate crystals?

*b10* *What colour is potassium permanganate when dissolved in water?*

**a11** Whose diary was actually written by Sue Townsend?

*b11* *Who, supposedly, wrote the 'Dear Bill' letters which appeared in the magazine* Private Eye?

**a12** Which cricket club's flag shows Prince of Wales' feathers?

*b12* *On a motor-racing track, what does a white flag indicate?*

# No. 83 Answers

**a1**  It was a swindle; not worth the money paid for it; cheat
*b1*  *A car with a sloping rear door opening upward*
**a2**  He/she talks at great length (irrelevantly or repetitively)
*b2*  *It has special architectural interest (no demolition without special authority)*
**a3**  VAT
*b3*  *One in which you can't win (because a circumstance will change to block any course of action you take)*
**a4**  Seller raising the price after agreeing to sell (before contract signed)
*b4*  *One event sparks off a chain of similar ones (e.g. one country turning to communism causes similar adjacent nations to follow suit)*
**a5**  Rhein
*b5*  *Seine*
**a6**  Luxembourg
*b6*  *Russian Federation*
**a7**  Switzerland's
*b7*  *France's*
**a8**  *Fame*
*b8*  *Dallas*
**a9**  Friction
*b9*  *Gravity*
**a10**  Blue
*b10*  *Purple/deep red*
**a11**  Adrian Mole's
*b11*  *Denis Thatcher*
**a12**  Surrey
*b12*  *There's a service car on the circuit*

---

## Tie-breaker

**Q**  What are the 10 events of the Olympic Decathlon?
**A**  *100m, 110m hurdles, 400m, 1,500m races, long jump, high jump, pole vault, shot put, javelin, discus*

---

# No. 84

**a1** What's another name for a meteorological area of low pressure?

*b1* *Which country's parliament is called the Knesset?*

**a2** In *EastEnders*, who was played by Leslie Grantham?

*b2* *Which television drama is set in Holby City Hospital?*

**a3** What type of electric light or lighting was introduced in 1910?

*b3* *When was poison gas first used?*

What are the capital cities of the following Australian states and territories?

**a4** New South Wales

*b4* *Victoria*

**a5** Queensland

*b5* *Western Australia*

**a6** Northern Territory

*b6* *South Australia*

**a7** Which university opened near Brighton in 1961?

*b7* *Which university opened near Colchester in 1964?*

**a8** Where might you find cueing and anti-skating devices?

*b8* *What familiar product is graded in ASA and/or DIN?*

**a9** Who had hits with 'The Real Thing' and 'This is the Right Time'?

*b9* *'Is this Love' and 'Love Resurrection' were hits for whom?*

**a10** Which body of men elects the Pope?

*b10* *Which French girl was canonized in 1920?*

**a11** Which novel features Ralph, Jack and Piggy?

*b11* *Which novelist created the character Gandalf the Wizard?*

**a12** What particular discovery was made by the physician anatomist William Harvey?

*b12* *Sir Ronald Ross won a Nobel prize for his discoveries connected with – which illness?*

# No. 84 Answers

a1     Depression/cyclone
*b1*     *Israel*
a2     Den Watts, Dirty Den
*b2*     *Casualty*
a3     Neon
*b3*     *First World War (1915)*
a4     Sydney
*b4*     *Melbourne*
a5     Brisbane
*b5*     *Perth*
a6     Darwin
*b6*     *Adelaide*
a7     University of Sussex
*b7*     *University of Essex*
a8     On a record player/turntable deck
*b8*     *Photographic film*
a9     Lisa Stansfield
*b9*     *Alison Moyet*
a10    The Sacred College of Cardinals; cardinals of the Roman Catholic church
*b10*   *Joan of Arc*
a11    *Lord of the Flies* (by William Golding)
*b11*   *J R R Tolkien*
a12    Circulation of the blood
*b12*   *Malaria*

---

## Tie-breaker

**Q**    How many of the seven Welsh counties created in 1974 can you name?

**A**    *Clwyd, Dyfed, Gwent, Gwynedd, Powys, Mid-Glamorgan, South Glamorgan and West Glamorgan*

# No. 85

**a1**   On television, what was the name of the waiter in *Fawlty Towers*?

*b1*   *Which American TV series had as its stars Sharon Gless and Tyne Daly?*

**a2**   In Moscow, what was the Lubyanka?

*b2*   *What is Izvestia?*

*a3*   *What do the figures '007' mean in the James Bond books?*

*b3*   *And what is the name of M's secretary in many of the Bond films and books?*

**a4**   What is the normal temperature of your body in degrees Celsius?

*b4*   *In physics, what do we call a quantity which has both magnitude and direction?*

**a5**   Which of the following metals does not react with water: calcium, copper, iron, potassium, sodium?

*b5*   *Can you name the three bones in the middle ear?*

**a6**   Which comedian had success in the pop charts with 'Tears', 'Happiness' and 'Love is Like a Violin'?

*b6*   *Which vocalist often used to sing while sitting in a rocking chair?*

**a7**   Besides the board and the pieces, what do you need to play Backgammon?

*b7*   *In which game might you land on Mayfair or a railway station?*

**a8**   Prior to 1974, what were the three Ridings of Yorkshire?

*b8*   *After the Second World War, which three countries occupied West Germany?*

**a9**   In 1921, what chemical gave hope to diabetics?

*b9*   *If you suffer from xenophobia, what do you dislike?*

**a10**   Which Adriatic country came into being at the end of the First World War?

*b10*   *To which country did the Ottoman Empire belong (till it was broken up in 1920)?*

**a11**   Which university in Staffordshire opened in 1962?

*b11*   *Which university opened in Birmingham in 1966?*

**a12**   Who was Major Buckley?

*b12*   *In which game was the third Lord Tennyson successful?*

# No. 85 Answers

**a1** Manuel
*b1* Cagney and Lacey
**a2** A notorious prison
*b2* *Russian newspaper*
**a3** He is licensed to kill
*b3* *Miss Moneypenny*
**a4** 36.9 (allow 36 or 37)
*b4* *A vector*
**a5** Copper
*b5* *Malleus, incus, stapes (also known as hammer, anvil, stirrup)*
**a6** Ken Dodd
*b6* *Val Doonican*
**a7** Dice
*b7* *Monopoly*
**a8** North, West, East
*b8* *United Kingdom, United States of America and France*
**a9** Insulin
*b9* *Foreigners, strangers, other countries*
**a10** Yugoslavia
*b10* *Turkey*
**a11** Keele
*b11* *University of Aston (in Birmingham)*
**a12** Manager of Wolverhampton Wanderers
*b12* *Cricket*

---

## Tie-breaker

**Q** Who is this actress? 'For several seasons, I was the leading lady in Miss Horniman's repertory company in Manchester. To celebrate our golden wedding, my husband and I appeared in *Eighty in the Shade*. Down in Leatherhead, they graciously named a theatre after me.'

**A** *Dame Sybil Thorndike (1882–1976)*

# No. 86

**a1**   In snooker, how many points are scored when you pot the pink?

*b1*   *And how many when you pot the blue?*

**a2**   Galerie Lafayette is a department store in which capital city?

*b2*   *Which is the most famous department store in London's Knightsbridge?*

**a3**   In which types of food do we find Vitamin C?

*b3*   *Can you name the type of food in which we find Vitamin D?*

**a4**   In which battle was Germany defeated in August and September 1940?

*b4*   *In which battle was Germany defeated in October and November 1942?*

**a5**   In which musical is everything 'up-to-date in Kansas City'?

*b5*   *In which musical is the song 'If I were a Rich Man'?*

**a6**   What kind of ship is sometimes described as a 'ro-ro'?

*b6*   *The world's largest ship was destroyed by rocket attack in 1976. What type of ship was it?*

**a7**   In which year was the first flight of the supersonic plane, Concorde? Was it 1969, 1972 or 1976?

*b7*   *And in which year did it enter scheduled service?*

**a8**   In which county is Welwyn Garden City?

*b8*   *Which major new town or city has been developed in Buckinghamshire since 1967?*

**a9**   Who wrote *The Spy Who Came in from the Cold*?

*b9*   *Who wrote* Where Eagles Dare *and* The Guns of Navarone*?*

**a10**   On which planet did the space ships Viking 1 and 2 land in 1975?

*b10*   *Which planet did Mariner 2 fly by in 1962?*

**a11**   Male members of which religion wear a turban to cover their uncut hair?

*b11*   *Shinto is the folk religion of which country?*

**a12**   What is the UPU?

*b12*   *What is GATT?*

# No. 86 Answers

**a1** 6
*b1* *5*
**a2** Paris
*b2* *Harrods*
**a3** Fruit, green vegetables
*b3* *Liver, dairy products, eggs, fish*
**a4** Battle of Britain
*b4* *El Alamein*
**a5** *Oklahoma!*
*b5* Fiddler on the Roof
**a6** Roll-on, roll-off car ferry
*b6* *Oil tanker (the 'Seawise Giant')*
**a7** 1969
*b7* *1976*
**a8** Hertfordshire
*b8* *Milton Keynes*
**a9** John Le Carré
*b9* *Alistair Maclean*
**a10** Mars
*b10* *Venus*
**a11** Sikhism
*b11* *Japan*
**a12** Universal Postal Union (Co-ordinates internation post)
*b12* *General Agreement on Tariffs and Trade*

---

## Tie-breaker

**Q** Which are the four open tennis competitions a player must win to achieve the 'Grand Slam'?

**A** *French, Australian, US, and Wimbledon Opens*

---

# No. 87

**a1**    What do we call a car built before 1918?

*b1*    *And what name is given to a car built between 1918 and 1930?*

**a2**    Where in London are most of the Henry Wood Promenade Concerts held?

*b2*    *What is the telephone dialling code for inner London?*

**a3**    On which part of the body does a cardiac surgeon specialize?

*b3*    *On which parts of the body do orthopaedic surgeons work?*

**a4**    About a million people died in which siege during the Second World War?

*b4*    *And in which country's civil war did another 1½ million die between 1967 and 1969?*

**a5**    As what did Ralph Vaughan Williams achieve fame?

*b5*    *As what did Bertrand Russell achieve fame?*

**a6**    At which university did St Catherine's, St Peter's and St Anthony's colleges open this century?

*b6*    *Which university opened at Guildford in 1966?*

**a7**    Chief Detective Superintendent Lockhart was the central character of which television series?

*b7*    *On television, Barry Foster played a Dutch detective called ...?*

**a8**    Which author created the fictional village of Thrush Green?

*b8*    *What was the title of Muriel Spark's novel about a distinctive Edinburgh teacher?*

**a9**    What is the name of the neck of water which separates European and Asian Turkey?

*b9*    *The Gulf of Bothnia separates which two northern countries?*

**a10**    On which London underground line is the longest tunnel?

*b10*    *Which northern city re-introduced a street tramway system in 1992?*

**a11**    About what would you consult *Grove's Dictionary*?

*b11*    *Which magazine, originally reprinting condensations of articles from other magazines, first appeared in 1922?*

**a12**    Which playwright wrote the line, 'Very flat, Norfolk'?

*b12*    *Which French playwright wrote the farces* A Flea in Your Ear *and* Look After Lulu?

# No. 87 Answers

**a1** A veteran
*b1* *Vintage*
**a2** Albert Hall
*b2* *0171*
**a3** The heart
*b3* *Bones (and joints)*
**a4** Siege of Leningrad (St Petersburg)
*b4* *Nigeria (accept: Biafra)*
**a5** Composer
*b5* *Philosopher (contributor to many radio programmes)*
**a6** Oxford
*b6* *University of Surrey*
**a7** *No Hiding Place*
*b7* *Van der Valk*
**a8** Miss Read
*b8* *The Prime of Miss Jean Brodie*
**a9** The Bosporus
*b9* *Sweden and Finland*
**a10** Northern (Morden – East Finchley via Bank) (17.3 miles)
*b10* *Manchester*
**a11** Music
*b11* *Reader's Digest*
**a12** Noël Coward
*b12* *Georges Feydeau*

## Tie-breaker

**Q**   Who wrote the novel *Catch-22*?
**A**   *Joseph Heller*

# No. 88

**a1** In which city is the department store called Macy's?

*b1* *And in which city is the department store called GUM?*

**a2** In Germany, what is the Bundesbahn (say: bun-des-barn)?

*b2* *What are or were Delta, Eastern and Braniff?*

**a3** Which is the largest civil engineering project this century?

*b3* *In the world of transport, what were Counties, Kings and Castles?*

**a4** On television's *New Avengers*, who played Purdey?

*b4* *Grace Metalious wrote a novel which inspired a film and a television series. It was called ...?*

**a5** Which country suffered most casualties in the Second World War?

*b5* *Where was the setting for television's* Enemy at the Door *series?*

**a6** In London, which title role in an Andrew Lloyd Webber musical did Michael Crawford create?

*b6* *Who wrote (and performed) the songs 'Mad Dogs and Englishmen' and 'Mrs Worthington'?*

**a7** In which year was the Wall Street Crash in America?

*b7* *Since its foundation in 1929, which has been the world's smallest independent country?*

**a8** Where in the north of England is the Metro Shopping Centre?

*b8* *Which major new town has been developed in Shropshire since 1963?*

**a9** Which glamorous male film star appeared in *The Four Horsemen of the Apocalypse* and *The Sheikh*?

*b9* *What was the nickname of the Hollywood star, Roscoe Arbuckle?*

**a10** The inventor of which rapid fire machine gun died in 1903?

*b10* *Which material was invented by Leo Baekeland in 1907?*

**a11** Which is the more flexible plastic – polystyrene, polypropylene or polyester?

*b11* *Which purified element is used to make the chips in microprocessors?*

**a12** Did Aspirin go on sale for the first time in 1905, 1923 or 1931?

*b12* *In which year was the first radio broadcast of speech and music? Was it in 1906, 1920 or 1923?*

# No. 88 Answers

| | |
|---|---|
| **a1** | New York |
| *b1* | *Moscow* |
| **a2** | Railway system |
| *b2* | *(American) airline companies* |
| **a3** | The new Hong Kong airport |
| *b3* | *(Express) steam locomotives (on the Great Western Railway)* |
| **a4** | Joanna Lumley |
| *b4* | *Peyton Place* |
| **a5** | Soviet Union |
| *b5* | *Channel Islands* |
| **a6** | *Phantom of the Opera* |
| *b6* | *Noël Coward* |
| **a7** | 1929 |
| *b7* | *Vatican City State* |
| **a8** | Gateshead |
| *b8* | *Telford* |
| **a9** | Rudolf Valentino |
| *b9* | *Fatty (Arbuckle)* |
| **a10** | (Richard) Gatling |
| *b10* | *Bakelite* |
| **a11** | Polyester |
| *b11* | *Silicon* |
| **a12** | 1905 |
| *b12* | *1906* |

---

## Tie-breaker

**Q** 1934 saw the introduction of high street shops offering a useful domestic service. What were they?

**A** *Launderettes*

---

# No. 89

**a1**   Which television series featured Del and Rodney?

*b1*   *In which television series did Penelope Keith play Mrs Forbes-Hamilton?*

**a2**   In which sport were Maureen Connolly and Margaret Court champions?

*b2*   *HRH Princess Anne excelled in which sport?*

**a3**   Which country is the world's largest producer of wool?

*b3*   *What is the principal business or industry of the tiny country of Monaco?*

**a4**   In which musical did we see the Ascot Gavotte?

*b4*   *In which musical was there a lonely goatherd?*

**a5**   Before transistors were used in radios, what did their job?

*b5*   *Was the first electric washing machine made in 1906, 1931 or 1948?*

**a6**   The 'Third World' includes the developing countries. Which is the 'First World'?

*b6*   *And which is (or was) the 'Second World'?*

**a7**   Which item of clothing was first put on the market in 1937 by a New York and London company?

*b7*   *On a clothing label, what symbol indicates a garment may be dry-cleaned?*

**a8**   Where, in 1918, did almost the entire German naval fleet sink itself?

*b8*   *In which building near Paris was the First World War peace treaty signed?*

**a9**   What do geiger counters measure?

*b9*   *To whom has insulin been especially beneficial?*

**a10**   About which fictional character's complaint did Philip Roth write a novel?

*b10*   *American author Anita Loos became popular with a novel about a blonde flapper – called ... what?*

**a11**   Who would receive training at RADA?

*b11*   *As a preparation for which job might you obtain the CQSW?*

**a12**   Which university opened in Greater Manchester in 1967?

*b12*   *Which university opened at Coleraine in Northern Ireland in 1965?*

# No. 89 Answers

**a1** *Only Fools and Horses*
**b1** To The Manor Born
**a2** Tennis
**b2** *Equestrianism*
**a3** Australia
**b3** *Tourism and/or gambling*
**a4** *My Fair Lady*
**b4** The Sound of Music
**a5** Valves
**b5** *1906*
**a6** Western Europe, North America and Australasia
**b6** *The Soviet Union and what was formerly communist eastern Europe (it is disputed whether China is in the 'Second' or 'Third' world)*
**a7** Nylons (NY – Lon)
**b7** *A circle*
**a8** Scapa Flow, Scotland
**b8** *Palace of Versailles*
**a9** (Nuclear) radiation
**b9** *People suffering from diabetics*
**a10** Portnoy's (*Portnoy's Complaint*)
**b10** Gentlemen Prefer Blondes
**a11** Actors/Actresses (Royal Academy of Dramatic Art)
**b11** *Social worker (Certificate of Qualification in Social Work)*
**a12** University of Salford
**b12** *New University of Ulster*

## Tie-breaker

**Q** Which was the first European country to give women the vote?
**A** *Finland (1906)*

# No. 90

**a1**  Chris Boardman rides. On what?
*b1*  *What would you watch at Sandown?*
**a2**  Who were 'White' Russians?
*b2*  *In 1906, what was a 'Silver Ghost'?*
**a3**  The invasion by Germany of which country brought Britain into the Second World War?
*b3*  *Which country was occupied by Germany in the 1938 'Anschluss'?*
**a4**  Of what is laurel an emblem?
*b4*  *Of which country is the peacock an emblem?*
**a5**  On television, in which series did we meet Inspector Jack Regan and Detective Sergeant Carter?
*b5*  *And what is meant by the underworld expression, 'the Sweeney'?*
**a6**  In which county is the new town of Crawley?
*b6*  *In which English county is the new town of Washington?*
**a7**  By what nickname was Wild West show owner William Cody generally known?
*b7*  *Which early film star became known as 'The World's Sweetheart'?*
**a8**  In the Spanish Civil War was the Falange Party fascist or communist?
*b8*  *On which island has tension between Tamil Indians and native inhabitants led to violence?*
**a9**  Which fictional detective lives in a village called St Mary Mead?
*b9*  *Which novelist invented the Drones Club?*
**a10**  Which Irishman wrote the mammoth novel *Ulysses*?
*b10*  *Which Czech-Jewish author wrote* The Trial*?*
**a11**  Alongside which West German river is a major coal mining, steel and industrial region?
*b11*  *Which important dam was completed on the River Nile in 1970?*
**a12**  What fraction of the human body is water?
*b12*  *In medicine, for what are gamma rays used?*

# No. 90 Answers

**a1**  A (bi)cycle
**b1**  *Horse racing*
**a2**  Non-Communists
**b2**  *A Rolls-Royce motor car*
**a3**  Poland
**b3**  *Austria*
**a4**  Victory
**b4**  *India*
**a5**  *The Sweeney*
**b5**  *The Flying Squad*
**a6**  (West) Sussex
**b6**  *Tyne and Wear*
**a7**  Buffalo Bill
**b7**  *Mary Pickford*
**a8**  Fascist
**b8**  *Sri Lanka*
**a9**  Miss Marple
**b9**  *P G Wodehouse*
**a10**  James Joyce
**b10**  *Franz Kafka*
**a11**  Ruhr
**b11**  *Aswan Dam*
**a12**  Two thirds
**b12**  *To kill cancer cells*

---

## Tie-breaker

**Q**  In which sport do you 'take the drop'?
**A**  *Surfing*

---

# No. 91: The First World War

**a1**  By when was the War meant to be all over?

*b1*  *What shocked the generals at Christmas 1914?*

**a2**  Which side won the Battle of Mons?

*b2*  *Which army was defeated at Tannenberg?*

**a3**  Where, according to Sir Edward Grey, were the lamps going out?

*b3*  *According to a famous recruiting poster, what did the women of Britain say to their menfolk?*

**a4**  Until his death in 1916, who was Britain's Secretary of State for War?

*b4*  *What was the name of the infamous sea-battle off Denmark in 1916?*

**a5**  Where was 'no man's land'?

*b5*  *Which new so-called 'Motor Monsters' were first used in 1916?*

**a6**  In which year did the Somme campaign begin?

*b6*  *Which Field Marshal directed the British at the start of this campaign?*

**a7**  In 1915, how were Norfolk towns hit by German fire?

*b7*  *On which peninsula in the Dardanelles did the Allies seek to establish a base?*

**a8**  Which English poet died en route to the Dardanelles?

*b8*  *What was the nickname of German airman Baron Manfred von Richthofen?*

**a9**  Who became British prime minister halfway through the war?

*b9*  *Who had been prime minister at the start of the war?*

**a10**  What were 'doughboys'?

*b10*  *What was 'Big Bertha'?*

**a11**  On what charge was the dancer Mata Hari put to death?

*b11*  *Into what were the Royal Flying Corps and Royal Naval Air Service merged in 1918?*

**a12**  For what are Siegfried Sassoon and Isaac Rosenberg remembered?

*b12*  *And for what are Sir John Sergeant and John Nash remembered?*

# No. 91 Answers

**a1** Christmas
*b1* *Brief peace in the trenches, fraternization between armies*
**a2** Germany
*b2* *Russia*
**a3** All over Europe
*b3* *'Go'*
**a4** Lord Kitchener
*b4* *Jutland*
**a5** Between the opposing front lines
*b5* *Tanks*
**a6** 1916
*b6* *Sir Douglas Haig*
**a7** By Zeppelin raids
*b7* *Gallipoli*
**a8** Rupert Brooke
*b8* *Red Baron*
**a9** Lloyd George
*b9* *Herbert Asquith*
**a10** American soldiers
*b10* *A huge German gun*
**a11** Spying
*b11* *RAF (Royal Air Force)*
**a12** Their war poetry
*b12* *Their war paintings*

---

## Tie-breaker

**Q** Who wrote the words, 'They shall not grow old as we that are left grow old'?
**A** *Laurence Binyon*

---

**a1**  What is Princess Margaret's second christian name?

*b1*  *Which member of the Royal Family was killed in a flying accident in 1942?*

**a2**  Of which American state is Sacramento the capital?

*b2*  *Which dance, popular in the twenties, was named after a city in South Carolina?*

**a3**  What is the usual word for a motorway in the United States of America?

*b3*  *And what is a motorway called in Germany?*

**a4**  What is sumo?

*b4*  *And where or what is Sumatra?*

**a5**  On television, who plays Ken Boon?

*b5*  *On television, who plays Hadleigh?*

**a6**  In which year did we see the first pocket calculators? Was it 1969, 1971 or 1974?

*b6*  *In which year did we see the first digital watches? Was it 1963, 1968 or 1971?*

**a7**  A gruelling 19 day cycle race was run for the first time in 1903. What was it called?

*b7*  *To see which sport would you be most likely to travel to Ripon in Yorkshire?*

**a8**  What is a Tristar? (say: try-star)

*b8*  *What are the Triads?*

**a9**  Which airport is sometimes known by the initials LHR?

*b9*  *Entebbe airport is in which African country?*

**a10**  In 1900, which empire stretched from Constantinople and Baghdad westwards through Egypt to Tripoli?

*b10*  *In which war early in the century did Britain imprison women and children in concentration camps?*

**a11**  Which American humourist wrote *Guys and Dolls*?

*b11*  *Which American novelist wrote the 'sex-change' novel* Myra Breckinridge*?*

**a12**  Which South American country was still a département of France in 1991?

*b12*  *In which country is there an area of grassland called the Mato Grosso?*

# No. 92 Answers

**a1** Rose
*b1* *(George) Duke of Kent*
**a2** California
*b2* *Charleston*
**a3** Freeway or highway
*b3* *Autobahn*
**a4** Japanese wrestling
*b4* *Largest island of Indonesia (south of Singapore)*
**a5** Martin Elphick
*b5* *Gerald Harper*
**a6** 1971
*b6* *1971*
**a7** Tour de France
*b7* *Horse racing*
**a8** (American) airliner
*b8* *Members of a Chinese secret society (said to be involved in drugs and gambling)*
**a9** London Heathrow
*b9* *Uganda (near Kampala)*
**a10** Turkish
*b10* *Boer War (in southern Africa)*
**a11** Damon Runyon
*b11* *Gore Vidal*
**a12** French Guiana
*b12* *Brazil*

---

## Tie-breaker

**Q** On which radio show did the presenter regularly ask, 'Are you courting?' or 'Tell us, have you had any embarrassing moments?'?

**A** Have A Go *(with Wilfred Pickles)*

# No. 93

**a1**  In which sport was Jack Hobbs a star?

*b1*  *Which sportsman, known as 'W G', died in October 1915?*

**a2**  Where were a group of part-time policemen known as B-Specials?

*b2*  *And to which religion or order did they belong?*

**a3**  Which American secret society used violence to defend white supremacy over Blacks and Jews?

*b3*  *Who said, 'There will be no white wash at the White House'?*

**a4**  Who was the star of the early film comedy *Cops*?

*b4*  *Who starred in the film* The Man Who Fell to Earth*?*

**a5**  The composer of the 'Savoy Operas' died in 1900. Who was he?

*b5*  *Who composed 'Rhapsody in Blue'?*

**a6**  Who wrote the thriller *The Eagle Has Landed*?

*b6*  *About which Roman emperor did Robert Graves write two novels?*

**a7**  As what did Alexander Skryabin (say: scree-a-bin) become famous?

*b7*  *As what did Professor A J 'Freddie' Ayer achieve fame?*

**a8**  Who was Geraldo?

*b8*  *And for playing which instrument did Semprini become famous?*

**a9**  Which political party held its first rally in 1923, led by an Austrian corporal and decorator?

*b9*  *And which world leader resigned in 1923, after a serious stroke?*

**a10**  Who was Tsar of Russia in the early years of the century?

*b10*  *Of which country was David Lange (say: longi) prime minister?*

**a11**  Which churchman became the first leader of independent Cyprus in 1960?

*b11*  *Who became the first president of the Turkish Republic in 1923?*

**a12**  In which year did Britain first have a Labour prime minister?

*b12*  *In which year were Australian Aborigines given the vote? Was it 1947, 1973 or 1981?*

# No. 93 Answers

**a1** Cricket
**b1** *W G Grace, the cricketer*
**a2** Northern Ireland
**b2** *Protestant, the Protestant Orange Order*
**a3** Ku Klux Klan
**b3** *President Nixon (during the Watergate affair)*
**a4** Buster Keaton
**b4** *David Bowie*
**a5** Sir Arthur Sullivan
**b5** *George Gershwin*
**a6** Jack Higgins
**b6** *Claudius (*I, Claudius*; *Claudius the God*)*
**a7** Composer
**b7** *Philosopher (member of television's original Brains Trust)*
**a8** Band leader (became famous in London in the thirties)
**b8** *Piano*
**a9** National Socialist (Nazi)
**b9** *(Vladimir) Lenin*
**a10** Nicholas II
**b10** *New Zealand*
**a11** Archbishop Makarios
**b11** *(Mustafa) Kemal Attaturk*
**a12** 1924
**b12** *1973*

## Tie-breaker

**Q** Which European city was the last to be liberated in the Second World War?

**A** *Prague*

# No. 94

**a1**  In the Second World War, what was the BEF?
*b1*  *And for what did the initials ARP stand?*
**a2**  What was Babe Ruth's sport?
*b2*  *And what was Wally Hammond's sport?*
**a3**  Which group recorded the album 'Urban Hymns'?
*b3*  *Name the lead singer of Catatonia.*
**a4**  As what did Lord Northcliffe achieve fame?
*b4*  *Who was the philanthropist who died in 1922, having founded a village for his workers called Bournville?*
**a5**  Where do the Masai people live?
*b5*  *And in which country do Sherpas live?*
**a6**  Which cat and mouse were invented in 1939 by Fred Quimby, William Hanna and Joseph Barbera?
*b6*  *Who are Laa Laa and Po?*
**a7**  In which country is the city of Isfahan?
*b7*  *In which capital city is there a royal enclave known as the 'Forbidden City'?*
**a8**  Antonio Salazar was dictator of which European country?
*b8*  *Which statesman was buried in the village of Colombey-les-Deux-Eglises in November 1970?*
**a9**  In which year did Britain introduce decimal currency?
*b9*  *And when that happened, what was the new value of the old 'florin' coin?*
**a10**  What was the name (or nickname) of the American woman who became a successful painter at the age of 78?
*b10*  *Which artist can be said to have invented Cubism?*
**a11**  Who wrote the novels *Howard's End* and *A Room With a View*?
*b11*  *Who wrote the novel* The Great Gatsby?
**a12**  Which radio family lived in Parkwood Hill?
*b12*  *In which long-running comedy radio programme did Richard Murdoch star with Kenneth Horne?*

# No. 94 Answers

**a1** British Expeditionary Force
*b1* *Air raid precautions*
**a2** Baseball
*b2* *Cricket*
**a3** The Verve
*b3* *Cerys (Matthews)*
**a4** Newspaper owner (died 1922, founded the *Daily Mail* in 1896)
*b4* *(George) Cadbury*
**a5** East Africa (highlands of Kenya and Tanzania)
*b5* *Nepal*
**a6** Tom and Jerry
*b6* *Two of the Teletubbies*
**a7** Iran
*b7* *Beijing (Peking), in China*
**a8** Portugal
*b8* *(Charles) de Gaulle*
**a9** 1971
*b9* *10p*
**a10** Grandma Moses (Anna Mary Robertson Moses)
*b10* *Picasso (also Braque)*
**a11** E M Forster
*b11* *F Scott Fitzgerald*
**a12** *The Dales* (originally called *Mrs Dale's Diary*)
*b12* Much-Binding-in-the-Marsh

---

## Tie-breaker

**Q** What were 'The Four Freedoms', the democratic ideals proposed jointly by Franklin D Roosevelt and Winston Churchill in 1941?

**A** *Freedom of Expression, Freedom of Worship, Freedom from Fear, Freedom from Want*

# No. 95

**a1** Which boy's comic, launched in 1950, featured Dan Dare?
*b1* *And, pre-war, which comic featured Corky the Cat?*
**a2** In which sport was Donald Budge a champion?
*b2* *Which was Sam Snead's sport?*
**a3** For which instrument was Harry James renowned?
*b3* *And Fats Waller?*
**a4** Julius, Arthur and Leonard were the real names of which film star brothers?
*b4* *What was the screen name of the actress V M Leigh Holman?*
**a5** Who attempted (in 1923) to start a revolution in a beer hall or cellar?
*b5* *Which capital city did the Russians capture on 13 April 1945?*
**a6** Which famous bomber of the Second World War was made by Boeing?
*b6* *Besides the Fortress, what was America's other main bomber in the same war?*
**a7** Which American president was assassinated in 1901?
*b7* *Which American politician was assassinated in 1968?*
**a8** Pre-war, as what did the Swiss known as Grock become famous?
*b8* *Which world-famous clown first appeared in Britain in Bertram Mills Circus in 1930?*
**a9** Was safety glass invented in 1905, 1935 or 1955?
*b9* *Was the first IBM word processor introduced in 1938, 1964 or 1974?*
**a10** Which comedian had the nickname 'The Prime Minister of Mirth'?
*b10* *What was the nickname of the American comedian, Jimmy Durante?*
**a11** What was the pen name of the creator of the fictional hero, Bulldog Drummond?
*b11* *Pelham Grenville were the first names of which novelist?*
**a12** What name was given to German air raids on historic or beautiful towns in the Second World War?
*b12* *In the Second World War, on which island did the British intern foreign nationals and those whose loyalty was suspect?*

# No. 95 Answers

**a1**  *The Eagle*
**b1**  The Dandy
**a2**  Lawn tennis
**b2**  *Golf*
**a3**  Trumpet
**b3**  *Piano*
**a4**  (Groucho, Harpo and Chico) Marx
**b4**  *Vivien Leigh*
**a5**  Adolf Hitler (and Erich van Ludendorff)
**b5**  *Vienna*
**a6**  Flying Fortress
**b6**  *Liberator*
**a7**  William McKinley
**b7**  *Bobby (Robert) Kennedy*
**a8**  Circus clown
**b8**  *Coco*
**a9**  1905
**b9**  *1964*
**a10**  George Robey
**b10**  *Schnozzle*
**a11**  Sapper
**b11**  *P G Wodehouse*
**a12**  Baedeker Raids
**b12**  *Isle of Man*

---

## Tie-breaker

**Q**  Who is this actress? 'I first acted in 1888 and was once described as "a glorious, impossible woman". It was I who said, "It doesn't matter what you do in the bedroom as long as you don't do it in the streets and frighten the horses." My great friend was Bernard Shaw.'

**A**  *Mrs Patrick Campbell (1865–1940)*

# No. 96

**a1**  In which sport did Phil de Glanville captain England?

*b1  What is South African Ernie Els' sport?*

**a2**  Which comedian had as his catch phrase, 'Can you hear me, mother?'?

*b2  Which diminutive comedian had as his catch phrases 'I thank you', pronounced 'Ay theng yow' and 'Before your very eyes'?*

**a3**  What was the name of Superman's girlfriend?

*b3  In the Walt Disney cartoons, who was Pluto?*

**a4**  'Tiger Rag' was the signature tune of which popular band-leader?

*b4  And whose signature tune was 'Say it with Music'?*

**a5**  In which country is the 'lost city' of the Incas, rediscovered in 1911?

*b5  In which country is the royal burial ground, the Valley of the Kings?*

**a6**  As what did the American Charles Manson become notorious?

*b6  Ethel Le Nève was mistress and accomplice to which famous murderer?*

**a7**  As what did Sir Frederick Ashton achieve fame?

*b7  Which scout became famous for organizing the scouting 'Gang Shows'?*

**a8**  Next to which city is Pearl Harbor naval base?

*b8  In the Second World War, which European capital did American troops liberate two days before D-Day?*

**a9**  Which organization once had its headquarters at London's Savoy Hill?

*b9  From where in London did the BBC transmit its first regular television programmes?*

**a10**  In the thirties, what was the 'China Clipper'?

*b10  And what was the 'Tiger Moth'?*

**a11**  Which American radio play caused panic in the streets in 1938?

*b11  Which cult television series invented a ministry for silly walks and featured a dead parrot?*

**a12**  Who wrote the science fiction anti-war novel *Slaughterhouse Five*?

*b12  Who wrote the book* The Female Eunuch?

# No. 96 Answers

**a1**    Rugby union
*b1*    *Golf*
**a2**    Sandy Powell
*b2*    *Arthur Askey*
**a3**    Lois Lane
*b3*    *The dog*
**a4**    Harry Roy
*b4*    *Jack Payne*
**a5**    Peru
*b5*    *Egypt*
**a6**    Murderer (of Sharon Tate and others)
*b6*    *Dr Crippen*
**a7**    Choreographer (accept: ballet dancer)
*b7*    *Ralph Reader*
**a8**    Honolulu
*b8*    *Rome*
**a9**    BBC
*b9*    *Alexandra Palace*
**a10**    A giant flying-boat
*b10*    *Bi-plane; training aircraft*
**a11**    *War of the Worlds* (produced by Orson Welles)
*b11*    Monty Python's Flying Circus
**a12**    Kurt Vonnegut
*b12*    *Germaine Greer*

---

## Tie-breaker

**Q**    In 1925, what was painted on British roads for the first time, in an attempt to reduce accidents?

**A**    *White lines*

# No. 97

**a1**   Which politician was born on 13th October 1925 in Grantham?

*b1*   *Which politician has been credited with advising the unemployed: 'On yer bike'?*

**a2**   What name was given to the hosts and entertainers at Butlins' Holiday Camps?

*b2*   *Which English seaside resort has the longest pier?*

**a3**   Which city is the Big Apple?

*b3*   *Which city is a holy city for three world religions?*

**a4**   In which daily paper did the picture strip 'Jane' appear?

*b4*   *In which comic did Lord Snooty first appear?*

**a5**   Which comedian reminisced about 'the day war broke out'?

*b5*   *By what name were Nervo and Knox, Naughton and Gold, and Flanagan and Allen known when they appeared together on stage?*

**a6**   In the post-war years, what was Godfrey Evans' great contribution to England's cricket?

*b6*   *The cricketer Denis Compton became famous for appearing in advertisements – for what?*

**a7**   Who wrote the hit of the thirties, 'Stardust'?

*b7*   *Which American musician was known as the 'King of Swing'?*

**a8**   Michael Collins was a politician and leader of which country?

*b8*   *Why did Bernadette Devlin become well-known in 1969?*

**a9**   Which French minister of war became famous for his 'line' of fortifications along the French-German frontier?

*b9*   *What name was given to the large balloons flown over towns and harbours in war-time to discourage enemy aircraft?*

**a10**   During the Second World War, why were Alvar Liddell, Frank Phillips and John Snagge household names?

*b10*   *In which radio series did we hear the catch phrase 'Don't forget the diver' and 'I don't mind if I do'?*

**a11**   As what did Josephine Baker win fame in the twenties?

*b11*   *Which famous series of paperback books was started by Sir Allen Lane?*

**a12**   In 1925, Eisenstein directed a film about which battleship?

*b12*   *In the world of films, for what do the initials MGM stand?*

# No. 97 Answers

**a1**  Margaret Thatcher (Lady Thatcher)
*b1*  *Norman Tebbit (Lord Tebbit)*
**a2**  Redcoats
*b2*  *Southend-on-Sea*
**a3**  New York
*b3*  *Jerusalem (Judaism, Christianity, Islam)*
**a4**  *Daily Mirror*
*b4*  The Beano
**a5**  Robb Wilton
*b5*  *The Crazy Gang*
**a6**  As wicket-keeper
*b6*  *Brylcream*
**a7**  Hoagy Carmichael
*b7*  *Benny Goodman*
**a8**  Ireland (Irish Free State)
*b8*  *Ulster MP, sentenced for incitement to riot*
**a9**  Maginot (say: maj-in-oh)
*b9*  *Barrage balloons*
**a10**  They were radio newsreaders
*b10*  ITMA *(Tommy Handley's* It's That Man Again*)*
**a11**  As a dancer (in French nightclubs)
*b11*  *Penguin Books*
**a12**  Potemkin (*The Battleship Potemkin*)
*b12*  *Metro-Goldwyn Mayer*

---

## Tie-breaker

**Q**  Who first said, 'We are all the president's men'?
*A*  *Dr Henry Kissinger (justifying the US invasion of Cambodia)*

---

# No. 98

**a1**    On television, whose catch phrase became 'Didn't he do well?'?

*b1*    *Which comedian and singer used to say, 'I've arrived and to prove it, I'm here'?*

**a2**    If you were on the 'Bluebell', how would you be travelling?

*b2*    *What is the name of the transcontinental railway across Russia, completed in 1904?*

**a3**    Which cartoon characters were created by Roger Hargreaves?

*b3*    *Who wrote about a bear called Winnie-the-Pooh?*

**a4**    What was the name of the first British aircraft carrier?

*b4*    *Which British liner made her maiden transatlantic voyage in 1936?*

**a5**    By which river do the Abu Simbel temples stand?

*b5*    *In which country is the Kruger National Park?*

**a6**    What was the surname of the entertainer 'Two-Ton Tessie'?

*b6*    *Which radio and television comedian was known for his schoolmasterly catch phrase, 'Wake up at the back, there!'?*

**a7**    Which international prizes were first awarded in Norway and Sweden in 1901?

*b7*    *The flag or sign of the International Red Cross is basically a reversal of which country's flag?*

**a8**    What was *Oh! Calcutta!*?

*b8*    *Which 'opera' includes the song 'Mack the Knife'?*

**a9**    In the Second World War, what was 'pool'?

*b9*    *What nickname was generally given to flying bombs in the Second World War?*

**a10**    Which poet was rude enough to write, 'Come friendly bombs and fall on Slough'?

*b10*    *Which 20th-century British prime minister's wife published a volume of her poems?*

**a11**    What was the name of the Communist family which savagely ruled Romania until 1989?

*b11*    *In which country was Adolf Eichmann executed in 1962?*

**a12**    Which Russian soccer team made a famous tour of Britain immediately after the Second World War?

*b12*    *At which Scottish football ground did 66 people die when a barrier collapsed in 1971?*

# No. 98 Answers

**a1**   Bruce Forsyth
*b1*   *Max Bygraves*
**a2**   By (steam) train; it's a preserved railway line
*b2*   *Trans-Siberian Railway*
**a3**   Mr Men
*b3*   *A A Milne*
**a4**   Ark Royal
*b4*   *The Queen Mary*
**a5**   Nile (Moved to avoid flooding during the building of the Aswan Dam)
*b5*   *South Africa*
**a6**   O'Shea
*b6*   *Jimmy Edwards*
**a7**   Nobel Prizes
*b7*   *Switzerland's*
**a8**   Theatrical sex revue (1970)
*b8*   *The Threepenny Opera*
**a9**   Unbranded petrol
*b9*   *Doodle bugs (or buzz bombs)*
**a10**   (Sir John) Betjeman
*b10*   *Mary Wilson*
**a11**   Ceausescu (say: chow-cheskew)
*b11*   *Israel*
**a12**   Moscow Dynamo
*b12*   *Ibrox Park (Glasgow Rangers)*

---

## Tie-breaker

**Q**   Which play by Peter Shaffer reconstructs the last ten years of the life of Mozart?
**A**   Amadeus

---

# No. 99

**a1**   What was the 'Tirpitz'?

*b1*   *Who or what was 'Arkle'?*

**a2**   In 1970, which British golfer became the first Briton to win the US Open for fifty years?

*b2*   *Nelli Kim was a champion at what?*

**a3**   Which 'layer' around the Earth prevents dangerous ultraviolet radiation from harming us?

*b3*   *In space exploration, what is linked with the name 'Hubble'?*

**a4**   Which ruler's real surname was Schickelgruber?

*b4*   *Where in Germany was the annual rally of the Nazi party held during the thirties?*

**a5**   The 1923 Cup Final was the first major event staged in which sporting stadium?

*b5*   *Of which football club did Matt Busby become manager in 1945?*

**a6**   Which major west European power left NATO in 1966?

*b6*   *Where are the headquarters of the Council of Europe?*

**a7**   'Buddy, Can You Spare a Dime' was a popular song during the American depression. Which singer made it a hit?

*b7*   *T H White's story of King Arthur, The Once and Future King, became a musical – under what title?*

**a8**   In British education, what is or was 'LMS'?

*b8*   *And in the world of transport, what was 'LMS'?*

**a9**   In which country is the city, Da Nang?

*b9*   *What is the capital of Slovakia?*

**a10**   Which Nazi propaganda minister was known as 'the Mouth'?

*b10*   *Who was head of the Gestapo and the SS, who committed suicide in 1945?*

**a11**   Just three aircraft were available to defend Malta in 1940. What were their names?

*b11*   *Which British pilot (who lost both legs before the war) became an ace pilot during the Second World War (before being taken prisoner)?*

**a12**   Which Frenchman wrote *A la Recherche du Temps Perdu*?

*b12*   *Which Polish author, writing in English, told many stories about the sea and the Far East?*

# No. 99 Answers

**a1** German battleship
*b1* *Race horse*
**a2** Tony Jacklin
*b2* *Gymnastics*
**a3** Ozone layer
*b3* *The Hubble Space Telescope (launched 1990)*
**a4** Adolf Hitler
*b4* *Nuremburg*
**a5** Wembley
*b5* *Manchester United*
**a6** France
*b6* *Strasbourg (in France)*
**a7** Bing Crosby
*b7* *Camelot*
**a8** Local management of schools
*b8* *London, Midland and Scottish Railway*
**a9** South Vietnam
*b9* *Bratislava*
**a10** Goebbels
*b10* *(Heinrich) Himmler*
**a11** 'Faith', 'Hope' and 'Charity'
*b11* *Douglas Bader*
**a12** (Marcel) Proust
*b12* *Joseph Conrad*

## Tie-breaker

**Q** Which country had an internal security force known as STASI?
**A** *East Germany (German Democratic Republic)*

# No. 100

**a1**    Where, in the United States, is Disney World?

*b1*    *And in which state in the USA is Disneyland?*

**a2**    Which part of the body is affected by dermatitis?

*b2*    *Which type of flu killed almost three thousand people in Britain in one week in 1970?*

**a3**    What, in the Second World War, were Weights and Capstan?

*b3*    *What were Grants, Shermans and Cromwells?*

**a4**    Of which country are Orange Free State and the Transvaal now parts?

*b4*    *Of what origin were the large group of people expelled from Uganda in 1972?*

**a5**    Who or what are gauchos?

*b5*    *And what is a gaudy?*

**a6**    Which Australian batsman made a sensational debut in England in 1930?

*b6*    *Who was Britain's champion racing jockey in the thirties (and after the Second World War)?*

**a7**    'Coco' was the nickname of which famous French fashion queen?

*b7*    *Besides being a dancer, who or what was Nijinsky?*

**a8**    What giant carving has been cut into the Black Hills of Dakota?

*b8*    *The merchant ship called 'The Savannah of America' was famous for its means of propulsion. Why?*

**a9**    From the 1920s onwards, which country embarked on a series of Five-Year Plans?

*b9*    *In 1948 and 1949, which city was saved by a huge, ongoing 'airlift' of its requirements?*

**a10**    'Older' and 'Faith' were albums issued by which male vocalist?

*b10*    *'Give Me a Little More Time' and 'Dreams' were hits for which female vocalist?*

**a11**    Which country was formed in 1963 by the merging of Malaya, Singapore, Sabah and Sarawak?

*b11*    *For what was Monte Bello island used in October 1952?*

**a12**    Which two countries fought at the Battle of Tsushima in 1905?

*b12*    *In 1935, where on the continent were British troops sent to keep the peace?*

# No. 100 Answers

**a1** Florida
*b1* *California*
**a2** The skin
*b2* *Hong Kong flu (Hong Kong A2 virus)*
**a3** Brands of cigarettes
*b3* *Tanks*
**a4** South Africa
*b4* *Asian ('Ugandan Asians')*
**a5** South American cowboys
*b5* *College or university reunion, entertainment*
**a6** Don Bradman
*b6* *Gordon Richards*
**a7** (Gabrielle) Chanel (say: sha-nell)
*b7* *Champion racing horse*
**a8** Statues of four American presidents (Washington, Jefferson, Roosevelt and Lincoln)
*b8* *First nuclear-powered merchant ship*
**a9** Soviet Union (USSR)
*b9* *Berlin*
**a10** George Michael
*b10* *Gabrielle*
**a11** Malaysia
*b11* *The testing of Britain's first atomic bomb*
**a12** Japanese and Russians
*b12* *The Saar*

---

## Tie-breaker

**Q** *Towards a New Architecture was written by which Swiss-French architect in 1923?*
**A** *Le Corbusier (Charles Edouard Jeanneret)*

# No. 101: More Modern Lingo

What is meant by the following words and phrases which have all entered the language in recent years?

**a1** Advertorial
*b1* *Affinity card*
**a2** Callanetics (say: cal-a-ne-ticks)
*b2* *The chattering classes*
**a3** On message
*b3* *A Denver boot*
**a4** 'E' or Ecstasy
*b4* *A graphic novel*
**a5** 'Fatwa' or 'Fatwah'
*b5* *Intifada*
**a6** A ligger
*b6* *Mondo*
**a7** A Sloane Ranger
*b7* *Quorn (as you might find it in a supermarket)*
**a8** 'Slo-mo' (as used in the media and the world of films)
*b8* *A sound bite*
**a9** A spin doctor (as used in the world of politics)
*b9* *Sampling (as practised in the world of music)*
**a10** A white knight (as used in the financial world)
*b10* *Black Monday (again, as in the financial world)*
**a11** Paintball
*b11* *A rah-rah skirt*
**a12** The Gaia theory
*b12* *Jojoba (say: ho-ho-ba)*

# No. 101 Answers

**a1** A newspaper advertisement written to look like an article
*b1 A credit card issued to a particular group*
**a2** A physical exercise programme
*b2 Members of the educated, middle classes who read the 'quality' newspapers and who hold opinions about topical matters*
**a3** Giving an approved opinion
*b3 A wheel clamp*
**a4** A drug
*b4 A book-length story in comic strip format*
**a5** A ruling given by an Islamic leader; a decree
*b5 An Arab uprising*
**a6** A 'sponger' or freeloader; a party-crasher
*b6 'Utterly', extremely (slang)*
**a7** An upper-class, very conventional young person
*b7 Vegetable protein, vegetarian meat substitute*
**a8** Slow motion
*b8 A short extract from a recorded speech or interview*
**a9** A spokesman employed to make news sound favourable
*b9 Re-using short pieces of music in a new composition*
**a10** A company that rescues one facing a hostile takeover bid
*b10 The day of the stock market crash (19 October 1987)*
**a11** A type of 'war-game' in which pellets of bright paint are fired at the 'enemy'
*b11 Type of skirt worn by American cheerleaders*
**a12** Theory that the Earth adapts itself in order to survive
*b12 A desert shrub; oil (from that shrub) used in cosmetics*

## Tie-breaker

**Q** On which Far Eastern island are there amusement parks called the Great World, the Gay World and the New World?
*A Singapore*

# No. 102

**a1**    What did the Diners' Club introduce in 1950?
*b1*    *What new means of cooking was patented in 1953?*
**a2**    Who crashed a car at Chappaquiddick in 1969?
*b2*    *And what was the name of his passenger, who drowned?*
**a3**    In which sport is the Calcutta Cup a trophy?
*b3*    *And which two countries compete for the Calcutta Cup?*
**a4**    Which building near Agra is said to look its best in moonlight?
*b4*    *In 1939, which country changed its name to Thailand?*
**a5**    Which disease is sometimes called 'MS'?
*b5*    *What is caries?*
**a6**    Which spaceship carried the first men to stand on the moon?
*b6*    *In space, what is thought to cause a 'black hole'?*
**a7**    In the Second World War, what did 'ack-ack' mean?
*b7*    *During the Second World War, what was 'bully beef'?*
**a8**    Of which country was Alexander Dubcek (say: dub-check) a ruler?
*b8*    *Of which country was John G Diefenbaker prime minister from 1957 to 1963?*
**a9**    What was the native country of Samuel Beckett (author of *Waiting for Godot*)?
*b9*    *Who wrote the farces* Rookery Nook, The Cuckoo in the Nest *and* Thark?
**a10**    On radio what is 'BFBS'?
*b10*    *Which radio station broadcast for many years on 208 metres?*
**a11**    What nationality was the composer Béla Bartok?
*b11*    *What nationality was the composer Arnold Bax?*
**a12**    In which year was the British electricity supply system privatized?
*b12*    *In which year did the nationalized British Railways come into being?*

# No. 102 Answers

**a1**  Credit cards
*b1*  *Microwave ovens*
**a2**  Senator Edward Kennedy
*b2*  *Mary Jo Kopechne*
**a3**  Rugby union
*b3*  *England and Scotland*
**a4**  Taj Mahal
*b4*  *Siam*
**a5**  Multiple sclerosis (say: skluh-roh-sis)
*b5*  *Tooth decay*
**a6**  Apollo 11
*b6*  *The explosion of a large star*
**a7**  Anti-aircraft
*b7*  *Corned beef*
**a8**  Czechoslovakia
*b8*  *Canada*
**a9**  Ireland
*b9*  *Ben Travers*
**a10**  British Forces Broadcasting Service
*b10*  *Radio Luxembourg*
**a11**  Hungarian
*b11*  *British*
**a12**  1990
*b12*  *1948*

---

## Tie-breaker

**Q**  *The Big Sleep, Farewell My Lovely and The High Window are novels by which American crime writer?*
**A**  *Raymond Chandler*

# No. 103

**a1**  In the film *Kind Hearts and Coronets*, who played eight different roles?

*b1*  *Who were the two stars of the 1946 film* Brief Encounter*?*

**a2**  On which sport does Peter Bromley commentate?

*b2*  *Which county cricket club did the commentator 'Aggers' formerly represent?*

**a3**  What is the purpose of a hospice?

*b3*  *What is a hologram?*

**a4**  Known as 'the hard man', what was Vinnie Jones sport?

*b4*  *Which civil rights leader did James Earl Ray shoot dead in 1968?*

**a5**  What is a herbivore?

*b5*  *Which kind of tree was ravaged by disease in the seventies?*

**a6**  Which sport (in Britain) do the Barbarians play?

*b6*  *In which sport might you compete for the Admiral's Cup?*

**a7**  In the Second World War, what was the WAAF?

*b7*  *Also in the Second World War, what was ENSA?*

**a8**  Who wrote the book *My Family and Other Animals*?

*b8*  *Who wrote books called* The Human Zoo *and* The Naked Ape*?*

**a9**  What is measured in ampères?

*b9*  *What is measured in watts?*

**a10**  Which South African doctor pioneered human heart transplant surgery?

*b10*  *Research by Enrico Fermi led to the building of the first nuclear ... what?*

**a11**  Who became chancellor of West Germany in 1969?

*b11*  *Sir Joshua Hassan was chief minister of which British colony?*

**a12**  As what did Arnold Schoenberg become famous?

*b12*  *Walter Sickert died in 1942. What was his trade or profession?*

# No. 103 Answers

**a1**   (Sir) Alec Guinness
*b1*   *Celia Johnson, Trevor Howard*
**a2**   Racing
*b2*   *Leicestershire (Jonathan Agnew)*
**a3**   To care for the dying, the terminally ill
*b3*   *A picture which appears to have depth; a 3-D picture*
**a4**   Soccer
*b4*   *Martin Luther King*
**a5**   An animal that feeds only on plants
*b5*   *Elm (Dutch elm tree disease)*
**a6**   Rugby Union
*b6*   *Yachting*
**a7**   Women's Auxiliary Air Force
*b7*   *Entertainments National Service Association (entertainment for the troops)*
**a8**   Gerald Durrell
*b8*   *Dr Desmond Morris*
**a9**   Electric current
*b9*   *Electrical power*
**a10**  Dr Christiaan Barnard
*b10*  *Reactor*
**a11**  Willi Brandt
*b11*  *Gibraltar*
**a12**  Composer (of 'modern' music)
*b12*  *Artist*

---

## Tie-breaker

**Q**   The films *Brighton Rock*, *Fame Is the Spur* and *Lucky Jim* were made by which pair of brothers?
**A**   *(John and Roy) Boulting*

# No. 104

**a1** On television, who originally presented *Take Your Pick*?

*b1* *And who presented* Double Your Money*?*

**a2** Which is the most westerly point on the English mainland?

*b2* *Which is the most important city in Scotland's Grampian region?*

**a3** Which theatrical satire, devised by Joan Littlewood, attacked aspects of the First World War?

*b3* *In which popular musical did the cast face the audience nude (in 1968)?*

**a4** In the Second World War slang, what were 'angels'?

*b4* *In the Second World War RAF slang, what were 'cookies'?*

**a5** For which soccer club did Jimmy Armfield play?

*b5* *For which country did Danny Blanchflower play soccer?*

**a6** What is particular about a 'geostationary' satellite?

*b6* *What is the source of 'geothermal' energy?*

**a7** Which British politician made a controversial speech in 1968 about 'rivers of blood'?

*b7* *Which British prime minister tried to be reassuring about 'the pound in your pocket'?*

**a8** What is the purpose of antibodies, medically speaking?

*b8* *In the human body, what is a capillary?*

**a9** Who composed a piece of music called 'On Hearing the First Cuckoo in Spring'?

*b9* *Who composed a suite of music called 'The Planets'?*

**a10** Which author created the character Horatio Hornblower?

*b10* *Which novelist created the private eye Philip Marlowe?*

**a11** Who directed the films *A Clockwork Orange* and *2001: A Space Odyssey*?

*b11* *Which stage actor directed himself in the films* Henry V, Hamlet *and* Richard III*?*

**a12** Which British painter created a huge tapestry for Coventry Cathedral and became famous for controversial portraits?

*b12* *Which English test cricketer became a bishop in the Church of England?*

# No. 104 Answers

**a1** Michael Miles (Des O'Connor hosted a later version)
*b1* *Hughie Green*
**a2** Land's End
*b2* *Aberdeen*
**a3** *Oh, What a Lovely War!*
*b3* Hair
**a4** Friendly aircraft
*b4* *Bombs*
**a5** Blackpool
*b5* *Northern Ireland*
**a6** It stays in the same place above the Earth
*b6* *The heat inside the Earth, found in rocks, geysers, etc.*
**a7** Enoch Powell
*b7* *Harold Wilson*
**a8** To protect us from disease; to fight disease
*b8* *A tiny blood vessel*
**a9** Frederick Delius
*b9* *(Gustav) Holst*
**a10** C S Forester
*b10* *Raymond Chandler*
**a11** Stanley Kubrick
*b11* *Laurence Olivier*
**a12** Graham Sutherland
*b12* *David Sheppard*

## Tie-breaker

**Q** For which sport do you need a loft, a basket or transporter crate and a special type of clock?

**A** *Pigeon racing*

# No. 105

**a1** American, Australian and Canadian are all codes of which sport?

*b1* *Which sport can be indoor, lawn or crown?*

**a2** In England which two counties surround the Wash?

*b2* *Which English city has road tunnels called Kingsway and Queensway?*

**a3** By what name was the comedian, Arthur Stanley Jefferson (who was born at Ulverston in England) internationally known?

*b3* *Which newspaper tycoon drowned in 1991?*

**a4** What is measured in ohms?

*b4* *Of what is a hertz a measure?*

**a5** Who was Che Guevara (say: chay gw-var-a)

*b5* *Who became leader of the Palestine Liberation Organization in 1969?*

**a6** Which county cricket team plays at home at Lords?

*b6* *Which county cricket team plays at home at the Oval?*

**a7** Which writer created William in the 'Just William' stories?

*b7* *Which writer's stories were televised as* Tales of the Unexpected*?*

**a8** In which film about two hustlers trying to live in New York did Dustin Hoffman star with Jon Voigt?

*b8* *In which film about a motor bike ride across America did Dennis Hopper star with Peter Fonda?*

**a9** What nationality was the composer Dmitri Shostakovich?

*b9* *What nationality was the composer Jean (say: jan) Sibelius?*

**a10** In which year was the treaty signed bringing into existence the Irish Free State (or Irish Republic)?

*b10* *In which year did the Spanish Civil War begin?*

**a11** Which long-running radio programme was regularly introduced by 'Uncle Mac'?

*b11* *With which radio programme was Jack de Manio associated?*

**a12** In the Second World War, what was the ATS?

*b12* *During the Second World War, where did 'Bevin Boys' work?*

# No. 105 Answers

**a1** Football
*b1* *Bowls*
**a2** Lincolnshire, Norfolk
*b2* *Liverpool (Merseyside)*
**a3** Stan Laurel
*b3* *Robert Maxwell*
**a4** Electrical resistance
*b4* *Wave frequency*
**a5** Latin American guerilla leader or revolutionary
*b5* *Yassir Arafat*
**a6** Middlesex
*b6* *Surrey*
**a7** Richmal Crompton
*b7* *Roald Dahl's*
**a8** *Midnight Cowboy*
*b8* Easy Rider
**a9** Russian
*b9* *Finnish*
**a10** 1921
*b10* *1936*
**a11** *Children's Hour* (Derek McCulloch – also *Children's Favourites*)
*b11* Today
**a12** Auxiliary Territorial Service
*b12* *Down mines (instead of in the forces)*

---

## Tie-breaker

**Q** Who is this composer? 'One of my earliest hits was the First World War song, "Keep the Home Fires Burning". After that, I became better known as the writer of romantic musicals. My career took off one glamorous night and my final word was gay.'

**A** *Ivor Novello*

---

# No. 106

**a1**   In what sport has Tiger Woods been a champion?

*b1*   *Where is the annual Oxford-Cambridge rugby match played?*

**a2**   Counting all its forms, which language is spoken by the most people?

*b2*   *Which two Chinese words symbolize male and female, day and night, sky and earth?*

**a3**   About which part of the world did the novelist Catherine Cookson write?

*b3*   *Daphne du Maurier wrote a famous novel about a Cornish inn called ...?*

**a4**   In politics, what is (or was) the CP?

*b4*   *In a computer, what is the CPU?*

**a5**   Pasolini, Polanski and Visconti were all ... what?

*b5*   *For which kind of film did the American director John Ford become especially famous?*

**a6**   Which one event brought the United States into the Second World War?

*b6*   *Did bread rationing begin in Britain in 1940, 1942 or 1946?*

**a7**   What was the name of the toy animal with whom Annette Mills appeared on early children's television programmes?

*b7*   *Who were the three central characters on television's* The Flowerpot Men?

**a8**   From what do we get ambergris?

*b8*   *Who or what was Alban Berg?*

**a9**   Is the element radon a metal, a gas or an alkali?

*b9*   *Is the element cadmium a gas, a metal or an alkali?*

**a10**   Why was Bikini Atoll in the news in 1946?

*b10*   *In the late sixties, what was Biba?*

**a11**   In which capital did Soviet tanks crush a movement for freedom in 1968?

*b11*   *Which country seized control of Albania in 1939?*

**a12**   In which year this century was the most serious flooding of Britain's east coast?

*b12*   *In which year was the British coal industry nationalized?*

# No. 106 Answers

**a1** Golf
**b1** *Twickenham*
**a2** Chinese
**b2** *Yin and yang*
**a3** Tyneside; northeast England
**b3** *Jamaica Inn*
**a4** Communist Party
**b4** *Central processing unit (the part that controls the circuits and holds the memory)*
**a5** Film directors
**b5** *Westerns (Stagecoach, The Man Who Shot Liberty Valance, etc.)*
**a6** Bombing of Pearl Harbor
**b6** *1946*
**a7** Muffin the Mule
**b7** *Bill and Ben and Little Weed*
**a8** The sperm-whale (it's used in perfumery)
**b8** *(Austrian) composer*
**a9** A gas
**b9** *A metal*
**a10** It was used for atom bomb tests
**b10** *Department store or boutique for young women*
**a11** Prague
**b11** *Italy*
**a12** 1953
**b12** *1947*

---

## Tie-breaker

**Q** In which group did pop guitarist Eric Clapton play 'Five Long Years' and 'Louise'?

**A** *The Yardbirds*

---

# No. 107

**a1** When was 'Put out that light' a slogan?
*b1* *What is a 'Black Box'?*
**a2** In which political party was Barbara Castle a key figure?
*b2* *By what first name was the Labour politician Cripps always known?*
**a3** For what does PAYE stand?
*b3* *As a human group, what are WASPs?*
**a4** In the television comedy series *Open All Hours*, who played Arkwright?
*b4* *On television, who was the star of* I Love Lucy?
**a5** What is measured by an ammeter?
*b5* *What does a hygrometer measure?*
**a6** In which sport was Jonah Barrington a champion?
*b6* *What was Rod Laver's sport?*
**a7** Who wrote *The Murder of Roger Ackroyd*?
*b7* *Which novelist wrote* Tender Is the Night?
**a8** In which year did Britain invade Suez?
*b8* *In which year did British troops first go into action in Belfast in the present troubles?*
**a9** In which country has been Salvador Allende (say: al-en-deh) a radical leader?
*b9* *What did Edwin 'Buzz' Aldrin achieve on July 21, 1969?*
**a10** Who directed the films *The Music Lovers*, *The Devils* and *Tommy*?
*b10* Blazing Saddles, Young Frankenstein *and* Silent Movie *were all comedies directed by ... whom?*
**a11** Which basketball team or troupe has toured the world and has the signature tune 'Sweet Georgia Brown'?
*b11* *In archery, what colour is the centre of the target?*
**a12** What post has been held by John Masefield and Cecil Day Lewis?
*b12* *What genetic structure was discovered by Francis Crick and James Watson?*

# No. 107 Answers

**a1** During the Black Out, in the Second World War
*b1 Flight recorder in an aircraft, designed to survive any accident*
**a2** Labour
*b2 Stafford (Sir Stafford Cripps)*
**a3** Pay As You Earn
*b3 White Anglo-Saxon Protestants*
**a4** Ronnie Barker
*b4 Lucille Ball*
**a5** The strength of an electrical current
*b5 The amount of moisture in the air*
**a6** Squash
*b6 Tennis*
**a7** Agatha Christie
*b7 F Scott Fitzgerald*
**a8** 1956
*b8 1969*
**a9** Chile
*b9 He was the second man to walk on the moon*
**a10** Ken Russell
*b10 Mel Brooks*
**a11** Harlem Globetrotters
*b11 Gold (accept: yellow)*
**a12** Poet Laureate
*b12 DNA (the molecule that contains genetic information)*

## Tie-breaker

**Q** Which British sculptor became famous (or infamous) for his smooth stone figures, sometimes of human torsos, sometimes of shapes which included holes in them?

**A** *Henry Moore*

# No. 108

**a1**  What was expected to be 'all over by Christmas'?
*b1*  *In the Second World War, what was a Dornier?*
**a2**  Which county cricket team plays at home at Old Trafford?
*b2*  *Which county cricket team plays at home at Edgbaston?*
**a3**  What is the BMA?
*b3*  *What is the BSI?*
**a4**  Which singer had hits with 'Mary's Boy Child' and 'Island in the Sun'?
*b4*  *And which British singer had hits with 'Someone Else's Baby' and 'What Do You Want If You Don't Want Money?'?*
**a5**  As what did Alexander Korda become famous?
*b5*  *As what did the American Aaron Copland become famous?*
**a6**  About which profession did Richard Gordon write a series of comic novels?
*b6*  *About which profession did Henry Cecil write comic novels?*
**a7**  In our cities, what is the major source of the poison, carbon monoxide?
*b7*  *In a car's exhaust system, what is the purpose of the baffle?*
**a8**  In which year did Sir Winston Churchill die? Was it 1958, 1964 or 1965?
*b8*  *Was the death penalty finally abolished in Britain in 1947, 1963 or 1969?*
**a9**  On television, for what was Eileen Fowler once famous?
*b9*  *Who was the first presenter in Britain of the television series* This Is Your Life?
**a10**  What is the biomass (say: bi-o-mass)?
*b10*  *What eventually happens to biodegradable matter?*
**a11**  Who wrote the novel *A Kind of Loving*?
*b11*  *Who wrote the science fiction novel* Fahrenheit 451?
**a12**  What is the currency of South Africa?
*b12*  *What is the currency of Mexico?*

# No. 108 Answers

**a1**    The First World War
*b1*    *German aircraft*
**a2**    Lancashire (at Manchester)
*b2*    *Warwickshire (Birmingham)*
**a3**    British Medical Association
*b3*    *British Standards Institution*
**a4**    Harry Belafonte
*b4*    *Adam Faith*
**a5**    Film producer and director
*b5*    *Composer*
**a6**    Doctors; the medical profession (*Doctor in the House*, etc.)
*b6*    *The law; barristers (*Brother-in-Law*, etc.)*
**a7**    Car exhausts
*b7*    *To reduce noise*
**a8**    1965
*b8*    *1969*
**a9**    Keep-fit programmes
*b9*    *Eamonn Andrews*
**a10**    Total amount of plant and animal life on Earth
*b10*    *It rots; is broken down by bacteria*
**a11**    Stan Barstow
*b11*    *Ray Bradbury*
**a12**    Rand
*b12*    *Peso*

---

## Tie-breaker

**Q**    In which sport do blue and black play against red and yellow?

**A**    *Croquet (blue and black balls always play against the red and yellow balls)*

# No. 109

**a1**  What is the currency of Japan?
*b1*  *What is the currency of Italy?*
**a2**  Which country built the ill-fated airship, the R101?
*b2*  *What kind of aircraft is a Tornado?*
**a3**  Which popular pianist always had as his 'trademark' a candelabra on his piano?
*b3*  *And which clean-cut American singer of the fifties had as his trademark his 'white bucks' (or shoes)?*
**a4**  Which country was the home of 'Tito-ism'?
*b4*  *Which country has been divided by the 38th Parallel?*
**a5**  What is or was a Poseidon C-3?
*b5*  *Of what is 'hydragas' a type?*
**a6**  What is aerodynamics?
*b6*  *What is an aileron?*
**a7**  What is cartography?
*b7*  *In business, what is a cartel?*
**a8**  Which Russian composed a 'Sabre Dance' and a ballet called 'Spartacus'?
*b8*  *Who composed the 'Liberty Bell' and 'Washington Post' marches?*
**a9**  Which country does not take part in cricket's World Cup: Kenya, Wales, or Bangladesh?
*b9*  *In or near which capital city does the soccer team Anderlecht play?*
**a10**  What is your profession if you have the letters ARIBA after your name?
*b10*  *And which musical instrument do you play if you can use the letters ARCO after your name?*
**a11**  Which woman crime writer created the character Mr Ripley?
*b11*  *Which author created the lawyer Perry Mason?*
**a12**  Athol Fugard is a famous South African. What is his profession?
*b12*  *What was the profession of the Italian, Federico Fellini?*

# No. 109 Answers

**a1** Yen
*b1* *Lira*
**a2** Britain
*b2* *(Jet) fighter*
**a3** Liberace
*b3* *Pat Boone*
**a4** Yugoslavia
*b4* *Korea*
**a5** Submarine-launched missile
*b5* *Car suspension system*
**a6** The study of the effect of moving gases; the forces that act on objects moving in the air
*b6* *Movable flap on an aircraft wing (which controls the movements of the aircraft)*
**a7** The making of maps or charts
*b7* *Union of manufacturers (etc.) to control production, prices, etc.*
**a8** (Aram) Khachaturian
*b8* *(John Philip) Sousa*
**a9** Wales
*b9* *Brussels*
**a10** Architect (Associate of the Royal Institute of British Architects)
*b10* *Organ (Associate of the Royal College of Organists)*
**a11** Patricia Highsmith
*b11* *Erle Stanley Gardner*
**a12** Playwright
*b12* *Film director*

---

## Tie-breaker

**Q** How did the first man in space, Yuri Gagarin, die?
**A** *He was killed in a plane crash in 1968 (a Mig fighter he was piloting crashed into the ground)*

---

# No. 110

**a1**  What is a derrick?
*b1*  *What is or was Prestel?*
**a2**  For what is fibreglass wool used?
*b2*  *What is fibrositis?*
**a3**  Which company developed the Xerox (say: zir-rox) copier?
*b3*  *Which company developed the Walkman?*
**a4**  What kind of books were written by Zane Grey?
*b4*  *Which character is the most famous creation of the novelist Edgar Rice Burroughs?*
**a5**  What nickname did 617 Squadron acquire after causing widespread flooding in the Ruhr Valley?
*b5*  *What was the nickname of the 7th Armoured Division which saw action in northern Africa?*
**a6**  Which county cricket team plays at home at Trent Bridge?
*b6*  *Which county cricket team plays at home on the St Lawrence ground?*
**a7**  Which disease was first noted when 34 people died at a convention of the American Legion in 1976?
*b7*  *For what has Papworth in Cambridgeshire become famous?*
**a8**  Who originally sang about Mr Wu cleaning windows?
*b8*  *Who was famous for singing 'Wish Me Luck', 'I Took My Harp to a Party' and 'Walter, Walter'?*
**a9**  What is an AGR?
*b9*  *What is the concern of the organization ASH?*
**a10**  As what did Fred Hoyle achieve fame?
*b10*  *What was the trade or profession of the German, Rainer Fassbinder?*
**a11**  In which country is the currency the zloty (say: zhwo-tee)?
*b11*  *And in which country is the currency the rupee?*
**a12**  On what day of the week are Mardi Gras (say: mar-dee grah) carnivals properly held?
*b12*  *What day of the week is Ascension Day?*

# No. 110 Answers

**a1** Framework of girders over an oilwell that supports the drilling machinery; a crane

*b1* *Information system accessed by phone and television set*

**a2** Insulation of buildings; to conserve heat

*b2* *Information of the muscles; rheumatic disorder*

**a3** Rank

*b3* *Sony*

**a4** Westerns

*b4* *Tarzan*

**a5** Dam Busters

*b5* *Desert Rats*

**a6** Nottinghamshire

*b6* *Kent (at Canterbury)*

**a7** Legionnaires' Disease

*b7* *It's a hospital (heart transplant surgery)*

**a8** George Formby

*b8* *Gracie Fields*

**a9** Advanced Gas-cooled Reactor

*b9* *It is against the ill-effects of smoking (Action on Smoking and Health)*

**a10** Astronomer and/or science fiction writer

*b10* *Film director (and actor)*

**a11** Poland

*b11* *India (and Pakistan, Sri Lanka)*

**a12** Tuesday (Shrove Tuesday; Mardi = Tuesday)

*b12* *Thursday*

---

## Tie-breaker

**Q** Which two American universities row a boat race on the Thames River in Connecticut?

**A** *Harvard, Yale*

---

# No. 111: A la Carte

Recent years have brought foreign restaurants to this country and many more people dine out than used to. But how much do you really know about the terms you see on the menu and in cookery books? What is the meaning of the following?

a1  Aspic
*b1  Au gratin*
a2  Bisque
*b2  Blanch*
a3  Borscht
*b3  Bouillabaisse*
a4  Bouquet garni
*b4  Canapé*
a5  Caviare
*b5  Chowder*
a6  Compote
*b6  Crêpe Suzette*
a7  Croûtons
*b7  Cutlets*
a8  Devilled
*b8  En brochette*
a9  Filet mignon
*b9  Fondue*
a10  Fricassée
*b10  Hollandaise*
a11  Lyonnaise
*b11  Marinade*
a12  Mignon
*b12  Petits fours*

# No. 111 Answers

**a1** Jelly made from gelatine and either meat, fish or vegetable stock

*b1* *Food cooked and covered with breadcrumbs*

**a2** A cream soup prepared from game, fish or vegetables

*b2* *Plunging into boiling water*

**a3** A Russian soup which includes beetroot and other vegetables

*b3* *A fish soup*

**a4** Mixed herbs tied in muslin and used to season foods

*b4* *A piece of toast which is topped with any savoury*

**a5** The roe of the sturgeon

*b5* *A thick soup made from vegetables or fish cooked in milk*

**a6** Fruit cooked slowly in a syrup, often served in a glass stemmed dish

*b6* *A thin pancake, often cooked in wine or spirits*

**a7** Small squares of toast

*b7* *Meat cut from the ribs or legs of beef, lamb, veal or pork*

**a8** Cooked with sauce or hot seasoning

*b8* *Food which is cooked on a skewer*

**a9** A small strip of meat – usually beef

*b9* *A dish made from breadcrumbs, cheese, eggs and milk*

**a10** Braised or sometimes stewed, as with chicken, etc.

*b10* *A sauce, served hot, made from the yolks of eggs and butter*

**a11** Food seasoned with parsley, onions, etc.

*b11* *A mixture of vinegar, wine, spices, in which meat or fish is left to soak to gain extra flavour*

**a12** A tender cut of beef, without any bone

*b12* *Small iced cakes cut into fancy shapes*

---

## Tie-breaker

**Q** In 1951, which novelist and historian edited the first edition of *The Good Food Guide*?

*A* *Raymond Postgate*

---

# No. 112

**a1**   Between which two cities did the Golden Arrow train run?
*b1*   *Which train did Agatha Christie use as a setting for a crime?*
**a2**   What was an 'Instamatic'?
*b2*   *What were 'Craven A'?*
**a3**   In which British city is Sauchiehall (say: sock-i-hall) Street?
*b3*   *And which city has streets called Dale Street, Paradise Street and Scotland Road?*
**a4**   Which American pop singer starred in the television series *The Partridge Family*?
*b4*   *Who had pop hits with 'Puppy Love' and 'Too Young'?*
**a5**   In which country would you be if you holidayed in the Dordoine (say: door-doyne)?
*b5*   *And in which country is the Algarve?*
**a6**   What product or technique was invented by Clarence Birdseye in 1930?
*b6*   *What gadget was first known as the 'Drunkometer'?*
**a7**   What composer is honoured at the Bayreuth (say: by-royt) Festival each summer?
*b7*   *Which saint is honoured at Lourdes in France each February?*
**a8**   Which American novelist wrote *Hotel* and *Airport*?
*b8*   *What was the name of the novel about a public school master written by James Hilton?*
**a9**   What was the trade or profession of John Huston?
*b9*   *Which French film actor and director created the character Monsieur Hulot?*
**a10**   Which western was based on the Japanese film *The Seven Samurai*?
*b10*   *In which film did John Wayne win an Oscar for playing a one-eyed marshal?*
**a11**   What abbreviated name is the explosive trinitrotoluene usually known?
*b11*   *And by what name are the Allied Powers in Europe's supreme headquarters known?*
**a12**   In which country do cricket teams compete for the Sheffield Shield?
*b12*   *Which country was re-admitted to international cricket in 1991?*

# No. 112 Answers

**a1** London and Paris
***b1*** *The Orient Express*
**a2** A small camera (which used small flash bulbs)
***b2*** *A type of cigarette*
**a3** Glasgow
***b3*** *Liverpool*
**a4** David Cassidy
***b4*** *Donny Osmond*
**a5** France
***b5*** *Portugal*
**a6** Frozen food
***b6*** *Breathalyser*
**a7** Wagner
***b7*** *St Bernadette*
**a8** Arthur Hailey
***b8*** Goodbye, Mr Chips
**a9** Film director (and writer) (*The African Queen*, etc.)
***b9*** *Jacques Tati*
**a10** *The Magnificent Seven*
***b10*** True Grit
**a11** TNT
***b11*** *SHAPE (Supreme Headquarters Allied Powers in Europe)*
**a12** Australia
***b12*** *South Africa*

---

# Tie-breaker

**Q** Can you give three examples of 'alternative energy'?
**A** *Solar power, wind power, hydroelectricity, power derived from tides*

---

# No. 113

**a1**  Who sang 'Congratulations' in the Eurovision Song Contest?

***b1***  *When the Beatles started their own record label, what did they call it?*

**a2**  Which car was nicknamed the 'Beetle'?

***b2***  *Of what make of car is or was the Robin a type?*

**a3**  Who led the miner's union in a strike in the eighties?

***b3***  *In Britain, in which year was the General Strike?*

**a4**  What is REME?

***b4***  *What is a QC?*

**a5**  Opened in 1937, the Golden Gate bridge crosses which bay?

***b5***  *Which bridge across a harbour opened in 1932?*

**a6**  First used to spray insecticides by the US Army, what invention came into use in 1941?

***b6***  *First used by Jacques Cousteau of the French Navy, what underwater device was invented in 1942?*

**a7**  What is the name of Tarzan's chimpanzee friend?

***b7***  *What was the name of the bear who sang 'The Bare Necessities' in the film of* The Jungle Book*?*

**a8**  Which company invented paper handkerchiefs in 1924?

***b8***  *What useful domestic or office product was first marketed by the 3M Company in 1928?*

**a9**  Which American comedian became famous for his 'driving instructor' and 'introducing tobacco' sketches?

***b9***  *On television, which couple were 'Happy Ever After'?*

**a10**  Which city is served by Orly Airport?

***b10***  *Which city is served by Ben Gurion International Airport?*

**a11**  Who wrote the novel *Lucky Jim*?

***b11***  *Who wrote the novels* First Among Equals *and* Kane and Abel*?*

**a12**  At the 1988 Seoul Olympics, two ball sports were added as 'demonstration events' – baseball and ...?

***b12***  *And also at the Seoul Olympics, which tennis player won Argentina's first medal for 16 years?*

# No. 113 Answers

**a1**  Cliff Richard
*b1*  *Apple*
**a2**  Volkswagen
*b2*  *Reliant*
**a3**  Arthur Scargill
*b3*  *1926*
**a4**  Royal Electrical and Mechanical Engineers
*b4*  *Queen's Counsel*
**a5**  San Francisco
*b5*  *Sydney Harbour Bridge*
**a6**  Aerosol cans
*b6*  *Aqualung*
**a7**  Cheetah
*b7*  *Balloo*
**a8**  Kleenex
*b8*  *Scotch tape (cellulose adhesive tape) (NB 'Cellotape' is the trade name of a later, rival product)*
**a9**  Bob Newhart
*b9*  *Terry and June (Terry Scott and June Whitfield played Terry and June Fletcher)*
**a10**  Paris
*b10*  *Tel Aviv*
**a11**  Kingsley Amis
*b11*  *Jeffrey Archer*
**a12**  Table tennis
*b12*  *Gabriela Sabatini*

---

## Tie-breaker

**Q**  913 people committed suicide together in Guyana in 1978. What did they have in common?

**A**  *All were members of a religious cult, the People's Temple (leader: Rev Jim Jones)*

---

# No. 114

**a1** On television, which cartoon or puppet characters were associated with Wimbledon?

*b1 And in which cartoon or puppet television series did we meet Dougal, Florence and Zebedee?*

**a2** In which English city is the Bull Ring?

*b2 In which university city is a street called the High?*

**a3** At which sport did Rachel Heyhoe-Flint captain England?

*b3 Athers. Whose sporting biography has this title?*

**a4** In the term 'street cred', what is 'cred' short for?

*b4 Who, cruelly, became known as 'Crumblies'?*

**a5** What is TM?

*b5 What is or was a UDC?*

**a6** Standard 8 and Super 8 are (or were) both types of ... what?

*b6 V-8 was a type of ... what?*

**a7** Which 1939 film featured the Cowardly Lion?

*b7 Which 1966 film was about Elsa the Lioness?*

**a8** Which event takes place in Oberammergau in Germany every 10 years?

*b8 Which event takes place at Llangollen (say: thllan-goth-len) in Wales each July?*

**a9** In 1963, who sang 'Take These Chains From My Heart'?

*b9 Which pop group had their first hit in 1964 with 'The House of the Rising Sun'?*

**a10** Who was Will Fyffe?

*b10 How did Clare Francis become famous?*

**a11** What type of transport flew successfully for the first time in 1936?

*b11 What useful device was first installed at a crossroads in Cleveland, Ohio in 1914?*

**a12** What was special about the steam locomotive 'Evening Star'?

*b12 And what was special about the steam locomotive 'Mallard'?*

# No. 114 Answers

a1   The Wombles
*b1*  *The Magic Roundabout*
a2   Birmingham
*b2*  *Oxford*
a3   Women's cricket
*b3*  *Mike Atherton*
a4   Credibility
*b4*  *Elderly people (in young people's slang)*
a5   Transcendental Meditation
*b5*  *Urban District Council*
a6   Home-movie (ciné) film
*b6*  *Car engine*
a7   *The Wizard of Oz*
*b7*  Born Free
a8   The Passion Play
*b8*  *International Eisteddfod a festival of music and other arts*
a9   Ray Charles
*b9*  *The Animals*
a10  Scottish comedian
*b10* *(Solo) yachtswoman*
a11  Helicopter (Focke Fa-61, in Germany)
*b11* *Traffic lights*
a12  It was the last one built for British Railways
*b12* *For many years, it held the speed record for steam locomotives*

---

## Tie-breaker

**Q**   Edvard Munch painted a famous picture of a person running towards us, hands clasped round the face and mouth open. What is it called?

**A**   The Scream *(also known as* The Cry*)*

---

# No. 115

**a1** Which sport is somewhat like bowls but is played on ice?
*b1* *And also in Scotland, which sport is played at Carnoustie?*
**a2** In which country are the Dolomites?
*b2* *And in which country are the Ardennes?*
**a3** Of what make of car were Sprites and Dolomites both types?
*b3* *Of what make of car were Consuls and Zephyrs both types?*
**a4** In London, what is 'the V and A'?
*b4* *And what is UCL?*
**a5** Which disc jockey was nicknamed 'Fluff'?
*b5* *Which pop group had hits with 'Shang-a-lang' and 'Summerlove Sensation'?*
**a6** In Britain, which tax replaced the rates?
*b6* *Who sends you a 'notice of coding'?*
**a7** Who wrote the novel *Casino Royale*?
*b7* *Who wrote the novel* The Thirty-Nine Steps?
**a8** Which city is served by Tempelhof Airport?
*b8* *Which city is served by a railway station called St Lazare (say: san la-zar)?*
**a9** Which comedian was known as 'the Cheekie Chappie'?
*b9* *Which female comedian was famous for her nursery school sketches?*
**a10** What twin disasters hit San Francisco in 1906?
*b10* *Which 'fault' makes the city vulnerable to earthquakes?*
**a11** On film, what was the name of Gene Autry's horse?
*b11* *And Tom Mix's horse?*
**a12** In which country was the French fortress Dien Bien Phu?
*b12* *In which country, principally, was the Ho Chi Minh trail?*

# No. 115 Answers

a1  Curling (played especially in Scotland)
*b1  Golf*
a2  Italy
*b2  Belgium (and France and Luxembourg)*
a3  Triumph
*b3  Ford*
a4  Victoria and Albert Museum
*b4  University College London*
a5  Alan Freeman
*b5  Bay City Rollers*
a6  Community charge (poll tax) (later replaced by Council Tax)
*b6  The Inland Revenue*
a7  Ian Fleming
*b7  John Buchan*
a8  Berlin
*b8  Paris*
a9  Max Miller
*b9  Joyce Grenfell*
a10  Earthquake and subsequent fire
*b10  San Andreas*
a11  Champion
*b11  Tony*
a12  Indo-China (accept: Vietnam)
*b12  Laos*

---

## Tie-breaker

**Q**  Who is this star of musical comedy? 'My last great role was in *Charley Girl* in 1969 but I'd also been in *The Belle of New York*. My greatest role was, however, in *The Merry Widow*.'

**A**  *Evelyn Laye*

---

# No. 116

**a1** What is a roadster?
*b1 In which country did Saab and Volvo cars originate?*
**a2** What is Godzilla?
*b2 And what is gazpacho?*
**a3** 'Back for Good', 'Never Forget' and 'Babe' were all hits for which group?
*b3 And who had hits with 'Wonderwall', 'Live Forever' and 'Stand By Me'?*
**a4** Which very tall building was opened in London in 1965?
*b4 Which tall skyscraper was opened by President Hoover in 1931?*
**a5** In which sport or entertainment did Henry Higgins become the first successful Englishman?
*b5 By what married name did the British tennis player Ann Haydon become well known?*
**a6** On television, what was *Crackerjack*?
*b6 On television, what was The Six Five Special?*
**a7** To which country does Ascension Island belong?
*b7 In which ocean is the island of Tristan da Cunha?*
**a8** What was ILEA?
*b8 For what is BNFL an abbreviation?*
**a9** Which woman was convicted of the so-called 'Moors Murders'?
*b9 And who was her male partner-in-crime?*
**a10** Which screen detective has been played by both Margaret Rutherford and Joan Hickson?
*b10 And which one by Peter Ustinov and David Suchet?*
**a11** Which general won power in China in 1927?
*b11 Who expelled Trotsky from the Soviet Communist Party?*
**a12** Which is the most north-easterly state in the USA?
*b12 Which Australian state forms the northeastern part of that country?*

# No. 116 Answers

**a1** An open car; often a two-seater
*b1* *Sweden*
**a2** Film monster
*b2* *(Spanish) soup, served hot or cold*
**a3** Take That
*b3* *Oasis*
**a4** Post Office Tower
*b4* *Empire State Building*
**a5** Bull-fighting
*b5* *Ann Jones (Ann Haydon-Jones)*
**a6** Children's variety show
*b6* *Pop music show*
**a7** United Kingdom (Britain)
*b7* *South Atlantic*
**a8** Inner London Education Authority
*b8* *British Nuclear Fuels*
**a9** Myra Hindley
*b9* *Ian Brady*
**a10** Miss Marple (Agatha Christie)
*b10* *Hercule Poirot*
**a11** Chiang Kai-Shek
*b11* *Joseph Stalin*
**a12** Maine
*b12* *Queensland*

## Tie-breaker

**Q** By what name did the 'pre-selective multiphone' invented by John C Danton in 1905 come to be known?
**A** *Juke box*

# No. 117

**a1** What was the Cakewalk?
*b1* *And what is a catwalk?*
**a2** According to Vera Lynn, where did a nightingale sing?
*b2* *In popular music, who was 'the Old Groaner'?*
**a3** What was Peter May's sport?
*b3* *In which sport is Dick Best a coach?*
**a4** For what has Dounreay in Scotland become famous?
*b4* *And what sort of buildings are known as Arndale Centres?*
**a5** In law, what is a legatee?
*b5* *What is the legal term for giving false testimony?*
**a6** On film, what was the name of the Lone Ranger's horse?
*b6* *Phoebe, Ross and Chandler are all ...?*
**a7** What type of craft was the SRN-1?
*b7* *Of what make of car was the 2CV a type?*
**a8** What is crêpe de chine?
*b8* *And what is crème de menthe?*
**a9** In Rhodesia, what was UDI?
*b9* *And which Rhodesian prime minister declared UDI?*
**a10** On whose side was Italy at the end of the First World War?
*b10* *In the First World War, on whose side was Holland?*
**a11** Which American state lies south of Alabama and Georgia?
*b11* *Which American state lies south of Oklahoma?*
**a12** Who wrote *The Grapes of Wrath*?
*b12* *Who wrote* The Maltese Falcon*?*

# No. 117 Answers

**a1** A dance (popular in 1900)
***b1*** *Narrow passageway or platform on which fashion shows are held (or platform surrounding a large machine)*
**a2** In Berkeley (say: barclay) Square
***b2*** *Bing Crosby*
**a3** Cricket
***b3*** *Rugby union*
**a4** Fast breeder reactor; nuclear power station
***b4*** *Shopping centres*
**a5** One to whom a legacy is bequeathed
***b5*** *Perjury*
**a6** Silver
***b6*** *Friends (characters in the TV series* Friends*)*
**a7** Hovercraft
***b7*** *Citroën*
**a8** A silk fabric
***b8*** *A (green) peppermint liqueur (drink) (accept: peppermint)*
**a9** Unilateral Declaration of Independence
***b9*** *Ian Smith*
**a10** The Allies; Britain's and France's
***b10*** *It was neutral*
**a11** Florida
***b11*** *Texas*
**a12** John Steinbeck
***b12*** *Dashiell Hammett*

---

## Tie-breaker

**Q** What was the name of the first type of wide-screen film?
**A** *Cinerama (1952) (CinemaScope appeared in 1953)*

---

# No. 118

**a1** For what did Mary Whitehouse start a campaign?
*b1* *Who is said to be 'infallible'?*
**a2** In which sport did Gentlemen play Players until 1963?
*b2* *Which sport is played by the Harlequins?*
**a3** What is meant by 'to go', when speaking of food?
*b3* *What is or was a 'closed shop'?*
**a4** For whom were 'Great Balls of Fire' and 'Whole Lotta Shakin'' hit records?
*b4* *Which pianist was known as 'Fats'?*
**a5** Which film studio created the cartoon rabbit, Bugs Bunny?
*b5* *And who provided the voice for Bugs Bunny?*
**a6** What is meant by Kamikaze?
*b6* *What were cami-knickers?*
**a7** Which well-meaning detective has been played on television by Michael Elphick?
*b7* *In which television series did we regularly meet Gary and Tony?*
**a8** What is a megaton?
*b8* *What is 0.125 expressed as a fraction?*
**a9** In 1914, in which country was Sarajevo (where the Archduke Ferdinand was assassinated)?
*b9* *In which country is Mons, the site of a the First World War battle?*
**a10** What is the everyday name for nitrous oxide?
*b10* *What is the chemical name for common salt?*
**a11** Which author, who died in 1928, wrote of an area he called Wessex?
*b11* *Who wrote a novel about an otter called Tarka?*
**a12** Of which country was Sukarno president?
*b12* *Of which country until his assassination was Dr Verwoerd prime minister?*

# No. 118 Answers

**a1** 'Cleaner' television
*b1* *The Pope*
**a2** Cricket
*b2* *Rugby union*
**a3** Take-away, 'eat out'
*b3* *An arrangement which required workers to be members of a trade union*
**a4** Jerry Lee Lewis
*b4* *Fats Domino (Antoine Domino) and Fats Waller*
**a5** Warner Brothers
*b5* *Mel Blanc*
**a6** Suicidal (from Japanese 'suicide pilots' who crash-landed bomb-laden planes)
*b6* *Woman's item of clothing, combining a camisole (worn on the top half of the body) and knickers*
**a7** Boon
*b7* Men Behaving Badly
**a8** One million tons
*b8* *One-eighth*
**a9** Austro-Hungary
*b9* *Belgium*
**a10** Laughing gas
*b10* *Sodium chloride*
**a11** Thomas Hardy
*b11* *Henry Williamson*
**a12** Indonesia
*b12* *South Africa*

---

## Tie-breaker

**Q** Which four American states border Mexico?
**A** *California, Arizona, New Mexico and Texas*

---

# No. 119

**a1** What is 'real estate'?

*b1* *The word 'nervy' has different meanings in Britain and America. What are they?*

**a2** In which television series did Gordon Kaye play Réné?

*b2* *And in which series did Ronnie Barker play a jailbird?*

**a3** Which honour did the Beatles receive at Buckingham Palace in 1965?

*b3* *And in which year did the Beatles split?*

**a4** In which country is the city of Poznan?

*b4* *In which country is the port of Chittagong?*

**a5** Which is André Agassi's sport?

*b5* *What was Ayrton Senna's sport?*

**a6** What or who is an apparatchik?

*b6* *Who or what is or was a Beatnik?*

**a7** Which 1982 hit film resulted in a catch phrase asking the central character to phone home?

*b7* *In which film is there an evil character called 'the Joker'?*

**a8** What is the motto of Girl Guides?

*b8* *When did we hear the slogan 'Not a penny off the pay, not a minute on the day'?*

**a9** In which country is the Ogaden region?

*b9* *Name one of the two countries which border Belize.*

**a10** A boy violinist (aged 10) became famous in 1927. In adult life, he was still a famous violinist – called ...?

*b10* *As what did Edward Ardizzone mainly achieve fame?*

**a11** In which year was the Six Day War (in the Middle East)?

*b11* *In which year did the first facsimile transmission of a picture take place? Was it 1907, 1957 or 1977?*

**a12** King Umberto I was shot dead in 1900. Of which country was he king?

*b12* *In which country did Marshal Pilsudski seize power in 1926?*

# No. 119 Answers

**a1** Property consisting of land and houses; houses to be bought/sold
*b1* *In Britain: nervous; in America: cheeky*
**a2** 'Allo 'Allo!
*b2* Porridge (Going Straight *showed him on his 'release'*)
**a3** The MBE (they later gave them back as a protest against the Vietnam War)
*b3* *1970*
**a4** Poland
*b4* *Bangladesh*
**a5** Tennis
*b5* *Motor-racing*
**a6** A bureaucrat, firmly entrenched in his/her post
*b6* *A hippy (term used in the fifties and sixties); person who opts out of traditional values*
**a7** *ET – The Extra-Terrestrial*
*b7* Batman
**a8** Be prepared
*b8* *During the General Strike (1926)*
**a9** Ethiopia
*b9* *Mexico, Guatemala*
**a10** Yehudi Menuhin
*b10* *Illustrator (children's books) (also an author)*
**a11** 1967
*b11* *1907*
**a12** Italy
*b12* *Poland*

---

## Tie-breaker

**Q** In electronics, what does a rectifier rectify?
*A* *An (alternating) electric current (a rectifier can change alternating current to direct current)*

# No. 120

**a1** What is a billboard?
*b1* *What is a helipad?*
**a2** In the sixties, which London street was the centre of the fashion scene?
*b2* *What is or was a Vespa?*
**a3** Who scored just after the commentator said 'they think it's all over'?
*b3* *Tim Rice and Mick Jagger are fans of which sport?*
**a4** In the original *Doctor Dolittle* film, which actor said 'you've got to talk to the animals'?
*b4* *Which lanky American comedian starred in the films* Chitty Chitty Bang Bang *and* Some Kind of a Nut?
**a5** On television, what is James Kavanagh's job?
*b5* *On television, who played Callan?*
**a6** For what was Harry Houdini famous?
*b6* *Who was Lenny Bruce?*
**a7** What was a Dakota?
*b7* *What kind of ship was the 'Torrey Canyon'?*
**a8** In which country was the revolutionary Baader-Meinhof (say: barder-mine-hof) gang active?
*b8* *In which country did the revolutionary Red Brigade (or Brigades) operate in the seventies?*
**a9** In which city is the Ballymurphy housing estate?
*b9* *In which city was the Sabra refugee camp?*
**a10** What was *The British Gazette*, edited by Winston Churchill?
*b10* *Under what name did William Connor start a crusading column in the* Daily Mirror?
**a11** In which country is Benghazi?
*b11* *In which country is the Kikuyu Reserve?*
**a12** What instrument was played by the jazz musician Bix Beiderbecke (say: by-der-beck)?
*b12* *And which instrument was played by Jack Teagarden?*

# No. 120 Answers

**a1** Advertising hoarding (American)
*b1* *Site for landing a helicopter (e.g. on a building's roof)*
**a2** Carnaby Street
*b2* *Motor-scooter*
**a3** Geoff Hurst
*b3* *Cricket*
**a4** Rex Harrison
*b4* *Dick van Dyke*
**a5** QC, barrister (accept: lawyer)
*b5* *Edward Woodward*
**a6** Escaping; escapologist
*b6* *American comedian*
**a7** Passenger aircraft (Douglas DC-3)
*b7* *Oil tanker (went aground off Cornwall, causing pollution)*
**a8** West Germany
*b8* *Italy*
**a9** Belfast
*b9* *Beirut*
**a10** Daily paper, published during the General Strike (1926)
*b10* *Cassandra*
**a11** Libya
*b11* *Kenya*
**a12** Cornet
*b12* *Trombone*

---

## Tie-breaker

**Q** Who were the people of India whom Gandhi called 'Harijans', the children of God?
*A* *Outcasts; lower caste people; or 'untouchables'*

---

# No. 121: Famous Buildings

For which building is each of the following especially famous?

**a1**  Balmoral
*b1*  *Osborne, Isle of Wight*
**a2**  Blackpool
*b2*  *York*
**a3**  Framlingham, Suffolk
*b3*  *Greenwich*
**a4**  Avebury, Wiltshire
*b4*  *Fountains, near Ripon, Yorkshire*
**a5**  Alnwick (say: annick), Northumberland
*b5*  *Furness, near Barrow, Cumbria*
**a6**  Blenheim, Oxfordshire
*b6*  *Haworth, Yorkshire*
**a7**  Alloway, Ayrshire
*b7*  *Ayot St Lawrence, Hertfordshire*
**a8**  Buckfast, Devon
*b8*  *Harlech, North Wales*
**a9**  Grasmere, in the Lake District
*b9*  *St Michael's, Cornwall*
**a10**  Drax, in Yorkshire
*b10*  *Sizewell, in Suffolk*
**a11**  Banbury, Oxfordshire
*b11*  *Kenilworth, Warwickshire*
**a12**  Woolwich Reach
*b12*  *Barton and Hessle*

# No. 121 Answers

**a1**  Castle; private home of the reigning monarch
*b1*  *Osborne House (Queen Victoria's home)*
**a2**  Blackpool Tower
*b2*  *York Minster*
**a3**  Framlingham Castle
*b3*  *Royal Naval College; National Maritime Museum*
**a4**  Stone circle (largest in the world)
*b4*  *Fountains Abbey (Cistercian)*
**a5**  Alnwick Castle
*b5*  *Furness Abbey*
**a6**  Blenheim Palace (birthplace of Winston Churchill)
*b6*  *Haworth Parsonage, home of the Bronte sisters*
**a7**  Burns' Cottage (birthplace of Robert Burns)
*b7*  *Home of Bernard Shaw*
**a8**  Buckfast Abbey
*b8*  *Harlech Castle*
**a9**  Dove Cottage (home of William Wordsworth)
*b9*  *St Michael's Mount (castle, monastery)*
**a10**  Power station
*b10*  *Nuclear power station*
**a11**  Banbury Cross (also a castle)
*b11*  *Kenilworth Castle*
**a12**  Thames (flood) barrier
*b12*  *Humber Bridge*

---

## Tie-breaker

**Q**  Which architect designed the controversial Lloyds building, opened in London in 1986?
*A*  *Richard Rogers*

---

# No. 122

**a1** In *EastEnders*, which character has been played by Barbara Windsor?

*b1* *And which character by Wendy Richard?*

**a2** What is the full name of the Scottish soccer club, 'Hearts'?

*b2* *Which sport is played by the Boston Red Sox?*

**a3** What is 'featherbedding'?

*b3* *What was meant by psychedelic?*

**a4** Within which country is the mouth of the River Plate?

*b4* *Off the north coast of which country is the White Sea?*

**a5** Who is the star of the pop video film *Moonwalker*?

*b5* *What item of clothing is sometimes used to mute a trumpet in a jazz or dance band?*

**a6** What is a conurbation?

*b6* *Who or what is a cinéaste (say: sin-ay-ast)?*

**a7** Who was 'Little Mo'?

*b7* *What was Reg Harris's sport?*

**a8** In 1957, what was the popular name for the type of flu which hit many people in Britain?

*b8* *What tragedy hit Aberfan in 1966?*

**a9** Svetlana was the daughter of which Soviet ruler?

*b9* *Who died when his boat 'Bluebird' somersaulted at 300 mph?*

**a10** Which cartoon rabbit invariably outwits Elmer Fudd?

*b10* *Which film cartoon character was supposedly based on 'boop-a-doop' singer Helen Kane?*

**a11** On BBC Television, what kind of show was *Monitor*?

*b11* *What was the name of ITV's regular Monday evening current affairs programme?*

**a12** In South African politics, what are or were 'Bantustans'?

*b12* *In which country was the Mujahideen a fighting force?*

# No. 122 Answers

**a1** Peggy Mitchell
*b1* *Pauline Fowler*
**a2** Heart of Midlothian FC
*b2* *Baseball*
**a3** Giving a group of people an easy time (through tax advantages, etc.)
*b3* *Mind-influencing; making the senses seem keener; of patterns and lights which have this effect*
**a4** Argentina
*b4* *Russia*
**a5** Michael Jackson
*b5* *A bowler or 'derby'*
**a6** A number of cities and/or towns which have spread to form one built-up area
*b6* *Connoisseur of films (or, in France, someone working in the film industry)*
**a7** Maureen Connolly (US tennis player)
*b7* *Cycling*
**a8** Asian flu
*b8* *A coal tip buried a village school (116 children were killed)*
**a9** Joseph Stalin
*b9* *Donald Campbell*
**a10** Bugs Bunny
*b10* *Betty Boop*
**a11** Arts programme
*b11* World in Action
**a12** Supposedly independent homelands
*b12* *Afghanistan*

---

## Tie-breaker

**Q** Which whitish powder results from the action of chlorine on slaked lime?

**A** *Bleaching powder or chloride of lime (consists mainly of calcium oxychloride)*

---

# No. 123

**a1**    What is a risotto?
*b1*    *What is meant by 'raffish'?*
**a2**    What is a retro-rocket?
*b2*    *What is the colour of a sodium flare?*
**a3**    What was the name of the cartoon pirate captain who became a popular children's television character?
*b3*    *On television, who was Andy Pandy's best friend?*
**a4**    For what is Woomera in Australia famous?
*b4*    *In which Northern Ireland county is Crossmaglen?*
**a5**    To which film was *The Empire Strikes Back* a sequel?
*b5*    *What is Superman's other name?*
**a6**    In which ocean are the Galapagos Islands?
*b6*    *To which country does the Pacific island of Guam belong?*
**a7**    Which American television situation comedy was set in a bar?
*b7*    *Who was BBC Television's main commentator on royal events in the fifties and early sixties?*
**a8**    In which country is the town of Maastricht?
*b8*    *Of which country is Hyderabad a part?*
**a9**    Alec and Eric both played cricket for Surrey, Alec being a record-breaking bowler. What was their surname?
*b9*    *Which England goalkeeper later managed Plymouth Argyle?*
**a10**    With what was the Plowden Report concerned?
*b10*    *And what was the Beeching Report about?*
**a11**    The Colts play football; the Orioles play baseball. In which American city do both teams play?
*b11*    *What were the British Commonwealth Games originally called?*
**a12**    Claude Monet (say: mon-ay) is said to have been what kind of painter or artist?
*b12*    *Which dancer was strangled by her own shawl when it caught in a car wheel?*

# No. 123 Answers

**a1** Dish made of rice plus meat and/or vegetables
*b1* *Happy, wild and not very respectable*
**a2** Rocket used to slow down a rocket or aircraft
*b2* *Yellow*
**a3** Captain Pugwash
*b3* *Teddy*
**a4** Rocket range, rocket testing
*b4* *Armagh*
**a5** *Star Wars*
*b5* *Clark Kent*
**a6** Pacific
*b6* *United States of America*
**a7** *Cheers*
*b7* *Richard Dimbleby*
**a8** The Netherlands (Holland)
*b8* *India*
**a9** Bedser
*b9* *Peter Shilton*
**a10** Primary school education
*b10* *British Railways*
**a11** Baltimore
*b11* *British Empire Games*
**a12** Impressionist
*b12* *Isadora Duncan*

---

## Tie-breaker

**Q** One of the two major Russian ballet companies is the Kirov company in St Petersburg. Which is the other?
**A** *The Bolshoi (in Moscow)*

---

# No. 124

**a1** Abbreviations: what is a CD?
*b1* *And what is CD?*
**a2** In London, what trade is conducted at Billingsgate Market (now held on the Isle of Dogs)?
*b2* *And what is sold at Smithfield?*
**a3** In film, what kind of creature is Dumbo?
*b3* *And what was Rin-Tin-Tin?*
**a4** What is Factor Eight?
*b4* *What is 'faction'?*
**a5** Which British pop star had a hit with 'Angels'?
*b5* *From which film was Celine Dion's song 'My Heart Will Go On' taken?*
**a6** Who was the first man to run a mile in under four minutes?
*b6* *What pioneer swim did Gertrude Ederle achieve in 1926?*
**a7** Of which city in America was Wyatt Earp a marshal?
*b7* *In which American city was there a gangland Valentine's Day massacre?*
**a8** For playing which television detective did John Nettles become famous?
*b8* *In which television comedy series did Michael Crawford play Frank Spenser?*
**a9** Who wrote the play *A View from the Bridge*?
*b9* *Who wrote the play* Educating Rita*?*
**a10** Which Canadian province borders the Pacific Ocean?
*b10* *What is Canada's national anthem or 'hymn'?*
**a11** Which high office did William Temple take over in 1942?
*b11* *And who was Archbishop of Canterbury throughout the eighties?*
**a12** The 1936 Olympics basketball finals saw an attempt to ban competitors over 1.9m high. True or false?
*b12* *Was Alex James transferred to Arsenal in 1929 for £9,000 or £12,000?*

# No. 124 Answers

**a1** A compact disc
*b1* *Civil Defence*
**a2** Fish
*b2* *Meat*
**a3** Flying elephant
*b3* *German Army dog; star of many silent films*
**a4** A substance in blood which helps it to coagulate
*b4* *A blend of fact and fiction – especially in a film, television play or novel*
**a5** Robbie Williams
*b5* *Titanic*
**a6** (Dr Roger) Bannister
*b6* *First woman to swim the English Channel*
**a7** Dodge City
*b7* *Chicago*
**a8** Bergerac
*b8* *Some Mothers Do 'Ave 'Em*
**a9** Athur Miller
*b9* *Willy Russell*
**a10** British Columbia
*b10* *'O, Canada'*
**a11** Archbishop of Canterbury
*b11* *Robert Runcie*
**a12** True
*b12* *£9,000*

---

## Tie-breaker

**Q** Can you name the four English counties which border Wales?

**A** *Cheshire; Shropshire (Salop); Hereford and Worcester (now one county); Gloucestershire*

# No. 125

**a1** In which country did the Caledonian Railway operate until 1923?

***b1*** *And in which country did the Cambrian Railway chiefly operate?*

**a2** What is a debriefing?

***b2*** *What is 'double-think'?*

**a3** On which sport is Richie Benaud a television commentator?

***b3*** *On television, on which sport have John Motson and Kenneth Wolstenholme been commentators?*

**a4** With which song did Sandie Shaw win the Eurovision Song Contest in 1967?

***b4*** *And in 1970, who won the contest with 'All Kinds of Everything'?*

**a5** What is the DFC?

***b5*** *What happens to you in the Army if you're 'CB'?*

**a6** What name or nickname is given to someone who buys shares in the hope of selling them when the price goes up?

***b6*** *And what name is given to someone who sells shares in the hope of buying them back at a lower price?*

**a7** Where in London is the Royal National Theatre?

***b7*** *Where is the London home of the Royal Shakespeare Company?*

**a8** Laura Davies and Alison Nicholas are English internationals. In which sport?

***b8*** *Whose name has been linked with Steve Redgrave's since 1992?*

**b9** Which gas is the 'greenhouse gas'?

**a9** What is damaged by CFCs?

**a10** Which Chinese American practitioner of the martial arts starred in *Enter the Dragon* and *Way of the Dragon*?

***b10*** *Which Oriental film detective has been played by Warner Oland, J Carrol Naish and, once, by Peter Ustinov?*

**a11** Which television comedy series starred Wendy Craig with Geoffrey Palmer as her dentist-husband?

***b11*** *In which television situation comedy series did Michael Williams play opposite Judy Dench?*

**a12** In which country is the city of Aleppo?

***b12*** *And in which country is the city of Casablanca?*

# No. 125 Answers

**a1** Scotland
*b1* *Wales*
**a2** Extracting all available information from a returned space-man, spy, soldier, etc.
*b2* *Believing two contradictory ideas at once*
**a3** Cricket
*b3* *Soccer*
**a4** 'Puppet on a String'
*b4* *Dana*
**a5** Distinguished Flying Cross
*b5* *You're confined to barracks*
**a6** Bull, bullish
*b6* *Bear, bearish*
**a7** On the South Bank (near Waterloo)
*b7* *The Barbican*
**a8** Golf
*b8* *Matthew Pinsent (both are oarsmen)*
**a9** The ozone layer
*b9* *Carbon dioxide*
**a10** Bruce Lee
*b10* *Charlie Chan*
**a11** *Butterflies*
*b11* A Fine Romance
**a12** Syria
*b12* *Morocco*

---

## Tie-breaker

**Q** Who is this composer? 'Gertrude Lawrence appeared in three of my works. Fred Astaire in two. I collaborated with various composers but especially with my brother. As for myself, when I say I got plenty of nothing, it ain't necessarily so.'

**A** *Ira Gershwin (brother of George, the composer)*

# No. 126

**a1**   For what is Petticoat Lane in London famous?
*b1*   *And for what is Savile Row famous?*
**a2**   Colloquially, who or what is a 'sab'?
*b2*   *What is a clip joint?*
**a3**   In the Eurovision Song Contest who sang 'Ooh Ahh Just a Little Bit'?
*b3*   *And who won the competition with 'What's Another Year'?*
**a4**   What does the drink Bucks Fizz consist of?
*b4*   *And what is a Bloody Mary?*
**a5**   Which television comedy series features Clegg, Compo and Nora Batty?
*b5*   *Which work-shy lad was played by Hywel Bennett in a television comedy series of the same name?*
**a6**   Sir Pelham ('Plum') Warner was famous in which sport?
*b6*   *Which country did Jean (say: jhan) Borotra represent at tennis?*
**a7**   What is BAFTA?
*b7*   *What is the BFI?*
**a8**   On which island is Famagusta?
*b8*   *Between which two countries is the Khyber Pass?*
**a9**   Who was the first ex-grammar school boy to lead the Conservative Party?
*b9*   *Which was Mrs Thatcher's parliamentary constituency?*
**a10**   Can you name one of the two male stars of the film *Some Like It Hot*?
*b10*   *Which Oriental master criminal was played on the screen by Harry Agar Lyons in the twenties and by Christopher Lee in the sixties?*
**a11**   For what did Dr Albert Schweitzer become famous?
*b11*   *As what did the Irishman W B Yeats (say: yates) achieve fame?*
**a12**   What was the title of Erich Maria Remarque's famous novel about the First World War?
*b12*   *And what was the title of R C Sherriff's play about the same war?*

# No. 126 Answers

**a1** Its street market
*b1* *Tailors' shops*
**a2** Saboteur (especially of blood sports)
*b2* *Restaurant or nightclub that charges too much (and which may be dishonest in other ways)*
**a3** Gina G
*b3* *Johnny Logan*
**a4** Champagne, orange juice
*b4* *A mixture of vodka and tomato juice (and possibly Worcestershire sauce)*
**a5** *Last of the Summer Wine*
*b5* Shelley
**a6** Cricket
*b6* *France*
**a7** British Academy of Film and Television Arts
*b7* *British Film Institute*
**a8** Cyprus
*b8* *Pakistan, Afghanistan*
**a9** Edward Heath
*b9* *Finchley*
**a10** Tony Curtis, Jack Lemmon
*b10* *Fu Manchu*
**a11** As a doctor in Equatorial Africa
*b11* *As a poet*
**a12** *All Quiet on the Western Front*
*b12* Journey's End

---

## Tie-breaker

**Q**  Which gas is produced by the action of water on calcium carbide?

*A*  *Acetylene (accept: Ethyne)*

---

# No. 127

**a1**  At the end of which London thoroughfare does Buckingham Palace stand?

*b1*  *And where in London is Nelson's Column?*

**a2**  In which television serial did we meet Adam Chance and Jill Harvey?

*b2*  *And in which serial did we meet Stan and Hilda Ogden?*

**a3**  Which sport would you be most likely to want to play if you visited Gleneagles?

*b3*  *In which sport has the Gillette Cup been a trophy?*

**a4**  Which newspaper cartoon hero saved the world in his first film, when he was played by Buster Crabbe?

*b4*  *In the world of film, what have the following in common: Nurse, Teacher, Constable, Regardless ...?*

**a5**  What is meant by 'Subtopia'?

*b5*  *What is the literal meaning of the word 'veto'?*

**a6**  In the Vietnam War, were the Viet Cong fighting with or against the Americans?

*b6*  *Who was crowned emperor of Japan in 1928?*

**a7**  Of which political party was George Brown a colourful member?

*b7*  *And of which party was Jeremy Thorpe a leader?*

**a8**  In music, what is the LSO?

*b8*  *And also in London, what is the LSE?*

**a9**  Who had a number one hit with 'Sleeping Satellite'?

*b9*  *What was the name of Eric Burdon's original group?*

**a10**  In which country is the Great Bear Lake?

*b10*  *And in which country is Mount Kilimanjaro?*

**a11**  Who wrote the play *The Royal Hunt of the Sun*?

*b11*  *And who wrote a trio of plays called* The Norman Conquests?

**a12**  In the world of finance, who issues 'gilts' or 'gilt-edged' securities?

*b12*  *Which was the first British credit card?*

# No. 127 Answers

**a1** The Mall
*b1* *Trafalgar Square*
**a2** *Crossroads*
*b2* Coronation Street
**a3** Golf
*b3* *Cricket*
**a4** Flash Gordon
*b4* *They are all* Carry On *films*
**a5** Ill-conceived building development; a sprawl of houses, etc.
*b5* *I forbid (from the Latin)*
**a6** Against (they were Communist forces)
*b6* *Hirohito*
**a7** Labour
*b7* *Liberal*
**a8** London Symphony Orchestra
*b8* *London School of Economics*
**a9** Tazmin Archer
*b9* *The Animals*
**a10** Canada
*b10* *Tanzania*
**a11** Peter Shaffer
*b11* *Alan Ayckbourn*
**a12** The Government
*b12* *Barclaycard*

---

## Tie-breaker

**Q** Which author wrote a book about the art of 'one-upman-ship'?
**A** *Stephen Potter*

---

# No. 128

**a1**  On television, who played the scarecrow, Worzel Gummidge?

*b1*  *On television, who played Arthur Daley's original 'Minder'?*

**a2**  Which is the home country of golfer Ian Woosnam?

*b2*  *Which is the main sport that takes place at Silverstone?*

**a3**  In which country is the ski resort of St Moritz?

*b3*  *In which country is the historic city of Granada?*

**a4**  What is broken at Mach 1?

*b4*  *What is the Maghreb?*

**a5**  In which year was John F Kennedy shot dead?

*b5*  *And in which city did it happen?*

**a6**  Which famous art gallery stands on Millbank in southwest London?

*b6*  *Whereabouts in London is the Science Museum?*

**a7**  What is or was the CEGB?

*b7*  *What is a country's GDP?*

**a8**  Which British comedy actor starred in the film *Dr Strangelove*?

*b8*  *Which television comedian starred in the cinema film* A Fish Called Wanda*?*

**a9**  'The Only One I Know' and 'North Country Boy' were hits for which group?

*b9*  *Which male singer had hits with 'Black or White' and 'Earth Song'?*

**a10**  To whom did the 'Balfour Declaration' promise a homeland?

*b10*  *Born Max Aitken, this Canadian became a newspaper baron – under what name?*

**a11**  Kingsley and Martin were father and son. Both have been novelists. Their surname is ...?

*b11*  *Who wrote the novels* Wilt *and* Blott on the Landscape*?*

**a12**  In which country is the Horn of Africa (its most easterly point)?

*b12*  *In which country is Stanleyville?*

# No. 128 Answers

a1  Jon Pertwee
*b1  Dennis Waterman*
a2  Wales
*b2  Motor-racing*
a3  Switzerland
*b3  Spain*
a4  Sound barrier
*b4  Northwest Africa*
a5  1963
*b5  Dallas, Texas*
a6  The Tate
*b6  Exhibition Road; Kensington; southwest London*
a7  Central Electricity Generating Board
*b7  Gross domestic product (or output)*
a8  Peter Sellers
*b8  John Cleese*
a9  The Charlatans
*b9  Michael Jackson*
a10  The Jewish people (in Palestine)
*b10  Lord Beaverbrook*
a11  Amis
*b11  Tom Sharpe*
a12  Somalia
*b12  Congo*

## Tie-breaker

**Q**  Which fly transmits African sleeping sickness?
**A**  *Tsetse fly*

# No. 129

**a1** In films, what was the first name of the cowboy called Cassidy?

*b1* *Who starred as a ruthless policeman in Dirty Harry?*

**a2** In the early sixties, which group of teenagers regularly fought Rockers at seaside resorts?

*b2* *Of which major crime was Ronald Biggs convicted?*

**a3** Which Sheffield theatre has become famous as a venue for snooker tournaments?

*b3* *Which London theatre boasted 'We never closed' during the Second World War?*

**a4** Which band leader was famous for his Tijuana (say: ti-wharna) Brass?

*b4* *What is tequila?*

**a5** You might have had the DTs, but what does DT stand for?

*b5* *What is ESP?*

**a6** Which was Paddy Hopkirk's sport?

*b6* *In which sport did Herbert Sutcliffe achieve fame?*

**a7** Which group issued the album 'What's the Story Morning Glory'?

*b7* *And which group sung about 'park life'?*

**a8** On ITV, who was the original and long-time presenter of *You've Been Framed*?

*b8* *And on BBC-TV, who has been the chief presenter of* Animal Hospital?

**a9** What is tinnitus?

*b9* *What is neuralgia?*

**a10** Which army was commanded by General Bramwell Booth?

*b10* *Which high religious office has been held by Basil Hume?*

**a11** In the world of finance, what are 'securities'?

*b11* *What is the difference between libel and slander?*

**a12** On radio and the stage, who was comedian Jimmy Jewel's long-time partner?

*b12* *Which organist's signature tune was 'I Do Like To Be Beside the Seaside'?*

# No. 129 Answers

**a1**  Hopalong (Cassidy)
**b1**  *Clint Eastwood*
**a2**  Mods
**b2**  *The Great Train Robbery*
**a3**  The Crucible
**b3**  *The Windmill*
**a4**  Herb Alpert
**b4**  *Mexican alcoholic drink*
**a5**  Delirium tremens ('the shakes')
**b5**  *Extra-sensory perception*
**a6**  Rally driving
**b6**  *Cricket*
**a7**  Oasis
**b7**  *Blur*
**a8**  Jeremy Beadle
**b8**  *Rolf Harris*
**a9**  A buzzing or ringing in the ear, heard only by the sufferer
**b9**  *Pain from a damaged nerve*
**a10**  Salvation Army
**b10**  *Archbishop of Westminster; leader of the Roman Catholic Church in England*
**a11**  Stocks and shares
**b11**  *Libel is written, slander is spoken*
**a12**  Ben Warris
**b12**  *Reg Dixon (at Blackpool)*

## Tie-breaker

**Q**  Wimbledon's new No. 1 tennis court opened in 1997. Is its capacity 6,500, 8,000 or 11,000?
**A**  *11,000*

# No. 130

**a1** In *Coronation Street*, which character has been played by Bryan Mosley?

*b1* *And which by Roy Barraclough?*

**a2** On television, what is the first name of the barrister called Rumpole?

*b2* *Which actor played Alf Garnett on television?*

**a3** Which country was captained by Ian Chappell?

*b3* *What are the surnames of two boxers called 'Sugar Ray'?*

**a4** Whom did Jack Ruby kill live on television in a police car park?

*b4* *Which American leader won the Nobel Peace Prize in 1964?*

**a5** Which chemical is found in coffee and tea and has a powerful action on the heart?

*b5* *Is chloroform a gas, a liquid or a salt?*

**a6** In which county are the Chislehurst Caves, used as air raid shelters in the Second World War?

*b6* *What was the last item to be freed from rationing after the Second World War?*

**a7** Which charge card advertised itself with the slogan 'That'll do nicely'?

*b7* *In financial jargon, what is the 'grey economy' or 'grey market'?*

**a8** Where is the official London residence of the Archbishop of Canterbury?

*b8* *And what address is the official home in London of the Chancellor of the Exchequer?*

**a9** Where would you see an ISBN?

*b9* *And which book is sometimes described as the AV?*

**a10** Which 'coloured' group sang about 'Stars'?

*b10* *Who had an instrumental hit with 'Children?'*

**a11** Which two countries were at war over claims to Kashmir in 1965?

*b11* *What two buildings were linked by a 'hot line' in 1963?*

**a12** In 1932, Vicki Baum's novel provided film roles for Garbo, the Barrymore brothers and Joan Crawford. What was it called?

*b12* *In which 1966 film did David Hemmings play a photographer who thinks he has witnessed a murder?*

# No. 130 Answers

**a1** Alf Roberts
*b1* *Alec Gilroy*
**a2** Horace
*b2* *Warren Mitchell*
**a3** Australia (cricket)
*b3* *Robinson and Leonard*
**a4** Lee Harvey Oswald (who was charged with President Kennedy's murder)
*b4* *Martin Luther King*
**a5** Caffeine
*b5* *A liquid*
**a6** Kent
*b6* *Meat (including bacon) in 1954*
**a7** American Express
*b7* *Income, earnings, profit which does not appear in official or public accounts; business done 'on the side'*
**a8** Lambeth Palace
*b8* *11 Downing Street*
**a9** On a book (International Standard Book Number)
*b9* *The Bible (Authorized Version)*
**a10** Simply Red
*b10* *Robert Miles*
**a11** India and Pakistan
*b11* *The Kremlin and the White House*
**a12** Grand Hotel
*b12* Blow-Up

---

## Tie-breaker

**Q** *Four Quartets, published during the Second World War, were considered by many to be the most important poems to appear in that period. Who wrote them?*
**A** *T S Eliot*

---

# No. 131: More Capitals

Another round of capital cities – and their countries, all of which have been in the headlines during the 20th century. Of which country is each of the following the capital city?

**a1**  Islamabad
*b1*  *Manila*
**a2**  Brazzaville
*b2*  *Luanda*
**a3**  Sofia
*b3*  *Bogota*
**a4**  Kinshasa
*b4*  *Lusaka*
**a5**  Mogadishu
*b5*  *Quito*
**a6**  Ventiane
*b6*  *Dodoma*

And what is the capital city of these countries?
**a7**  Israel
*b7*  *South Korea*
**a8**  Switzerland
*b8*  *Burma*
**a9**  Taiwan
*b9*  *Lithuania*
**a10**  United Arab Emirates
*b10*  *Oman*
**a11**  Georgia
*b11*  *Estonia*
**a12**  Senegal
*b12*  *Papua New Guinea*

# No. 131 Answers

**a1** Pakistan
*b1 Philippines*
**a2** Congo
*b2 Angola*
**a3** Bulgaria
*b3 Colombia*
**a4** Zaire
*b4 Zambia*
**a5** Somalia
*b5 Ecuador*
**a6** Laos
*b6 Tanzania*
**a7** Jerusalem (not recognized by the United Nations)
*b7 Seoul*
**a8** Berne
*b8 Rangoon*
**a9** Taipei
*b9 Vilnius*
**a10** Abu Dhabi
*b10 Muscat*
**a11** Tbilisi (Tiflis)
*b11 Tallinn*
**a12** Dakar
*b12 Port Moresby*

---

## Tie-breaker

**Q** What is the capital of Burkina Faso?
*A Ouagadougou*

---

# No. 132

**a1** What or who is an MFH?
*b1* *What is an MTB?*
**a2** In golf, what is an Eagle?
*b2* *What is the Tote?*
**a3** Which black American with a Mohawk hairstyle starred in television's *The A-Team*?
*b3* *In the sixties television series, who played Dr Kildare?*
**a4** Which jazz band was famous for playing 'Midnight in Moscow'?
*b4* *And who played 'Stranger on the Shore'?*
**a5** Who famously said 'Ich bin ein Berliner'?
*b5* *Who originally said 'Non' to British membership of the Common Market?*
**a6** Which film by Walt Disney is a visualization of musical classics?
*b6* *What was the screen name of the intelligent collie dog which began its film career in 1940?*
**a7** What does a carcinogen cause?
*b7* *Which germ-killing mould was discovered by accident (by Professor Fleming) in 1928?*
**a8** After Burgess and Maclean (say: ma-klane), who was the 'Third Man' in the spy ring?
*b8* *Why did Greville Wynne become famous?*
**a9** As what did the American Robert Frost achieve fame?
*b9* *And as what did the Frenchman Francis Poulenc achieve fame?*
**a10** Which two seas are linked by the Kiel Canal?
*b10* *Which two English counties border Scotland?*
**a11** Who wrote the children's novel *Ballet Shoes*?
*b11* *And who wrote the children's novel* Swallows and Amazons*?*
**a12** What happened to Britain's currency in both 1949 and 1967?
*b12* *What was the major financial change in Britain in 1931?*

# No. 132 Answers

**a1** Master of Foxhounds
*b1* *Motor torpedo boat*
**a2** A hole completed in two strokes under 'par' or 'bogey'
*b2* *Machine (totalizator) which shows amounts bet on a race, and amounts to be paid out*
**a3** Mr T
*b3* *Richard Chamberlain*
**a4** Kenny Ball
*b4* *Acker Bilk*
**a5** President Kennedy (in Berlin in 1963)
*b5* *President de Gaulle (of France)*
**a6** *Fantasia*
*b6* *Lassie*
**a7** Cancer
*b7* *Penicillin*
**a8** Kim Philby
*b8* *He was jailed in Moscow as a spy*
**a9** Poet
*b9* *Composer*
**a10** North Sea, Baltic Sea
*b10* *Cumbria and Northumberland*
**a11** Noel Streatfeild
*b11* *Arthur Ransome*
**a12** It was devalued
*b12* *Britain abandoned the Gold Standard*

## Tie-breaker

**Q** Which Pete Seeger song did Marlene Dietrich record in 1962?
**A** *'Where Have All the Flowers Gone?'*

# No. 133

**a1** For what is 'white spirit' mainly used?

*b1* *For what is the alloy 'solder' generally used?*

**a2** In which sport was His Highness the Aga Khan a sponsor and competitor?

*b2* *Which soccer club rose from bottom to top division under manager Graham Taylor?*

**a3** In film classifications, for what does 'PG' stand?

*b3* *And away from films, what is a PG?*

**a4** Which former Radio One DJ became famous for 'Our Tune'?

*b4* *Which former Pirate Radio DJ, now on Radio Two, starts all his shows with a jingle 'He's in, he's on'?*

**a5** In which country is Gallipoli?

*b5* *In which country is Arnhem?*

**a6** Which Labour leader died unexpectedly in 1963?

*b6* *And who succeeded him?*

**a7** Which actor played Henry VIII, Captain Bligh and the Hunchback of Notre Dame?

*b7* *What does an actor do if he 'corpses'?*

**a8** Can you complete this American quartet: Crosby, Stills ...?

*b8* *And can you complete this quintet: Dave Dee, Dozy, Beaky ...?*

**a9** Which important national museum faces onto Great Russell Street in London?

*b9* *And which other national museum is in Lambeth Road in southeast London?*

**a10** Until 1923, which railway was known as the LNWR?

*b10* *And which railway was the LBSCR?*

**a11** Who played the female lead in the film *Mary Poppins*?

*b11* *And who wrote the novel* Mary Poppins*?*

**a12** Which British prime minister bought Polaris missiles from America?

*b12* *Which Secretary of State for War had to resign in 1963 after a scandal involving call girls?*

# No. 133 Answers

**a1** To dissolve paint
*b1* *Joining metals (including wires)*
**a2** Horse-racing
*b2* *Watford*
**a3** Parental Guidance
*b3* *Paying guest*
**a4** Simon Bates
*b4* *Johnnie Walker*
**a5** Turkey
*b5* *Netherlands (Holland)*
**a6** Hugh Gaitskell
*b6* *Harold Wilson*
**a7** Charles Laughton
*b7* *Breaks into laughter, accidentally*
**a8** ... Nash and Young
*b8* *... Mick and Tich*
**a9** British Museum
*b9* *(Imperial) War Museum*
**a10** London and North Western Railway
*b10* *London, Brighton and South Coast Railway*
**a11** Julie Andrews
*b11* *P L Travers*
**a12** Harold Macmillan
*b12* *John Profumo*

## Tie-breaker

**Q** The first-ever soccer World Cup was played in 1930 in Montevideo. Who won it?

**A** *Uruguay*

# No. 134

**a1** What was the NCB?

*b1* *In government, what is the FCO?*

**a2** In London, what are the Garrick, the Globe and the Savoy?

*b2* *And what are the Garrick, the Savage and the Savile?*

**a3** Which American band's theme was 'Moonlight Serenade'?

*b3* *During the Second World War, for which musical instrument was Sandy Macpherson famous?*

**a4** Which French female singer had no regrets when she sang 'Je ne regrette rien'?

*b4* *Which pop singer sang 'Living Doll'?*

**a5** Viscount Stansgate gave up his peerage to remain an MP. What name did he resume?

*b5* *Prime minister Lord Home (say: hume) was also known as ...?*

**a6** In which European country is the port of Brindisi?

*b6* *In which country is the port of Dunkerque (Dunkirk)?*

**a7** What did Molesworth, Aldermaston and Greenham have in common?

*b7* *Calder Hall opened in 1956. Why was this a newsworthy event?*

**a8** Who was made into an international star by her role in the 1930 film *The Blue Angel*?

*b8* *Who played the female lead in the film* Dr Zhivago?

**a9** Which small Scottish town became the site of a tragic aviation crime towards the end of 1988?

*b9* *In which Yugoslav city was there a major earthquake in 1963?*

**a10** Which television drama series features real-life adventures of a bomb disposal squad?

*b10* *In which television series did Jeremy Irons play an Evelyn Waugh hero?*

**a11** George Wallace (who tried to defy new race laws) was governor of which American state?

*b11* *In America, what was Alcatraz?*

**a12** What did American John De Lorean dream of building in Belfast?

*b12* *Chris Bonington was the first Briton to conquer the North Face of which mountain?*

# No. 134 Answers

**a1** National Coal Board
*b1 Foreign and Commonwealth Office*
**a2** (London) theatres
*b2 (London) clubs*
**a3** Glenn Miller
*b3 Organ; theatre organ*
**a4** Edith Piaf
*b4 Cliff Richard*
**a5** Tony Benn (Anthony Wedgwood Benn)
*b5 Sir Alec Douglas-Home (say: hume)*
**a6** Italy
*b6 France*
**a7** All were Cruise (nuclear) missile bases (USAF bases)
*b7 It was the world's first nuclear power station*
**a8** Marlene Dietrich
*b8 Julie Christie*
**a9** Lockerbie
*b9 Skopje*
**a10** *Danger UXB*
*b10* Brideshead Revisited
**a11** Alabama
*b11 Prison; a jail built on a rocky island*
**a12** Luxury sports cars
*b12 The Eiger (say: eye-ger)*

---

## Tie-breaker

**Q** Which film star's first line in 'talking pictures' was 'Gimme a vhisky with ginger ale on the side – and don't be stingy, baby'?
**A** *Greta Garbo*

---

# No. 135

**a1**  In which London park is the Round Pond?
*b1*  *And in which park is Speakers' Corner?*
**a2**  In which radio serial do we meet Eddie Grundy?
*b2*  *In which radio comedy show did we meet Eccles, Bluebottle and Henry Crun?*
**a3**  Which island was the focus of a 'missile crisis' in 1962?
*b3*  *Which country installed the missiles?*
**a4**  Who was the leader who backed down and removed the missiles?
*b4*  *Which American president claimed a victory over the Soviet Union?*
**a5**  Which television satire show in the early sixties annoyed politicians but won huge late Saturday night audiences?
*b5*  *And who was the compère of the shows?*
**a6**  Which two countries are separated by the Ionian Sea?
*b6*  *Which two countries are separated by the Kattegat?*
**a7**  With what is NASA concerned?
*b7*  *And what is meant by VTOL?*
**a8**  In a series of cartoons and films, who was Dagwood Bumstead's wife?
*b8*  *Which was the Beatles' first film?*
**a9**  In which city were the 1948 Olympics held?
*b9*  *In which city were the 1900 Olympic Games held?*
**a10**  What is RSI?
*b10*  *What is HIV?*
**a11**  Which pop group sang 'Part of the Union'?
*b11*  *Once with the Faces; later he sang 'Sailing'. Who is this pop star?*
**a12**  Who became Poet Laureate in 1984?
*b12*  *Who composed a 'War Requiem' based on poems by Wilfred Owen?*

# No. 135 Answers

**a1**  Kensington Gardens
*b1*  *Hyde Park*
**a2**  *The Archers*
*b2*  The Goon Show
**a3**  Cuba
*b3*  *Soviet Union*
**a4**  Mr Khrushchev (of the USSR)
*b4*  *President Kennedy*
**a5**  *That Was the Week That Was*
*b5*  *David Frost*
**a6**  Italy and Greece
*b6*  *Denmark and Sweden*
**a7**  Space travel (National Aeronautics and Space Administration)
*b7*  *Vertical take-off and landing*
**a8**  Blondie
*b8*  A Hard Day's Night
**a9**  London
*b9*  *Paris*
**a10**  Repetitive strain injury (incurred by spending too long at a keyboard)
*b10*  *Human immunodeficiency virus (breakdown of the body's immune system)*
**a11**  The Strawbs
*b11*  *Rod Stewart*
**a12**  Ted Hughes
*b12*  *Benjamin Britten*

---

## Tie-breaker

**Q**  Who is this singer? 'I was born in Austria in 1900 but later settled in New York. I became famous for what was once described as my "steel-like" voice, and appeared in cabaret.

**A**  *Lotte Lenya*

---

# No. 136

**a1** Which was Peter Thomson's sport?
*b1* *And what was Douglas Jardine's sport?*
**a2** Who topped the pop charts with his 'Long-Haired Lover From Liverpool'?
*b2* *And which nineties boy band came from Walthamstow?*
**a3** Which product was advertised by a group of monkeys?
*b3* *And which brand of tea bags were famous for their 'little perforations'?*
**a4** On television, on which subject have 'Saint' and 'Greavsie' presented programmes?
*b4* *On which subject has Barry Norman presented programmes?*
**a5** As what did Sir David Low achieve fame?
*b5* *How did Yves St Laurent (say: eve san lo'ron) achieve fame?*
**a6** In which county is the town of Barrow-in-Furness?
*b6* *And in which county was it prior to 1974?*
**a7** With which other European country did Britain attack Egypt in 1956?
*b7* *Which country did the Soviet Union crush while Britain was attacking Egypt?*
**a8** Which action provoked the Suez invasion?
*b8* *Which Egyptian town did the British bomb heavily during the Suez invasion?*
**a9** What sort of displays were given at Hendon in the thirties?
*b9* *What was a 'de-mob' suit?*
**a10** Which country very roughly now covers the area called Tripolitania at the start of the century?
*b10* *At the beginning of the century, which country lay immediately to the north of Greece?*
**a11** If you were travelling on a 'Routemaster', what means of transport would you be using?
*b11* *And if you were travelling in an 'Islander', how would you be travelling?*
**a12** Peter, Susan, Edmund and Lucy first appeared in which children's story?
*b12* *And which kingdom do they visit (to meet a White Witch and Aslan the Lion)?*

# No. 136 Answers

**a1**   Golf
*b1*   *Cricket*
**a2**   Jimmy Osmond
*b2*   *East 17*
**a3**   P G Tips tea
*b3*   *Quick Brew tea*
**a4**   Soccer
*b4*   *Films*
**a5**   (Political) cartoonist
*b5*   *As a fashion designer*
**a6**   Cumbria
*b6*   *Lancashire*
**a7**   France
*b7*   *Hungary*
**a8**   Egypt's nationalization of the Suez Canal
*b8*   *Port Said*
**a9**   Aviation (Royal Air Force)
*b9*   *Suit issued to servicemen when 'demobilized' after the Second World War (i.e. when leaving the army, etc.)*
**a10**   Libya
*b10*   *Macedonia (part of the Turkish Empire)*
**a11**   Bus (London double-decker)
*b11*   *By aircraft*
**a12**   *The Lion, the Witch and the Wardrobe*
*b12*   *Narnia*

---

## Tie-breaker

**Q**   What 1904 American invention was later to make it possible to build the first tanks?

**A**   *Caterpillar tread/caterpillar-tracked vehicles*

---

# No. 137

**a1**    At which game or sport has Stephen Hendry been a champion?

*b1*    *Which sportsman popularized the phrase 'I am the greatest'?*

**a2**    In films, whose preferred drink is 'a martini – shaken, not stirred'?

*b2*    *Which was the first James Bond film?*

**a3**    What make of car are the Nova, Astra and Carlton?

*b3*    *The Anglia and Sierra were both models of which make of car?*

**a4**    Which children's television programme featured a dog called Petra?

*b4*    *The television play* Cathy Come Home *highlighted the plight of which group of people?*

**a5**    Out of which two counties was Tyne and Wear carved in 1974?

*b5*    *Into which English county was Huntingdonshire absorbed in 1974?*

**a6**    Were tea bags invented in 1920, 1955 or 1965?

*b6*    *In the fifties, which drink was dispensed from Gaggia machines?*

**a7**    Which television comedian was famous for playing a character who said 'Oo, you are awful – but I like you'?

*b7*    *Which glove puppet was famous for saying 'Boom, boom!' after his own jokes?*

**a8**    Who became president of the United States when John F Kennedy was assassinated?

*b8*    *In America, what post was held by Dean Rusk?*

**a9**    In 1991, which prime minister was (like his mother) assassinated?

*b9*    *Of which country has Mrs Bandaranaike been prime minister?*

**a10**    What nationality was the composer Béla Bartók?

*b10*    *And what nationality was Percy Grainger, who composed 'Country Gardens' and 'Brigg Fair'?*

**a11**    What kind of cell is used in most 'electric eyes' that work automatic doors?

*b11*    *Where are you most likely to have a Quartz crystal?*

**a12**    How did Sir Alexander Korda become famous?

*b12*    *And how did C P Scott become well known?*

# No. 137 Answers

**a1**  Snooker
*b1*  *Muhammed Ali (formerly Cassius Clay)*
**a2**  James Bond
*b2*  Dr No
**a3**  Vauxhall
*b3*  *Ford*
**a4**  *Blue Peter*
*b4*  *The homeless*
**a5**  Northumberland and Durham
*b5*  *Cambridgeshire*
**a6**  1920 (by Joseph Krieger in San Francisco)
*b6*  *(Frothy) coffee*
**a7**  Dick Emery
*b7*  *Basil Brush*
**a8**  Lyndon B Johnson
*b8*  *Secretary of State*
**a9**  Rajiv Gandhi (in India)
*b9*  *Sri Lanka*
**a10**  Hungarian
*b10*  *Australian*
**a11**  Photoelectric cell
*b11*  *In you watch*
**a12**  As a film producer
*b12*  *As a newspaper editor (of the then* Manchester Guardian*)*

---

## Tie-breaker

**Q**  Who were the four stars of the theatrical revue *Beyond the Fringe*?

**A**  *Alan Bennett, Peter Cook, Jonathan Miller, Dudley Moore*

---

# No. 138

**a1** Which domestic item was advertised with the slogan 'Prolongs Active Life'?

*b1* *And which item was said to help you work, rest and play?*

**a2** What is CJD?

*b2* *On which island was the Bay of Pigs invasion?*

**a3** In which stories is Mrs Goggins a postmistress?

*b3* *Who wrote the children's books* Fantastic Mr Fox *and* The BFG?

**a4** In which sport has Kriss Akabusi been a champion?

*b4* *Which has been Will Carling's sport?*

**a5** What is controlled by a thermostat?

*b5* *What does a humidifier add to the air?*

**a6** Wardour Street is said to be the London home of which industry?

*b6* *Which film comedian has his statue in London's Leicester Square?*

**a7** Which American rock singer joined the army in March 1958?

*b7* *Which football team lost seven members in a 1958 air crash?*

**a8** Sharon's and Tracey's husbands are in prison – in which television comedy series?

*b8* *In which television series has Mike Baldwin been a key character?*

**a9** In which county is Milton Keynes?

*b9* *In which county is Telford?*

**a10** In which Western did we first hear the song 'Raindrops Keep Falling on my Head'?

*b10* *Which film features the song 'Bright Eyes'?*

**a11** What have the following in common: Swindon, Crewe and Doncaster?

*b11* *What have the following in common: Cowley, Longbridge and Dunstable?*

**a12** Which political party was the surprise winner of a 1962 by-election in Orpington?

*b12* *When the British Labour government failed in 1931, how was Britain governed?*

# No. 138 Answers

**a1**    PAL dog food
*b1*    *Mars bars*
**a2**    Human form of BSE (Creuzfeldt-Jakob's Disease)
*b2*    *Cuba*
**a3**    The 'Postman Pat' stories
*b3*    *Roald Dahl*
**a4**    Athletics (track)
*b4*    *Rugby Union*
**a5**    The temperature of something (e.g. a room, oven or refrigerator)
*b5*    *Moisture; water vapour*
**a6**    Film
*b6*    *Charlie Chaplin*
**a7**    Elvis Presley
*b7*    *Manchester United*
**a8**    *Birds of a Feather*
*b8*    Coronation Street
**a9**    Buckinghamshire
*b9*    *Shropshire*
**a10**    *Butch Cassidy and the Sundance Kid*
*b10*    Watership Down
**a11**    All are 'railway towns'; all have had important locomotive works
*b11*    *All have major car plants*
**a12**    Liberal
*b12*    *By a coalition (the 'National Government')*

---

## Tie-breaker

**Q**    What useful domestic appliance was invented in 1906 by Alva J Fisher?
**A**    *Electric washing machine*

# No. 139

**a1**  Which sport is played at Murrayfield?

*b1*  *For which sport is Epsom well known?*

**a2**  In which television show did Bob Monkhouse say 'Bernie, the bolt!'?

*b2*  *On television, which singer introduced* The Record Breakers?

**a3**  Which ruling duo was known as 'B and K'?

*b3*  *On which day of the year in 1991 did President Gorbachev resign?*

**a4**  Which 1970 film, made in the north of England, featured steam trains?

*b4*  *Which real-life children's author was portrayed on screen by Danny Kaye?*

**a5**  With which industry has Port Talbot been associated?

*b5*  *Which industry has traditionally been associated with Kettering?*

**a6**  Which comedian had the catch phrases 'A good idea, son!' and 'I've arrived and to prove it I'm here'?

*b6*  *Which comedian used the phrase 'Aye, aye, that's yer lot'?*

**a7**  Which vitamin can help people to see in the dark?

*b7*  *What 'perk' for Britons flying abroad was introduced in 1959?*

**a8**  According to the song, who regrets she's unable to lunch today?

*b8*  *In a song, who goes out in the midday sun?*

**a9**  Which motorway would you use to travel to London from Oxford?

*b9*  *And which motorway would you use to reach London from Cambridge?*

**a10**  What did Hans Geiger invent in 1908?

*b10*  *An inventor gave his name to a type of emergency bridge which could be built quickly. His name was ...?*

**a11**  Walter Mondale was vice-president to which American president?

*b11*  *Nelson A Rockefeller was vice-president to which American president?*

**a12**  Which country's move to independence provoked a right-wing secret army (known as the OAS) into action in 1962?

*b12*  *In which South African township did police shoot 56 people dead in 1960?*

# No. 139 Answers

**a1** Rugby union (Edinburgh)
*b1* *Racing (horse-racing)*
**a2** *The Golden Shot*
*b2* *Roy Castle*
**a3** Marshall Bulganin (prime minister) and Mr Kruschev (Communist party leader), in the Soviet Union
*b3* *Christmas Day (December 25)*
**a4** *The Railway Children*
*b4* *Hans Christian Andersen*
**a5** Steel
*b5* *Footwear; shoe-making*
**a6** Max Bygraves (on radio in *Educating Archie*)
*b6* *Jimmy Wheeler*
**a7** Vitamin A
*b7* *Duty-free drink*
**a8** Miss Otis (by Cole Porter)
*b8* *Mad Dogs and Englishmen (Noël Coward)*
**a9** M40
*b9* *M11*
**a10** The geiger counter (which detects radiation)
*b10* *Bailey (Sir D Bailey)*
**a11** Jimmy Carter
*b11* *Gerald Ford*
**a12** Algeria
*b12* *Sharpeville*

---

# Tie-breaker

**Q** What is the CIS?
**A** *Commonwealth of Independent States (the former Soviet Union)*

---

# No. 140

**a1** Which ex-soap star sang 'Torn'?

*b1* *Name the song Babylon Zoo took to number one.*

**a2** What is the capital of the American state of Oklahoma?

*b2* *Salt Lake City is the capital of which American state?*

**a3** Which disc jockey has often asked, 'How's about that, then, guys and gals?'?

*b3* *In which disc jockey's programmes did we regularly hear the voice of a small boy saying ''Ello, darlin'!'?*

**a4** With which game is John Parrott associated?

*b4* *Which is Nick Faldo's sport?*

**a5** In which county is Salisbury Plain?

*b5* *In which country is Cannock Chase?*

**a6** Eddie Valiant appears in a film with which cartoon character?

*b6* *In which film does an eccentric scientist help a teenager to travel back to the fifties to meet his parents?*

**a7** In its adverts, which soap promised 'a schoolgirl complexion'?

*b7* *And also in the adverts, which pills were supposedly worth a guinea a box?*

**a8** When the Dalai Lama escaped from Tibet, which country gave him sanctuary?

*b8* *What was the name of the U-2 pilot shot down over the Soviet Union and imprisoned as a spy?*

**a9** What is an enzyme?

*b9* *What is a base metal?*

**a10** In Sherlock Holmes' 'Final Problem', who was described as 'the Napoleon of crime'?

*b10* *Which thriller writer (of 170 books, including* The Four Just Men*) died in 1932?*

**a11** For which city is Aldergrove the airport?

*b11* *And for which city is Dyce the airport?*

**a12** Which British prime minister sacked seven members of his cabinet in what became known as 'the night of the long knives'?

*b12* *In Britain, which Labour minister resigned in 1930 and started his own extreme right-wing party?*

# No. 140 Answers

**a1** Natalie Imbruglia
*b1* *'Spaceman'*
**a2** Oklahoma City
*b2* *Utah*
**a3** Jimmy Savile
*b3* *Ed Stewart's*
**a4** Snooker
*b4* *Golf*
**a5** Wiltshire
*b5* *Staffordshire*
**a6** Roger Rabbit
*b6* *Back to the Future*
**a7** Palmolive
*b7* *Beecham's Pills*
**a8** India
*b8* *Gary Powers*
**a9** A biological catalyst; a substance which speeds up a reaction or digests starch or fats
*b9* *A non-precious metal*
**a10** (Professor) Moriarty
*b10* *Edgar Wallace*
**a11** Belfast
*b11* *Aberdeen*
**a12** Harold Macmillan (1962)
*b12* *Sir Oswald Mosley*

## Tie-breaker

**Q** Name the seven dwarfs.
*A* *Sleepy, Grumpy, Sneezy, Happy, Dopey, Doc and Bashful*

# No. 141 Who Wrote That?

Who wrote the following 20th-century literary works?

**a1**   *The History of Mr Polly*
**b1**   Blandings Castle
**a2**   *Tinker, Tailor, Soldier, Spy*
**b2**   *The Maigret novels*
**a3**   *Of Mice and Men*
**b3**   An Inspector Calls
**a4**   *Women in Love*
**b4**   The Moon and Sixpence
**a5**   *Clayhanger*
**b5**   Finnegans Wake
**a6**   *Doctor Zhivago*
**b6**   The Gulag Archipelago
**a7**   *Brideshead Revisited*
**b7**   The Road to Wigan Pier
**a8**   *The Trial*
**b8**   The Satanic Verses
**a9**   *Goodbye to All That*
**b9**   A Shropshire Lad
**a10**   *Mapp and Lucia*
**b10**   The Forsyte Saga
**a11**   *Goodbye to Berlin*
**b11**   Lolita
**a12**   'Sea Fever' and 'Cargoes'
**b12**   The Go-Between

# No. 141 Answers

**a1** H G Wells
*b1 P G Woodhouse*
**a2** John le Carré
*b2 Georges Simenon*
**a3** John Steinbeck
*b3 J B Priestley*
**a4** D H Lawrence
*b4 Somerset Maugham*
**a5** Arnold Bennett
*b5 James Joyce*
**a6** Boris Pasternak
*b6 Alexander Solzhenitsyn*
**a7** Evelyn Waugh
*b7 George Orwell*
**a8** Franz Kafka
*b8 Salman Rushdie*
**a9** Robert Graves
*b9 A E Housman*
**a10** E F Benson
*b10 John Galsworthy*
**a11** Christopher Isherwood
*b11 Vladimir Nabokov*
**a12** John Masefield
*b12 L P Hartley*

## Tie-breaker

**Q** Who wrote the novels *Point Counter Point*, *Chrome Yellow* and *Eyeless in Gaza*?
**A** *Aldous Huxley*

# No. 142

**a1**   What make of car are the Polo and the Jetta?
*b1*   *What make of car are the Civic and the Accord?*
**a2**   Which television comedian regularly said, 'Hello, my darlings'?
*b2*   *Which comedian is associated with such words as 'tattifilarious', 'plumptiousness' – and also had trouble with the Inland Revenue?*
**a3**   In which sport has Liz McColgan won a gold medal?
*b3*   *Which snooker star was, for a time, thought to be 'boring'?*
**a4**   Which Italian story about a wooden puppet became a major Walt Disney film in 1940?
*b4*   *Which cartoon character plays the Sorcerer's Apprentice in the film* Fantasia?
**a5**   Out of which two counties was Avon created in 1974?
*b5*   *Into which new county was Westmorland absorbed in 1974?*
**a6**   What invention, linked with the number $33^{1}/_{3}$, first went on sale in 1931?
*b6*   *What domestic item was invented by Tefal in Paris in 1955?*
**a7**   What was the middle name of American Secretary of State Dulles?
*b7*   *Which American president started a work programme which promised a 'new deal'?*
**a8**   Who composed the Enigma Variations?
*b8*   *Which pianist became famous for her war-time recitals in the National Gallery?*
**a9**   Which actress (who starred in the film *A Passage to India*) has a theatre named after her in Croydon?
*b9*   *Which new theatre was opened in 1932 with performances of Shakespeare's* Henry IV, *parts 1 and 2?*
**a10**   Which two countries signed on 'Entente Cordiale' in 1904?
*b10*   *In which country (in the early sixties) was Patrice Lumumba a leader?*
**a11**   Which tube line can you take to Heathrow Airport?
*b11*   *On a London Underground map, what colour is the Circle Line?*
**a12**   In which radio programme did we regularly hear the announcement, 'We stop the roar of London's traffic ...'?
*b12*   *Which radio show introduced us to the Angus Prune tune?*

# No. 142 Answers

**a1** Volkswagen
*b1* *Honda*
**a2** Charlie Drake
*b2* *Ken Dodd*
**a3** Athletics (10,000 metres)
*b3* *Steve Davis*
**a4** *Pinocchio*
*b4* *Mickey Mouse*
**a5** Gloucestershire; Somerset
*b5* *Cumbria*
**a6** Long-playing records (revolving at 33⅓ rpm)
*b6* *Non-stick pans*
**a7** Foster (John Foster Dulles)
*b7* *Franklin Roosevelt*
**a8** (Edward) Elgar
*b8* *Dame Myra Hess*
**a9** Dame Peggy Ashcroft
*b9* *Shakespeare Memorial Theatre, Stratford upon Avon*
**a10** Britain, France
*b10* *The Congo*
**a11** Piccadilly
*b11* *Yellow*
**a12** *In Town Tonight*
*b12* I'm Sorry I'll Read That Again

---

## Tie-breaker

**Q** Why was Europe at Sixes and Sevens in 1959?
**A** *Six countries were in the Common Market (France, Germany, Italy, Belgium, Netherlands and Luxembourg) and seven were in EFTA or the European Free Trade Association (UK, Norway, Sweden, Denmark, Switzerland, Austria and Portugal)*

---

# No. 143

**a1**   Which satirical television show was dependent on latex rubber?

**b1**   *Which television character regularly said, 'Silly old moo'?*

**a2**   In its adverts, which beer promised to work wonders?

**b2**   *And which one reached parts other ones could not reach?*

**a3**   Chris Lowe and Neil Tennant make up which famous duo?

**b3**   *Who was the lead singer of the group Culture Club?*

**a4**   Which was athlete Herb Elliott's principal track event?

**b4**   *Which rugby league club did Andy Gregory coach when he stopped playing?*

**a5**   In what is carbon tetrachloride often used?

**b5**   *What is made from potassium nitrate?*

**a6**   Who was the male star of the film *Grease*?

**b6**   *Who played Gandhi in the film of that name?*

**a7**   Which post in a Tory cabinet is Selwyn Lloyd best remembered for holding?

**b7**   *Which Labour politician was nicknamed 'Nye'?*

**a8**   In which county is Stevenage?

**b8**   *In which county is Basingstoke?*

**a9**   Santa Fé is the capital of which American state?

**b9**   *Of which American state is Lincoln the capital?*

**a10**  In which George Orwell novel are there a 'Two Minutes Hate', Thought Police and a language called Newspeak?

**b10**  *In a poem, T S Eliot suggests the way the world ends is not with a bang but with a ... what?*

**a11**  Which city has railway stations called Interchange and Forster Square?

**b11**  *In which Yorkshire cathedral city are railway stations called Kirkgate and Westgate?*

**a12**  Which important building was destroyed by fire on the night of February 28, 1933?

**b12**  *In which Northern Ireland town did the IRA kill 11 people on Remembrance Day in 1987?*

# No. 143 Answers

**a1**  *Spitting Image*
**b1**  *Alf Garnett*
**a2**  Double Diamond
**b2**  *Heineken*
**a3**  The Pet Shop Boys
**b3**  *Boy George*
**a4**  The mile (1,500 metres)
**b4**  *Salford*
**a5**  Cleaning
**b5**  *Matches, fireworks*
**a6**  John Travolta
**b6**  *Ben Kingsley*
**a7**  Chancellor of the Exchequer
**b7**  *Aneurin Bevan*
**a8**  Hertfordshire
**b8**  *Hampshire*
**a9**  New Mexico
**b9**  *Nebraska*
**a10**  *1984*
**b10**  *Whimper*
**a11**  Bradford
**b11**  *Wakefield*
**a12**  The German Reichstag (say: rike-starg) or parliament building
**b12**  *Enniskillen*

## Tie-breaker

**Q**  Which pop music manager said, 'I want to manage those four boys. It wouldn't take me more than two half-days a week'?

**A**  *Brian Epstein, about the Beatles (he did become their manager)*

# No. 144

**a1** What make of car are Pandas, Unos (say: u-nose) and Tipos (say: tee-pose)?

*b1* *What make of car are the Micra, Sunny and the Primera?*

**a2** In which sport did Terry Spinks win an Olympic gold medal?

*b2* *Which was heavyweight boxer Ingemar Johansson's home country?*

**a3** Weatherfield is the fictional location of which television serial?

*b3* *Which television serial is set in the borough of Walford?*

**a4** Which part of London saw race riots in 1958 and, later, an annual carnival?

*b4* *And also in London in 1958, who 'came out' (officially) for the last time?*

**a5** Near which town or city is Devonport naval dockyard?

*b5* *Off which mainland port lies the area of sea known as Spithead?*

**a6** In the films, what is Rambo's first name?

*b6* *What is Crocodile Dundee's first name?*

**a7** Who composed the piano piece 'Claire de Lune'?

*b7* *Which pianist played 'old ones, new ones'?*

**a8** George Bush was vice-president to which American president?

*b8* *Which famous American dramatist was accused of being 'unAmerican' during a Communist witch-hunt?*

**a9** What is a saline solution?

*b9* *What is gun cotton?*

**a10** Whom did Von Hindenburg beat in the 1932 German presidential election?

*b10* *What was Soviet President Kruschev's first name?*

**a11** *Cavalcade* is a play chronicling a family's life from 1899 to 1930. Who wrote it?

*b11* *In 1913, who wrote the play* Androcles and the Lion*?*

**a12** In which wartime comedy show did Mona Lott always gloomily announce, 'It's being so cheerful as keeps me going'?

*b12* *In which radio panel game did we regularly hear the phrase 'And the next object is ...'?*

# No. 144 Answers

**a1** Fiat
*b1 Nissan*
**a2** Boxing
*b2 Sweden*
**a3** *Coronation Street*
*b3* EastEnders
**a4** Notting Hill Gate
*b4 Debutantes (the last time young ladies were 'presented' at court)*
**a5** Plymouth
*b5 Portsmouth*
**a6** John
*b6 Mick*
**a7** (Claude) Debussy
*b7 Semprini*
**a8** Ronald Reagan
*b8 Arthur Miller*
**a9** Liquid containing salt
*b9 An explosive (nitro cellulose)*
**a10** Hitler
*b10 Nikita*
**a11** Noël Coward
*b11 George Bernard Shaw*
**a12** ITMA
*b12* Twenty Questions

---

## Tie-breaker

**Q**  Which was Britain's first stretch of motorway?
*A   The Preston bypass (now part of the M6)*

---

# No. 145

**a1**  With which means of transport is Westland associated?
*b1*  *What are (or were) trolley buses?*
**a2**  As what did Anna Pavlova achieve fame?
*b2*  *And what kind of food is Pavlova?*
**a3**  In an advert, which product were you asked to 'tell' from butter?
*b3*  *And which product promised to make you a little lovelier each day?*
**a4**  With which country was Britain in disagreement during the so-called 'Cod War'?
*b4*  *Which subject caused violent scenes during a debate in the House of Commons in 1902?*
**a5**  Which prime minister regularly holidayed on the Scilly Isles?
*b5*  *Which Welsh writer lived in Laugharne near Carmarthen?*
**a6**  In which war film did Michael Caine lead a team of German commandos trying to assassinate Churchill?
*b6*  *In which film epic did Charlton Heston go chariot racing?*
**a7**  Did Liverpool FC first win the Cup Final in 1925, 1935 or 1965?
*b7*  *Which soccer club did Danny Blanchflower captain to success in the League and the Cup Final in 1961?*
**a8**  Charleston is the capital of which American state?
*b8*  *Of which American state is St Paul the capital?*
**a9**  Which heavy, silvery white metal is more precious than gold?
*b9*  *In what is plutonium used?*
**a10**  Which female singer had hits with 'You Don't Have to Say You Love Me' and 'Son of a Preacher Man'?
*b10*  *Which singer had her greatest hit with 'These Boots Are Made for Walkin''?*
**a11**  In a wartime broadcast, Winston Churchill said to America 'we will finish the job' provided America were to do what?
*b11*  *According to Dorothy Parker, at whom do men seldom make passes?*
**a12**  Which cartoonist created the characters Fungus the Bogeyman, the Snowman and drew a popular 'Father Christmas'?
*b12*  *When the Noddy books were re-published in 1987, what did gnomes replace?*

# No. 145 Answers

**a1** Helicopters
*b1* *Buses powered by electricity (drawn from overhead wires through roof-mounted trolley poles)*
**a2** Ballet dancer (ballet mistress)
*b2* *A dessert with meringues and fruit*
**a3** Stork margarine
*b3* *('Fabulous pink') Camay soap*
**a4** Iceland
*b4* *Ireland*
**a5** Harold Wilson
*b5* *Dylan Thomas*
**a6** *The Eagle Has Landed*
*b6* Ben Hur
**a7** 1965
*b7* *Tottenham Hotspur*
**a8** West Virginia
*b8* *Minnesota*
**a9** Platinum
*b9* *Nuclear reactors, atomic weapons*
**a10** Dusty Springfield
*b10* *Nancy Sinatra*
**a11** 'Give us the tools'
*b11* *Girls who wear glasses*
**a12** Raymond Briggs
*b12* *Golliwogs*

## Tie-breaker

**Q** Which prime minister said, 'We are not at war with Egypt. We are in an armed conflict'?
**A** *Sir Anthony Eden*

# No. 146

**a1**  In which county is Clacton-on-Sea?
*b1*  *In which county is the inland resort of Buxton?*
**a2**  Of which make of car was the E-type a famous model?
*b2*  *What make of car was the Silver Cloud?*
**a3**  Which television policeman always said 'Mind how you go'?
*b3*  *Which comedian regularly said 'Now there's a funny thing'?*
**a4**  Which soccer club did Alex Ferguson manage before Manchester United?
*b4*  *Which club side did Glenn Hoddle manage before England?*
**a5**  Alma Ata is the capital of which former Soviet republic?
*b5*  *Kiev is the capital of which former Soviet republic?*
**a6**  Where did Dr Vivian Fuchs lead an expedition in 1958?
*b6*  *Who was the first American to orbit the Earth in space?*
**a7**  In which film musical (starring Grace Kelly) did Bing Crosby and Frank Sinatra sing 'Did You Evah?'?
*b7*  *Which American musical is set partly in Deadwood City's Golden Garter saloon?*
**a8**  Which Sunday newspaper was advertised with the slogan 'All human life is there!'?
*b8*  *Britain's first 'colour supplement' was published in 1962 – with which Sunday newspaper?*
**a9**  Ryan O'Neal starred with his daughter in the film *Paper Moon*. What is her name?
*b9*  *Who 'dragged up' to play the lead in the film* Tootsie?
**a10**  In 1971, Anthony Marriott and Alistair Foot wrote a long-running sex farce called ... what?
*b10*  *Which Terence Rattigan play features a translation of a Greek text?*
**a11**  What memorable phrase did Commander Tommy Woodrooffe utter several times on radio in 1937 when describing a Spit-head naval review?
*b11*  *From which radio comedy comes the line 'He's fallen in the water'?*
**a12**  Of which country was Sir Roy Welensky prime minister?
*b12*  *Of which country was Imre Nagy (say: naje) prime minister?*

# No. 146 Answers

**a1** Essex
**b1** *Derbyshire*
**a2** Jaguar
**b2** *Rolls-Royce*
**a3** Dixon of Dock Green (P C George Dixon)
**b3** *Max Miller*
**a4** Aberdeen
**b4** *Chelsea*
**a5** Khazakstan
**b5** *Ukraine*
**a6** Across the Antarctic
**b6** *Lieutenant-Colonel John Glenn*
**a7** *High Society*
**b7** Calamity Jane
**a8** *News of the World*
**b8** The Sunday Times
**a9** Tatum O'Neal
**b9** *Dustin Hoffman*
**a10** *No Sex Please – We're British*
**b10** The Browning Version
**a11** 'The fleet's lit up' (many listeners though he was drunk)
**b11** The Goon Show
**a12** Central African Federation (accept: Rhodesia)
**b12** *Hungary*

---

## Tie-breaker

**Q** In 1932 a British law was passed which abolished a previously legal punishment for children. What was it?
**A** *Whipping*

---

292

# No. 147

**a1** According to the adverts, with which cigarette were you never alone?

*b1* *And which lager was (or is) 'probably the best lager in the world?'*

**a2** What is the ex-West Indian cricketer Sobers' first name?

*b2* *Which sport or game does Eric Bristow play?*

**a3** In which film does Dick Van Dyke dance with four penguins?

*b3* *In which film is the Pushmipullyou?*

**a4** In which television series did Jim do battle with Sir Humphrey?

*b4* *Which television programme made the one-word answer 'pass' into a catch phrase?*

**a5** What is meant by 'synthetic'?

*b5* *What is sucrose?*

**a6** Which former Conservative leader accused the Conservative party (under Mrs Thatcher) of 'selling the family silver'?

*b6* *How many general elections did Mrs Thatcher win as leader of the Conservative party?*

**a7** In which county is Sizewell Nuclear Power Station?

*b7* *Why has Daventry in the English Midlands become known world-wide?*

**a8** Which city has railway stations called New Street and Snow Hill?

*b8* *Which town has railway stations called North, South and Pleasure Beach?*

**a9** 'End of the Road' was a hit for which nineties Motown group?

*b9* *Once in the TV series* Neighbours, *he starred on stage in* Joseph and the Amazing Technicolor Dreamcoat. *Who is he?*

**a10** Which has been the principal industry in the Rhondda (say: rhon-tha) Valley for much of the century?

*b10* *Which northeastern 'new' county disappeared in 1997?*

**a11** Of which American state is Jackson the capital?

*b11* *Of which American state is Sacramento the capital?*

**a12** Which 'beat generation' American wrote the book *On the Road*?

*b12* *Which French novelist wrote* The Outsider *(L'Etranger)?*

# No. 147 Answers

**a1**   Strand
*b1*   *Carlsberg*
**a2**   Garfield (Garry)
*b2*   *Darts*
**a3**   *Mary Poppins*
*b3*   Dr Dolittle
**a4**   *Yes, Minister* (and in *Yes, Prime Minister*)
*b4*   Mastermind
**a5**   Not natural; made from chemicals (by humans)
*b5*   *Pure white sugar (obtained from sugar beet or sugar cane)*
**a6**   Harold Macmillan
*b6*   *Three*
**a7**   Suffolk
*b7*   *Because of its radio transmission mast ('Daventry calling ...')*
**a8**   Birmingham
*b8*   *Blackpool*
**a9**   Boyz II Men
*b9*   *Jason Donovan*
**a10**  Coal-mining
*b10*  *Cleveland*
**a11**  Mississippi
*b11*  *California*
**a12**  Jack Kerouac
*b12*  *Albert Camus*

---

## Tie-breaker

**Q**  Why was the first American to cross the finishing line in the Marathon in the 1904 Olympics disqualified?

**A**  *He took a lift on a lorry for part of the course*

---

# No. 148

**a1** Which television star calls her friends 'possum'?

*b1* *On which television show is it possible to hear the line, 'And the same question to number two'?*

**a2** Which Russian dancer defected to the West in 1961?

*b2* *Who was born Jan Ludvik Hock and died in the sea near the Canaries?*

**a3** Which Eskimo word (meaning a jacket of skin or cloth, with a fur-lined hood) has come into the English language?

*b3* *In Russia, what is a 'dacha'?*

**a4** Into which area of maritime water does the River Hamble flow?

*b4* *In which county are the Mendip Hills?*

**a5** What became the official United States anthem in 1931?

*b5* *Which American musician composed the ballet* Billy the Kid*?*

**a6** Which motorway goes north from Preston to Scotland?

*b6* *Which motorway crosses the Pennines from north Manchester to Leeds?*

**a7** 'Nation shall speak peace unto nation' is a motto of which organization?

*b7* *In radio's* Children's Hour, *who always said, 'Good night, children, everywhere!'?*

**a8** Which English fast bowler was at the centre of the 'bodyline' controversy in 1933?

*b8* *Which bowler was paired with Ray Lindwall?*

**a9** What new building material was invented by a French civil engineer in 1904?

*b9* *What was the 'Flying Bedstead'?*

**a10** What post or title was Hitler given in 1933?

*b10* *Who was elected president of France in 1958?*

**a11** Which Norwegian playwright (who died in 1906) wrote the play *Peer Gynt*?

*b11* *And which composer (who died in 1907) wrote incidental music for* Peer Gynt*?*

**a12** Of which European country was Angola a colony?

*b12* *In which Tibetan city did the Dalai Lama have his palace?*

# No. 148 Answers

**a1** Dame Edna Everage (Barry Humphries)
*b1* *Blind Date*
**a2** (Rudolf) Nureyev
*b2* *Robert Maxwell*
**a3** Anorak (anoraq, originally)
*b3* *Country house; summer home (a privilege of party officials in Communist times)*
**a4** Southampton Water
*b4* *Somerset*
**a5** 'The Star-Spangled Banner'
*b5* *(Aaron) Copland*
**a6** M6
*b6* *M62*
**a7** BBC
*b7* *Uncle Mac (Derek McCulloch)*
**a8** Harold Larwood (also Bill Voce)
*b8* *Keith Miller*
**a9** Pre-stressed concrete (invented by Eugene Freyssinet)
*b9* *Early vertical take-off aircraft (Rolls-Royce TMR)*
**a10** Chancellor (of the German Reich or state)
*b10* *General de Gaulle*
**a11** (Henrik) Ibsen
*b11* *(Edvard) Grieg*
**a12** Portugal
*b12* *Lhasa*

---

## Tie-breaker

**Q** There are three main classes of food needed by the human body. Fats and carbohydrates are two. What is the third?

**A** *Proteins*

---

# No. 149

**a1** On screen, what make of car was Herbie?
*b1 In the cartoon films, what kind of creature is Goofy?*
**a2** What (in an advert) was said to be 'full of Eastern Promise'?
*b2 According to the advert, which chocolates 'grow on you'?*
**a3** For what construction is Jodrell Bank in Cheshire famous?
*b3 For which industry was Corby in Northamptonshire famous for part of the century?*
**a4** Which aircraft company builds the TriStar?
*b4 What public transport vehicles were manufactured by Leyland, Bristol and Crossley?*
**a5** About which boxer did Mike Tyson say, 'He should come back. All Americans love beating up poor old Frank'?
*b5 In 1991, which boxer went into a long coma after a fight against Chris Eubank?*
**a6** On television, what was the setting of the soap opera *Compact*?
*b6 Tannochbrae was the setting of which television series?*
**a7** In the story and the film, why did Cruella de Vil want to steal 101 dalmatians?
*b7 Ring of Bright Water principally features which mammals?*
**a8** Who was the first King of Britain to broadcast?
*b8 Which British Royal gave up the Royal Marines in 1987?*
**a9** 'I'm A Believer' and 'Daydream Believer' were hits for which television pop group?
*b9 Which pop group sang 'Dedicated Follower of Fashion', 'Sunny Afternoon' and 'Lola'?*
**a10** When did the last steam train run on London's Underground? Was it in 1911, 1931 or 1971?
*b10 In Europe, was the first motorway opened in 1921, 1935 or 1955?*
**a11** In which Eastern state was Mr Gomulka a leading politician?
*b11 Of which country was King Feisal monarch until his murder in 1958?*
**a12** As bishop of which diocese did David Jenkins become a controversial figure?
*b12 By what name or nickname was Lieutenant General John Glubb known when commanding the Arab Legion?*

# No. 149 Answers

**a1**  A Volkswagen
*b1*  *A dog*
**a2**  Fry's Turkish Delight
*b2*  *(Cadbury) Roses*
**a3**  Radio telescope
*b3*  *Steel*
**a4**  Lockheed
*b4*  *Buses*
**a5**  Frank Bruno
*b5*  *Michael Watson*
**a6**  The editorial offices of a women's magazine (called *Compact*)
*b6*  Dr Finlay's Casebook
*a7*  To make fur coats
*b7*  *Otters*
**a8**  King George V
*b8*  *Prince Andrew*
**a9**  The Monkees
*b9*  *The Kinks*
**a10**  1971
*b10*  *1921, in Berlin*
**a11**  Poland
*b11*  *Iraq*
**a12**  Durham
*b12*  *Glubb Pasha*

---

## Tie-breaker

**Q**  In the Second World War, for what was PLUTO an abbreviation?

**A**  *Pipe line under the ocean (actually across the English Channel, supplying oil to Allied forces after D-Day)*

# No. 150

**a1**  With which television entertainer is the line 'I'm in charge' associated?

*b1*  *In the fifties, whose catch phrase was 'I only arsked'?*

**a2**  Dame Nellie Melba died in 1931. How did she become famous?

*b2*  *And what food was named after her?*

**a3**  In which county is the container port of Felixstowe?

*b3*  *In which county is Leyland, the home of Leyland trucks and buses?*

**a4**  Which organization advertised itself with the statement 'We're getting there'?

*b4*  *And which airline advertised itself by promising 'We'll take good care of you'?*

**a5**  Which human organ can be regulated by an electronic pacemaker?

*b5*  *When does a doctor use a spatula?*

**a6**  What make of car were the Hawk and the Super Snipe?

*b6*  *What make of car were Imps and Huskies?*

**a7**  From what is polythene made?

*b7*  *What percentage of 18-carat gold is actually gold?*

**a8**  Which boy singer sang 'Walking in the Air' in the cartoon film *The Snowman*?

*b8*  *Which cartoon character said 'I taut I taw a puddy tat'?*

**a9**  In which city were the 1956 Olympics held – the first to take place south of the Equator?

*b9*  *Which tennis player's lover or partner was Nancy Lieberman?*

**a10**  Who created the character Miss Joan Hunter Dunn?

*b10*  *In Rupert Brooke's poem 'The Old Vicarage, Grantchester', the poet asks if the church clock still stands at ... what time?*

**a11**  How did United Nations Secretary – General Dag Hammarskjöld (say: hammer-shold) die?

*b11*  *Who died in a French prison and was known as the 'Butcher of Lyons'?*

**a12**  From which film comes the song 'Have Yourself a Merry Little Christmas'?

*b12*  *Which Harvey Fierstein musical features a St Tropez (say: san tro-pay) drag club?*

# No. 150 Answers

**a1** Bruce Forsyth
*b1* *Bernard Bresslaw's*
**a2** As a singer
*b2* *Peach Melba (peach served with ice cream and raspberry juice) and/or Melba toast*
**a3** Suffolk
*b3* *Lancashire*
**a4** British Rail
*b4* *British Airways*
**a5** The heart
*b5* *To hold down your tongue, when examining your throat*
**a6** Humber
*b6* *Hillman*
**a7** Oil
*b7* *75%*
**a8** Aled Jones
*b8* *Tweetie Pie*
**a9** Melbourne
*b9* *Martina Navratilova*
**a10** John Betjeman (poet)
*b10* *Ten to three*
**a11** In an aircrash
*b11* *Klaus Barbie*
**a12** Meet Me in St Louis
*b12* La Cage Aux Folles

---

## Tie-breaker

**Q** Fungicides get rid of fungi. Which pest is attacked with formicide?
**A** *Ants*

---

# No. 151 Singles

Which soloist, group or band had a hit with each of these pop and rock singles?

**a1** 'Glad All Over'
*b1* *'Strawberry Fields Forever'*
**a2** 'Think Twice'
*b2* *'Goodnight Girl'*
**a3** 'The Sound of Silence'
*b3* *'Imagine'*
**a4** 'Anticipation'
*b4* *'Brown Sugar'*
**a5** 'Every Beat of My Heart'
*b5* *'Reach Out, I'll Be There'*
**a6** 'All or Nothing'
*b6* *'Don't Stop the Carnival'*
**a7** 'Catch a Falling Star'
*b7* *'With or Without You'*
**a8** 'Why Do Fools Fall in Love?'
*b8* *'Will You Love Me Tomorrow?'*
**a9** 'I Want You Back'
*b9* *'Pretty Flamingo'*
**a10** 'California Dreamin''
*b10* *'Maggie May'*
**a11** 'Chorus'
*b11* *'Drive'*
**a12** 'Rocky Mountain High'
*b12* *'School's Out'*

# No. 151 Answers

**a1** The Dave Clark Five
*b1* *The Beatles*
**a2** Celine Dion
*b2* *Wet Wet Wet*
**a3** Simon and Garfunkel (or The Batchelors)
*b3* *John Lennon*
**a4** Carly Simon
*b4* *The Rolling Stones*
**a5** Gladys Knight and the Pips (accept: Rod Stewart)
*b5* *The Four Tops*
**a6** The Small Faces
*b6* *Alan Price*
**a7** Perry Como
*b7* *U2*
**a8** Frankie Lymon and the Teenagers (accept: Diana Ross)
*b8* *The Shirelles*
**a9** The Jackson Five
*b9* *Manfred Mann*
**a10** The Mamas and the Papas
*b10* *Rod Stewart*
**a11** Erasure
*b11* *REM*
**a12** John Denver (accept: James Galway)
*b12* *Alice Cooper*

---

# Tie-breaker

**Q** Which singer presented the history of rock music on a single called 'American Pie'?

**A** *Don Maclean*

---

# No. 152

**a1** With what sort of television programmes is David Attenborough principally associated?

*b1* *Which television police series introduced us to Detective Chief Inspector Barlow?*

**a2** What was first painted on London's streets in June 1958?

*b2* *Which athletic craze kept many people spinning in 1959?*

**a3** There are Compton and Edrich stands at Lord's. Who did Edrich play for?

*b3* *What was Billy Boston's sport?*

**a4** Which character in *Brookside* has been played by Paul Usher?

*b4* *And in which village is* Emmerdale *set?*

**a5** Which then-unspoiled Spanish seaside village became a famous holiday resort in the late fifties?

*b5* *In which city is Gorky Park?*

**a6** As what did Augustus John achieve fame?

*b6* *Ronald Searle created an infamous girls' school – called ...?*

**a7** In which unexpected place did a 19-year-old West German land a plane in 1987?

*b7* *In which country or countries is the airline SAS based?*

**a8** 1991 was the bicentenary of the death of which famous Austrian composer?

*b8* *Which musician composed a symphony 'From the New World'?*

**a9** Known as 'Hollywood's mermaid', she starred in *Bathing Beauty* in 1944. Who was she?

*b9* *Which child star sang 'On the Good Ship Lollipop'?*

**a10** Which Asian country was beset by civil war in 1971?

*b10* *And which African country suffered civil war from 1967–70?*

**a11** On which radio show did we hear the catch phrases 'The answer lies in the soil' and 'Thirty-five years'?

*b11* *During the Second World War, which two comediennes played the characters Gert and Daisy?*

**a12** Which pop song includes the lines, 'Well, it's a one for the money, two for the show'?

*b12* *Whose pop song includes the lines, 'Hop on the bus, Gus, don't need to discuss much'?*

# No. 152 Answers

**a1**  Natural history or wildlife programmes
*b1*  Z Cars
**a2**  Yellow no-parking lines
*b2*  *The hula hoop*
**a3**  Middlesex (and England)
*b3*  *Rugby league*
**a4**  Barry Grant
*b4*  *Beckindale*
**a5**  Benidorm
*b5*  *Moscow*
**a6**  Painter (especially of portraits)
*b6*  *St Trinian's*
**a7**  Red Square, Moscow (Mathias Rust)
*b7*  *Scandinavia (Denmark, Sweden, Norway)*
**a8**  Mozart
*b8*  *Dvorak (say: vor-jak)*
**a9**  Esther Williams
*b9*  *Shirley Temple*
**a10**  Pakistan
*b10*  *Nigeria*
**a11**  *Beyond Our Ken* and *Round the Horne*
*b11*  *Elsie and Doris Waters*
**a12**  'Blue Suede Shoes'
*b12*  *Paul Simon ('50 Ways to Leave Your Lover')*

---

## Tie-breaker

**Q**  What was abandoned in January 1975, after having made only three miles' progress in 93 years?

**A**  *(Construction of) the Channel Tunnel*

---

# No. 153

**a1**  Which television comedian regularly said, 'It's the way I tell them'?

*b1*  *Which characters on television originally uttered the command 'Exterminate'?*

**a2**  From which town does the anonymous 'Disgusted' traditionally write to newspapers?

*b2*  *Which Sussex town is famous for its theatre and theatre festival?*

**a3**  Which seaside resort has been advertised as 'so bracing' (on posters showing a jolly fisherman)?

*b3*  *What implement was said to 'beat as it sweeps as it cleans'?*

**a4**  What name is given to a sea-going vessel which has angled wings under the hull to lift it clear of the waves?

*b4*  *What form of transport is the 'Sea King'?*

**a5**  From 1956, what government scheme offered the public promises of £1,000 prizes?

*b5*  *Which coin was a joey?*

**a6**  James Hanratty was hanged in 1962 for murder. By what name was the murder widely known?

*b6*  *Which drug began to be suspected as the cause of many serious defeats in new born babies from 1958 onwards?*

**a7**  'I love to go a-wandering, my knapsack on my back.' What was the title of Frank Weir's hit song?

*b7*  *Which singer (later a radio presenter) had a hit with 'The Man from Laramie'?*

**a8**  Which Royal broke his arm playing polo?

*b8*  *Of which country was Alfonso king until 1931?*

**a9**  Which musical instrument did Jacqueline du Pré (say: pray) play?

*b9*  *What was composer Vaughan Williams' first name?*

**a10**  What is meant by 'protocol'?

*b10*  *What is a 'seminar'?*

**a11**  In the film of that name, who was the 'rebel without a cause'?

*b11*  *Which swash-buckling Hollywood hero played Captain Blood and Robin Hood – and died in 1959?*

**a12**  In which year was the Berlin Wall erected?

*b12*  *And in which year was it torn down?*

# No. 153 Answers

**a1**  Frank Carson
*b1*  *The Daleks (in* Dr Who*)*
**a2**  Tunbridge Wells
*b2*  *Chichester*
**a3**  Skegness
*b3*  *Hoover vacuum*
**a4**  Hydrofoil (accept: jetfoil)
*b4*  *Helicopter*
**a5**  Premium Bonds
*b5*  *A threepenny bit (3d) – pre-decimal coinage*
**a6**  The A6 Murder
*b6*  *Thalidomide*
**a7**  'The Happy Wanderer'
*b7*  *Jimmy Young*
**a8**  Prince Charles
*b8*  *Spain*
**a9**  Cello
*b9*  *Ralph*
**a10** Diplomatic etiquette; a correct way of doing things (in diplomacy)
*b10* *Small class or group meeting (usually at a university, etc.) for discussion or research*
**a11** James Dean
*b11* *Errol Flynn*
**a12** 1961
*b12* *1989*

---

## Tie-breaker

**Q**  In electronics, what are the two electrodes contained in a diode?
*A*  *A cathode and an anode*

---

# No. 154

**a1**    What form of transport is the One-Eleven?

*b1*    *Which country's airline is called Iberia?*

**a2**    When Germany was divided, was Saxony in West or East Germany?

*b2*    *And was Bavaria in East or West Germany?*

**a3**    Who compete between Putney and Mortlake?

*b3*    *And which two cricketing countries play each other for the F M Worrell Trophy?*

**a4**    Which instrument did the jazz musician Miles Davis play?

*b4*    *Which kind of music was played on a guitar, washboard and tea-chest?*

**a5**    Which radio and television personality used to say, 'Stop messing about'?

*b5*    *Which northern comedian regularly said, 'Right, monkey'?*

**a6**    What construction was killed off by Parliament in 1907, on grounds of national security?

*b6*    *With Mrs Thatcher, which French president gave the go-ahead to the Channel Tunnel?*

**a7**    Which American statue celebrated its 100th birthday in 1986?

*b7*    *In which American state did Blacks boycott buses in 1955, because of race laws?*

**a8**    Which puppet characters live on Tracey Island?

*b8*    *In which park does Yogi Bear live?*

**a9**    With which New Forest town is Lord Montagu connected?

*b9*    *In which British city is there an area known as Bogside?*

**a10**    Lord Rix (formerly Brian Rix) was leading man at which London theatre?

*b10*    *By what name was the stage revue* The Follies of 1907 *popularly known?*

**a11**    As what did Sir Stanley Spencer achieve fame?

*b11*    *As what did Toscanini become famous?*

**a12**    About which outdoor activity did A E Wainwright produce many guides?

*b12*    *Who wrote the best-selling book* A Year in Provence*?*

# No. 154 Answers

**a1** Passenger aircraft
*b1* *Spain*
**a2** East Germany (Lower Saxony, another province, was in West Germany)
*b2* *West Germany*
**a3** Oxford and Cambridge (in the Boat Race)
*b3* *West Indies and Australia*
**a4** Trumpet
*b4* *Skiffle*
**a5** Kenneth Williams
*b5* *Al Read*
**a6** The Channel Tunnel
*b6* *President Mitterand*
**a7** Statue of Liberty
*b7* *Alabama*
**a8** The Thunderbirds
*b8* *Jellystone Park*
**a9** Beaulieu (say: bew-lee)
*b9* *Londonderry/Derry*
**a10** Whitehall Theatre
*b10* *'The Ziegfeld Follies' (after Florenz Ziegfeld, the producer)*
**a11** Artist
*b11* *Conductor*
**a12** (Fell) walking
*b12* *Peter Mayle*

---

## Tie-breaker

**Q**  In which Marx Brother's film, made in 1937, did they cause havoc at a race course?

**A**  *A Day At the Races*

---

# No. 155

**a1**  What was the rallying cry of German Nazis?

***b1***  *Which military alliance came into being in Eastern Europe in 1955?*

**a2**  Which gangster movie features only children?

***b2***  *How does Dorothy give her classmates a major surprise in the film* Gregory's Girl?

**a3**  Why did Ruth Ellis hit the headlines in 1955?

***b3***  *In which city was James Anderton a controversial policeman?*

**a4**  If you face the sea at Ilfracombe in Devon, are you looking north, south, east or west?

***b4***  *Which Isle of Wight town is famous for its regatta?*

**a5**  As what did Gilbert Harding achieve fame?

***b5***  *Who was the first Director-General of the BBC?*

**a6**  In the 1932 hit, what had got his hat on and was coming out to play?

***b6***  *'20 tiny fingers, 20 tiny toes' went the popular song – but which group sang it?*

**a7**  As a result of which novel and film did the line 'I'm going to make him an offer he can't refuse' become popular?

***b7***  *In a 1946 speech, what did Winston Churchill say had descended across the continent of Europe?*

**a8**  Jesse Owens held a world record for 25 years. In which event?

***b8***  *What was Olympic swimmer Linda Ludgrove's best stroke?*

**a9**  After travelling north through the Channel Tunnel, which is the first English town your train might stop at?

***b9***  *92 died and nearly 200 were injured in Lewisham, south London, in 1957. How?*

**a10**  From 1933, what was the LPTB?

***b10***  *What large building became part of the Battersea skyline in 1933?*

**a11**  Who wrote the books *Another Country* and *The Fire Next Time*?

***b11***  *Jaroslav Hasek wrote a famous wartime novel – about a good soldier called ...?*

**a12**  In which year did various self-governing colonies join together as the Commonwealth of Australia?

***b12***  *Which country annexed (or took control of) Korea in 1910?*

# No. 155 Answers

**a1** 'Sieg Heil!' (accept: 'Heil, Hitler!')
*b1* *The Warsaw Pact*
**a2** *Bugsy Malone*
*b2* *She gets on the football team*
**a3** For murdering her (unfaithful) lover
*b3* *Manchester*
**a4** North
*b4* *Cowes*
**a5** Radio and television personality (in quiz shows)
*b5* *Sir John Reith (later Lord Reith)*
**a6** The sun
*b6* *The Stargazers*
**a7** *The Godfather*
*b7* *An iron curtain*
**a8** Long-jump
*b8* *Backstroke*
**a9** Ashford (Kent)
*b9* *Two trains crashed (in fog)*
**a10** London Passenger Transport Board
*b10* *Battersea Power Station*
**a11** James Baldwin
*b11* *Svejk (or Schweik)*
**a12** 1901
*b12* *Japan*

---

## Tie-breaker

**Q** 'F-numbers' on a camera indicate the size of ... what?
**A** *The size of the lens aperture*

---

# No. 156

**a1**  Which manufacturer used the advertising slogan, 'Don't forget the fruit gums, mum!'?

***b1***  *About which toothpaste did an advert say, 'You'll wonder where the yellow went'?*

**a2**  Near which royal residence is there a forest and a Great Park?

***b2***  *Kemp Town and Preston Park are both suburbs of which south coast town?*

**a3**  What have the following in common: Marston, Mildenhall and Mawgan?

***b3***  *Which city has railway stations called Parkway and Temple Meads?*

**a4**  Which sport, principally, is played at Fenner's?

***b4***  *For which sport is Indianapolis famous?*

**a5**  Traditionally, which branch of the Christian church is dominant in Russia?

***b5***  *Which important religious documents were found in Jordanian caves in 1947?*

**a6**  In which magazine did the 'Dear Bill' letters appear?

***b6***  *Which newspaper ran a gossip column called William Hickey?*

**a7**  What, notably, was founded by Dame Marie Rambert?

***b7***  *In the thirties, who were Harry Roy, Jack Jackson and Ambrose?*

**a8**  King Juan (say: huan) Carlos is King of Spain. His wife is Queen ...?

***b8***  *Of which country did King Constantine II become ruler in 1964?*

**a9**  In a film, which pop star was 'the man who fell to Earth'?

***b9***  *To which century (in the future) did Buck Rogers travel?*

**a10**  Which pop song includes the lines, 'One of 16 Vestal Virgins/ Who are leaving for the coast'?

***b10***  *Who was the singing half of the pop duo 'T' Rex?*

**a11**  In which northern city were the 1952 Olympics?

***b11***  *In which capital city was the 1900 World Exhibition?*

**a12**  Who wrote the book *Eminent Victorians*?

***b12***  *Who wrote a collection called* The Garden Party and Other Stories?

# No. 156 Answers

**a1** Rowntree
*b1* *Pepsodent*
**a2** Windsor Castle
*b2* *Brighton*
**a3** All have airfields (mainly military)
*b3* *Bristol*
**a4** Cricket (Cambridge University)
*b4* *Motor-racing*
**a5** Orthodox
*b5* *Dead Sea Scrolls*
**a6** *Private Eye* (supposedly written by Denis Thatcher)
*b6* Daily Express
**a7** The Rambert Dance Company (ballet company)
*b7* *All were bandleaders*
**a8** Sophia
*b8* *Greece*
**a9** David Bowie
*b9* *25th Century*
**a10** 'A Whiter Shade of Pale'
*b10* *Marc Bolan*
**a11** Helsinki
*b11* *Paris*
**a12** Lytton Strachey
*b12* *Katherine Mansfield*

---

# Tie-breaker

**Q** Chromium is never found alone naturally. Which metal is usually found combined with it?

**A** *Iron*

---

# No. 157

**a1**  What make of car were the Velox, Victor and Cresta?
*b1*  *What form of transport is the Chinook?*
**a2**  What were the 'H line' and the 'A line'?
*b2*  *What were A, AA, U and X?*
**a3**  Which was Johnny Leach's sport?
*b3*  *Which was Patsy Hendren's sport?*
**a4**  Which comic actor directed the film *Annie Hall*?
*b4*  *What is the name of the disaster movie in which a small fire gets out of control in a high-rise building?*
**a5**  By what name is a cluster of towns around Stoke-on-Trent known?
*b5*  *By what name are the towns of Rochester, Chatham and Gillingham collectively known?*
**a6**  In which part of which country is Walloon the traditional language?
*b6*  *In which part of Spain is Catalan the traditional language?*
**a7**  Which male singer was associated with a babbling brook?
*b7*  *Who was the other half of the pop duo, Nina and ...?*
**a8**  According to Peter Pan, what happens every time a child says 'I don't believe in fairies'?
*b8*  *Which fictional character regularly says 'Oh crikey' and Yaroooo!'?*
**a9**  Which country was ruled this century by King Frederick IX?
*b9*  *King Michael is claimant of which country's throne?*
**a10**  In which year did commercial television start in Britain?
*b10*  *And in which year did the BBC Television Service officially start?*
**a11**  On the London Underground map, what colour is the Metropolitan line?
*b11*  *And what colour is the Victoria line?*
**a12**  Who wrote the novel about university life called *The History Man*?
*b12*  *Who wrote the series of novels called* Alms for Oblivion*?*

# No. 157 Answers

**a1**  Vauxhall
*b1*  *Helicopter*
**a2**  Fashion styles (in the fifties, created by Christian Dior)
*b2*  *Film classifications (i.e. age groups allowed to see them)*
**a3**  Table tennis
*b3*  *He played cricket*
**a4**  Woody Allen
*b4*  The Towering Inferno
**a5**  The Potteries; or the Five Towns
*b5*  *The Medway towns*
**a6**  Southern Belgium (a French dialect)
*b6*  *Northeast (Catalonia)*
**a7**  Donald Peers ('By a Babbling Brook' was his theme song)
*b7*  *Frederick*
**a8**  A little fairy falls down dead
*b8*  *Billy Bunter*
**a9**  Denmark
*b9*  *Romania*
**a10**  1955
*b10*  *1936*
**a11**  Purple
*b11*  *(Light) blue*
**a12**  Malcolm Bradbury
*b12*  *Simon Raven*

---

## Tie-breaker

**Q**  Linus Carl Pauling won the Nobel Prize for Chemistry in 1954, for his work on the structure of molecules. Which Nobel Prize did he win in 1962?

**A**  *Nobel Peace Prize (for his efforts to secure a ban on nuclear testing)*

# No. 158

**a1** What make of car was the Elan?

*b1* *What is a Cessna?*

**a2** Who sang 'It's So Good' ('C'est si Bon' in French) (say: say see bon) and wanted an 'old-fashioned millionaire'?

*b2* *Paisley Park, Minneapolis has been the headquarters of which pop star?*

**a3** In which country does the *Picnic at Hanging Rock* take place?

*b3* *About which war was the film* Platoon*?*

**a4** As what did Annigoni become famous?

*b4* *Which district of Paris was often painted by Maurice Utrillo?*

**a5** Which rugby player's nickname is 'Chariots'?

*b5* *Which cricketer's nickname is 'Beefy'?*

**a6** Which television comedy show originated the catch phrases 'Sock it to me', 'Very interesting ... but stupid' and 'the fickle finger of fate'?

*b6* *Which character on television's* The Muppet Show *often said 'Kissy, kissy' when pursuing Kermit?*

**a7** Which country suffered the greatest losses (in number of lives) in the First World War?

*b7* *Which of the Allies suffered the greatest shipping losses in the First World War?*

**a8** Into which then 'new' country was the kingdom of Montenegro incorporated after 1918?

*b8* *Of which country did the island of Crete become a part in 1913?*

**a9** Which Japanese car company opened a factory near Sunderland in 1986?

*b9* *In which British city is the Harland and Wolff shipyard?*

**a10** Which was the only British colony on the South American mainland?

*b10* *Which South American soccer star claimed (in the World Cup) to have been helped 'by the hand of God'?*

**a11** *Bonjour Tristesse* was written by which female French novelist?

*b11* *Which German novelist wrote* Death in Venice*?*

**a12** Before the Second World War, Boris III was King of which country?

*b12* *Which country was ruled by King Zog from 1928?*

# No. 158 Answers

**a1**  Lotus
**b1**  *Small (or light) aircraft*
**a2**  Eartha Kitt
**b2**  *(the artist formerly known as) Prince*
**a3**  Australia
**b3**  *Vietnam*
**a4**  Painter (especially of portraits)
**b4**  *Montmartre*
**a5**  Martin Offiah
**b5**  *Ian Botham*
**a6**  *Rowan and Martin's Laugh-In*
**b6**  *Miss Piggy*
**a7**  Germany
**b7**  *Great Britain (7.8 million tons; next was France which lost .9 million)*
**a8**  Yugoslavia
**b8**  *Greece*
**a9**  Nissan
**b9**  *Belfast*
**a10**  British Guiana
**b10**  *(Diego) Maradona*
**a11**  Françoise Sagan
**b11**  *Thomas Mann*
**a12**  Bulgaria
**b12**  *Albania*

---

## Tie-breaker

**Q**  In a children's novel, which race of little people live under the kitchen floor of an old house in Bedfordshire?

**A**  *The Borrowers – in* The Borrowers *by Mary Norton*

---

# No. 159

**a1**  Who said of herself, 'The lady's not for turning'?

*b1  And who (after being re-elected in 1984) said, 'You ain't seen nothing yet'?*

**a2**  In modern times, which English holiday resort had the first nude bathing beach?

*b2  And which Kentish holiday resort has an amusement centre called Dreamland?*

**a3**  Which member of the Royal Family came close to marrying Group Captain Townsend?

*b3  To what did a branch of the Germanic Royal Family Battenberg change its name?*

**a4**  Which motor car manufacturer produced a Baby and a Seven?

*b4  What name was given to aircraft which landed on water?*

**a5**  What is 'software'?

*b5  What is meant by 'toxic'?*

**a6**  Why did some people wear red-and-green lensed glasses in 1955?

*b6  How did BBC Radio steal commercial television's thunder on the night the latter started up?*

**a7**  Of which political party was Herbert Morrison a leading member?

*b7  For which political party was David Icke once a spokesman?*

**a8**  Which European country occupied Lebanon from 1918?

*b8  Which European country conquered Libya in 1911?*

**a9**  Who took 'The Hustle' into the charts in the seventies?

*b9  Which pop group sang 'The Winner Takes It All'?*

**a10**  In 1933, who wrote the book *The Shape of Things to Come*?

*b10  And who wrote the music for the film of the book?*

**a11**  Which major sporting event did Angela Mortimer win (in Britain) in 1961?

*b11  Bombardier Billy Wells was a British title holder from 1911 to 1919. In which sport?*

**a12**  In which film (based on John Braine's novel) did Laurence Harvey star with Simone Signoret?

*b12  Who co-starred with Lauren Bacall in the Hollywood classic The Big Sleep?*

# No. 159 Answers

**a1** Margaret Thatcher
*b1* *Ronald Reagan*
**a2** Brighton
*b2* *Margate*
**a3** Princess Margaret
*b3* *Mountbatten*
**a4** Austin (Baby Austin, Austin 7)
*b4* *Flying boats*
**a5** Computer programmes, discs and cassettes
*b5* *Poisonous*
**a6** To help see films in '3-D'
*b6* *Grace Archer (a popular character in the radio serial* The Archers) *was killed off in a fire*
**a7** Labour
*b7* *Green Party*
**a8** France
*b8* *Italy*
**a9** Van McCoy
*b9* *ABBA*
**a10** H G Wells
*b10* *Sir Arthur Bliss*
**a11** Ladies Singles, Wimbledon
*b11* *Boxing (heavyweight)*
*a12* *Room at the Top*
*b12* *Humphrey Bogart*

---

## Tie-breaker

**Q** Neon in lamps is naturally red. What colour does it become when a few drops of mercury are added?
**A** *Bright blue*

---

318

# No. 160

**a1** Which exam was once widely used to decide which children should go to grammar schools?

*b1* *Also in education: what was the CSE?*

**a2** In the 1933 hit tune, where did smoke get?

*b2* *And in a 1965 hit tune, where would you have gone for a walk?*

**a3** Which was Henry Cotton's sport?

*b3* *And in which sport was Joe Davis a champion?*

**a4** In *Star Trek*, who is Captain Kirk's second-in-command?

*b4* *In* Thunderbirds Are Go, *what was the name of Lady Penelope's butler?*

**a5** On television, what job has been done by Nicholas Owen, Dermot Murnaghan and John Suchet?

*b5* *And what job has been done by Sian Lloyd, Peter Cockcroft and John Kettley?*

**a6** Which comedian regularly said, 'You lucky people'?

*b6* *Which film star is supposed to have said, 'You dirty rat, you'?*

**a7** In which year did Churchill resign as prime minister?

*b7* *In which year did Harold Wilson first become prime minister?*

**a8** Which steeplechase was won in consecutive years by Early Mist, Royal Tan and Quare Times?

*b8* *Which version of rugby was invented in 1924?*

**a9** Which pianist originally said 'I cried all the way to the bank'?

*b9* *And which American president said (two days before declaring war on Germany), 'The world must be made safe for democracy'?*

**a10** Until 1991, who was King of Norway?

*b10* *Who is the present King of Norway?*

**a11** As what did Isaac Albéniz (say: al-bay-nith) become famous?

*b11* *The 'Karelia (say: ca-ray-li-ah) Suite', which introduced the* This Week *programme on television was written by which Finnish composer?*

**a12** White Russia is now part of which country or state?

*b12* *Into which other country was Bessarabia absorbed in 1918?*

# No. 160 Answers

**a1** The Eleven Plus
*b1* *Certificate of Secondary Education*
**a2** In your eyes ('Smoke Gets in Your Eyes')
*b2* *In the Black Forest ('A Walk in the Black Forest')*
**a3** Golf
*b3* *Snooker*
**a4** Mr Spock
*b4* *Parker*
**a5** Newsreading (on ITN) (accept: reporting)
*b5* *Weather forecasting/presenting*
**a6** Tommy Trinder
*b6* *James Cagney*
**a7** 1955
*b7* *1964*
**a8** The Grand National (1953–5)
*b8* *Rugby union sevens (seven a side)*
**a9** Liberace
*b9* *Woodrow Wilson*
**a10** King Olav V (accept: Olav)
*b10* *King Harald V (accept: Harald)*
**a11** Composer (Spanish)
*b11* *Sibelius*
**a12** Belorussia
*b12* *Romania*

## Tie-breaker

**Q** By what nickname was the American criminal Charles Arthur Floyd known (he was shot by FBI agents in 1934)?
**A** *'Pretty Boy' Floyd*

# No. 161: Curtain Up!

Who wrote the following 20th-century plays?

**a1**    *Waiting for Godot*
**b1**    The Caretaker
**a2**    *The Mousetrap*
**b2**    The Entertainer
**a3**    *Blithe Spirit* and *Hay Fever*
**b3**    Loot *and* Entertaining Mr Sloane
**a4**    *An Inspector Calls*
**b4**    Journey's End
**a5**    *Rosencrantz and Guildenstern Are Dead*
**b5**    Chips With Everything
**a6**    *Barefoot in the Park*
**b6**    Who's Afraid of Virginia Woolf?
**a7**    *Major Barbara*
**b7**    The Cherry Orchard
**a8**    *Bedroom Farce* and *How the Other Half Loves*
**b8**    Not Now Darling *and* Run For Your Wife
**a9**    *A Taste of Honey*
**b9**    Blood Brothers
**a10**    *The Family Reunion* and *The Cocktail Party*
**b10**    The Browning Version *and* The Deep Blue Sea
**a11**    *Cat On a Hot Tin Roof*
**b11**    All My Sons
**a12**    *A Man for All Seasons*
**b12**    Equus *and* Amadeus

# No. 161 Answers

**a1** Samuel Beckett
*b1* *Harold Pinter*
**a2** Agatha Christie
*b2* *John Osborne*
**a3** Noël Coward
*b3* *Joe Orton*
**a4** J B Priestly
*b4* *R C Sherriff*
**a5** Tom Stoppard
*b5* *Arnold Wesker*
**a6** Neil Simon
*b6* *Edward Albee*
**a7** George Bernard Shaw
*b7* *Anton Chekhov*
**a8** Alan Ayckbourn
*b8* *Ray Cooney*
**a9** Shelagh Delaney
*b9* *Willy Russell*
**a10** T S Eliot
*b10* *Terence Rattigan*
**a11** Tennessee Williams
*b11* *Arthur Miller*
**a12** Robert Bolt
*b12* *Peter Shaffer*

---

## Tie-breaker

**Q**  *Long Day's Journey Into Night, Mourning Becomes Electra* and *Desire Under the Elms* were all written by which famous dramatist?

**A**  *Eugene O'Neill*

---

# No. 162

**a1**  What is the TA?
*b1*  *Which charity is known as SCF?*
**a2**  Whose pop album was titled 'The Immaculate Collection'?
*b2*  *Which singer's best-selling album and CD were called 'But Seriously'?*
**a3**  In the police and aviation alphabet, A is alpha. What is C?
*b3*  *In the same alphabet, what is F?*
**a4**  And I?
*b4*  *And what is G?*
**a5**  Which was the home country of the motor-racing driver Ayrton Senna?
*b5*  *And which was the home country of the tennis player Arthur Ashe?*
**a6**  What is 'bhangra'?
*b6*  *And what is 'salsa'?*
**a7**  For what has Jeff Banks become famous?
*b7*  *And as what did Geoff Capes become famous?*
**a8**  From which one town did 200 men march to London in 1936?
*b8*  *And, also in 1936, who was involved in the 'Battle of Cable Street' in London's East End?*
**a9**  What was stolen from Westminster Abbey on Christmas Day in 1950?
*b9*  *And which group claimed they were responsible?*
**a10**  In which country has Walter Sisulu been a national leader?
*b10*  *And who became president of South Africa in 1989?*
**a11**  How did Tory MP Ian Gow die in 1990?
*b11*  *Eric Heffer MP represented a parliamentary constituency in which English city?*
**a12**  From which year was the Soviet Union at war with Germany?
*b12*  *In which year were West and East Germany formally reunified?*

# No. 162 Answers

**a1**   Territorial Army
*b1*   *Save the Children Fund*
**a2**   Madonna
*b2*   *Phil Collins*
**a3**   Charlie
*b3*   *Foxtrot*
**a4**   India
*b4*   *Golf*
**a5**   Brazil
*b5*   *United States of America*
**a6**   Pop music, derived from traditional Punjabi (Indian) music
*b6*   *(Latin) (big-band) dance music (popularized by Puerto Ricans in New York)*
**a7**   Design (clothes, interiors)
*b7*   *Strongman (shot putter)*
**a8**   Jarrow
*b8*   *Fascists (plus local inhabitants and police)*
**a9**   The 'Coronation Stone' (or 'Stone of Scone')
*b9*   *Scottish Nationalists*
**a10**  South Africa
*b10*  *F W de Klerk*
**a11**  Killed by an IRA bomb at his home
*b11*  *Liverpool*
**a12**  1941 (–45)
*b12*  *1990 (October)*

---

## Tie-breaker

**Q**   In the world of publishing, what are OUP and CUP?
**A**   *Oxford University Press and Cambridge University Press*

---

# No. 163

**a1** In which cartoon strip do Lucy and Linus appear?
***b1*** *What is the name of the dog in the same cartoons?*
**a2** In 1954, Humphrey Bogart starred with Ava Gardner in *The Barefoot ...* what?
***b2*** *Which film and musical feature the song 'Tomorrow'?*
**a3** Which is Nancy Lopez's sport?
***b3*** *Which was Mark Spitz's sport?*
**a4** What is a manifesto?
***b4*** *And what is a mandate?*
**a5** For what has the American Calvin Klein become famous?
***b5*** *In which field did Art Blakey achieve fame?*
**a6** Which clarinetist was nicknamed 'the King of Swing'?
***b6*** *Who originally sang about 'lipstick on your collar'?*
**a7** Where in southern England was an opera house built in the grounds of a country house, in 1936?
***b7*** *Where in Buckinghamshire did a country house film studio open in 1936?*
**a8** Which two British diplomats disappeared from their posts in 1951 – and were later revealed as spies?
***b8*** *1931–5 and 1937–45 saw which two Eastern nations at war with each other?*
**a9** In which part of the world is CARICOM an organization for economic co-operation?
***b9*** *By what name is the International Bank for Reconstruction and Development popularly known?*
**a10** What does the abbreviation TIR mean?
***b10*** *For what is CFC an abbreviation?*
**a11** Of which country did Ion Iliescu become president in 1990?
***b11*** *Which Irish party leader was at the centre of a telephone tapping scandal in 1992?*
**a12** In 1954, which Asian country was divided along the 17th Parallel?
***b12*** *Which former British colony was invaded by the United States in 1983?*

# No. 163 Answers

**a1**   'Peanuts'
*b1*   *Snoopy*
**a2**   ... *Contessa* (*The Barefoot Contessa*)
*b2*   Annie
**a3**   Golf
*b3*   *Swimming*
**a4**   A political party's prospectus; an outline of the proposals it intends to carry out, if elected
*b4*   *An authority; the right to do something*
**a5**   Fashion; clothes designing (including sportswear and underwear)
*b5*   *Jazz (jazz drummer)*
**a6**   Benny Goodman
*b6*   *Connie Francis*
**a7**   Glyndebourne, Sussex
*b7*   *Pinewood (near Iver)*
**a8**   (Guy) Burgess and (Donald) Maclean
*b8*   *China and Japan*
**a9**   The Caribbean; West Indies
*b9*   *The World Bank*
**a10**   International Road Transport (Transports Internationaux Routiers)
*b10*   *Chlorofluorocarbon*
**a11**   Romania
*b11*   *(Charles) Haughey*
**a12**   Vietnam
*b12*   *Grenada*

---

## Tie-breaker

**Q**   In 1935, what did police do when they spotted a car breaking the speed limit?

**A**   *They sounded a gong on the police car*

---

# No. 164

**a1**  Of what did the singer have 'a lovely bunch', in the 1950 popular hit?

***b1***  *Who was 'Momma kissing' in the 1952 popular hit tune?*

**a2**  Which darts player is nicknamed 'the Crafty Cockney'?

***b2***  *Which soccer manager has been called 'Tank' and 'Bojangles'?*

**a3**  What is a 'gulag'?

***b3***  *What is a 'putsch'?*

**a4**  In films and comics, whose assistant is known as 'the boy wonder'?

***b4***  *In a film, who drives an Ectomobile?*

**a5**  Who said he needed 'the help and support of the woman I love'?

***b5***  *In 1934, which British politician claimed 'We have never been so defenceless as now'?*

**a6**  Which trade union is known as the RMT?

***b6***  *Which industries does the AEEU operate in?*

**a7**  In which country was Jan Smuts a politician?

***b7***  *Of which country was Prince von Bulow a statesman before the First World War?*

**a8**  For what has the Italian Giorgio Armani become famous?

***b8***  *For what has Henri Cartier-Bresson become famous?*

**a9**  Who has a summer palace or villa at Castel Gandolfo?

***b9***  *Which is England's tallest building?*

**a10**  What was 405 and is now 625?

***b10***  *And what is a 125?*

**a11**  Where, in England, was an Anglo-Saxon ship-burial treasure found in 1939?

***b11***  *Which primitive man's skull, discovered in 1911, was proved a fake in 1949?*

**a12**  What is GATT (say: gatt)?

***b12***  *What is G7?*

# No. 164 Answers

**a1** Coconuts ('I've got a lovely bunch of coconuts')
*b1* *Santa Claus ('I saw Momma Kissing Santa Claus')*
**a2** Eric Bristow
*b2* *Ron Atkinson*
**a3** Soviet labour or prison camp
*b3* *Violent seizure of political power*
**a4** Batman's (Robin)
*b4* *The Ghostbusters*
**a5** King Edward VIII
*b5* *Sir Winston Churchill*
**a6** National Union of Rail, Maritime and Transport Workers
*b6* *Engineering and Electrical (Amalgamated Engineering and Electrical Union)*
**a7** South Africa
*b7* *Germany*
**a8** Fashion designer; clothes
*b8* *Photography*
**a9** The Pope
*b9* *Canary Wharf (in Docklands) (250 metres/800 feet high)*
**a10** The number of lines that make up a (British) television picture (it changed with the introduction of colour and a move from VHF to UHF)
*b10* *An Inter-City (diesel)(high-speed) train*
**a11** Sutton Hoo
*b11* *Piltdown Skull*
**a12** The General Agreement on Tariffs and Trade (a United Nations organization)
*b12* *The Group of Seven (wealthiest nations in the world)*

## Tie-breaker

**Q** What did Bryan Allen achieve in 'Gossamer Albatross' in 1979?
**A** *First human-powered flight across the English Channel*

# No. 165

**a1**  On screen, what do doctors Venkman, Stante and Spengler hunt?

*b1*  *Which 1968 cartoon film featured the songs and voices of the Beatles?*

**a2**  Which group sang about Mandela Day and the Belfast Child?

*b2*  *Which English rock singer and song writer had the Attractions as a backing group and sang about 'Oliver's Army'?*

**a3**  In military terms, which is larger: a battalion or a brigade?

*b3*  *And which is larger: a corps or a division?*

**a4**  Of which country was Andreas Papandreou (say: pap-an-dray-oo) prime minister?

*b4*  *János Kádár was a communist leader in which country?*

**a5**  What nationality is racing-driver Jacques Villeneuve?

*b5*  *What nationality is tennis star Michael Stich?*

**a6**  What are SERPS?

*b6*  *What is SIS?*

**a7**  Which cartoon character was created by the artist Mary Tourtel in 1920 and later drawn by Alfred Bestall?

*b7*  *Which newspaper cartoonist created the character Maudie Littlehampton?*

**a8**  What was the Russian city of Volgograd called until 1961?

*b8*  *And what was the Russian city of Tsaritsyn renamed in 1925?*

**a9**  In the thirties, who asked the British people to elect him as a Fascist dictator?

*b9*  *In which country was Engelbert Dollfuss a political leader?*

**a10**  In which year did the present Queen Elizabeth and Prince Philip marry?

*b10*  *Where was Princess Elizabeth when she became queen?*

**a11**  In America, for what is the Pulitzer Prize awarded?

*b11*  *In America, in what area might you win a 'Tony' (or Tony Award)?*

**a12**  A J P Taylor became famous for what?

*b12*  *For what did Norman Parkinson become famous?*

# No. 165 Answers

**a1** Ghosts (in *Ghostbusters*)
*b1* Yellow Submarine
**a2** Simple Minds
*b2* Elvis Costello
**a3** Brigade
*b3* Corps
**a4** Greece
*b4* Hungary
**a5** French-Canadian
*b5* German
**a6** (State Earnings-Related) Pension Schemes
*b6* Special Intelligence Service
**a7** Rupert Bear
*b7* Osbert Lancaster
**a8** Stalingrad
*b8* Stalingrad
**a9** Sir Oswald Mosley
*b9* Austria
**a10** 1947
*b10* In Kenya (Treetops Hotel, or a game reserve)
**a11** Novels/fiction
*b11* The theatre
**a12** His television programmes; historical lectures on television
*b12* Fashion (and portrait) photography

---

## Tie-breaker

**Q** In which year last century did Poland first become an independent republic?

**A** *1918*

# No. 166

**a1** In the alphabet used by the police and in aviation, V is Victor, T is Tango. What is Z?

*b1* And what is Y?

**a2** And in the same alphabet, what is W?

*b2* And what is J?

**a3** What is a referendum?

*b3* What is a federation?

**a4** Which left-handed cricketer played for Leicestershire, Hampshire and England before becoming a commentator?

*b4* Which South African-born cricketer played for England in 79 tests and captained Northants?

**a5** For what is 'wpm' a standard abbreviation?

*b5* In science or mathematics, what is meant by 'ppm'?

**a6** Which singer and record producer, associated with Motown records, had solo hits with 'Cruisin'' and 'Being With You'?

*b6* Which jazz pianist's 'standards' included 'Round Midnight' and 'Blue Monk'?

**a7** In 1989 in Britain, which party surprised many people by winning two million votes in the European elections?

*b7* In Europe, what is the CAP?

**a8** Which American politician did Jacqueline Lee Bouvier marry in 1953?

*b8* As what did William Randolph Hearst become famous?

**a9** Of which country were the Philippines a colony until this century?

*b9* Until 1966, of which country was Botswana a colony?

**a10** On which ridge in Flanders did 400,000 British soldiers die in 1917?

*b10* Off the coast of which country was the naval battle of Jutland fought in 1916?

**a11** Of which country was Manuel Noriega the ruler?

*b11* And on what charges was he arrested in 1989 by the United States?

**a12** Who said, on losing her job, 'It's a funny old world'?

*b12* Which King of Britain said, 'I don't like abroad, I've been there'?

# No. 166 Answers

**a1** Zulu
*b1* *Yankee*
**a2** Whiskey
*b2* *Juliet*
**a3** A vote by the people on a particular issue
*b3* *When two or more countries or states combine under one government, but keep some independence*
**a4** David Gower
*b4* *Allan Lamb*
**a5** Words per minute
*b5* *Parts per million*
**a6** Smokey Robinson
*b6* *Thelonius Monk*
**a7** Green Party
*b7* *Common Agricultural Policy*
**a8** John F Kennedy
*b8* *As a newspaper publisher*
**a9** Spain
*b9* *Britain/United Kingdom*
**a10** Passchendaele
*b10* *Denmark*
**a11** Panama
*b11* *Drug-trafficking*
**a12** Mrs Thatcher
*b12* *King George V*

---

## Tie-breaker

**Q** To the military, what is NBC?
**A** *Nuclear, biological and chemical warfare*

---

# No. 167

**a1** Which cartoonist depicted the TUC as a carthorse?

*b1* *Which newspaper cartoonist became famous for drawing a family that included a black-coated Grandma?*

**a2** In what field has Helen Mirren become famous?

*b2* *For what did Kathleen Ferrier achieve fame?*

**a3** For what is IBM an abbreviation?

*b3* *When talking of milk, what is UHT?*

**a4** Who did John Wayne play in the frontier film *The Alamo*?

*b4* *Which actor played Professor Higgins in the film of* My Fair Lady?

**a5** Bob Cousy perfected the 'behind the back dribble'. In which sport?

*b5* *Franz Klammer achieved speeds over 80 mph. In which sport?*

**a6** Whose home was Fort Belvedere?

*b6* *Why did Rillington Place in London become infamous in 1953?*

**a7** What is white-water rafting?

*b7* *What is Scuba?*

**a8** Who wrote the popular hit tune 'Cheek to Cheek'?

*b8* *Alain Boublil was co-writer of a musical called* Miss ...?

**a9** When did rationing end in Britain after the Second World War? Was it 1947, 1950 or 1954?

*b9* *In which year did Britain's first North Sea oil flow ashore? Was it 1967, 1971 or 1975?*

**a10** Where is the International Court of Justice based?

*b10* *In which two cities is the European Parliament based?*

**a11** Which Secretary-General of the United Nations later became president of Austria?

*b11* *Of which country did Mary Robinson become president in 1990?*

**a12** Which building (including a banqueting hall) is the civic headquarters of the City of London?

*b12* *What is the Lord Mayor of London's official residence?*

# No. 167 Answers

**a1** (David) Low
***b1*** *Giles*
**a2** Acting
***b2*** *As a singer (contralto)*
**a3** International Business Machines
***b3*** *Ultra heat-treated milk*
**a4** Davy Crockett
***b4*** *Rex Harrison*
**a5** Basketball
***b5*** *Ski-ing*
**a6** Prince Edward's (the Prince of Wales; later King Edward VIII)
***b6*** *Because of a series of murders (by John Christie)*
**a7** Travelling by raft in fast-moving water
***b7*** *Self-Contained Underwater Breathing Apparatus (used by divers)*
**a8** Irving Berlin
***b8*** *... Saigon (Miss Saigon)*
**a9** 1954
***b9*** *1975*
**a10** The Hague (in the Netherlands)
***b10*** *Luxembourg and Strasbourg*
**a11** Kurt Waldheim
***b11*** *Ireland*
**a12** Guildhall
***b12*** *Mansion House*

---

## Tie-breaker

**Q** Which two countries joined the European Community in 1985?
***A*** *Portugal and Spain*

---

# No. 168

**a1**  In which industry or service do members of BIFU work?
*b1*  *In which area do members of the NASUWT work?*
**a2**  Which war involved Operation Desert Shield?
*b2*  *By what name was America's Strategic Defense Initiative popularly known?*
**a3**  *Steamboat Willie* was the first cartoon film to feature which character?
*b3*  *'Ars gratia artis' is the Latin motto of which film studio?*
**a4**  In film-making, what is 'dubbing'?
*b4*  *Can you name a major children's television series created by Jim Henson, apart from* The Muppet Show*?*
**a5**  What is an 'espadrille'?
*b5*  *What is 'bonsai'?*
**a6**  A far-reaching tournament started at the Waterloo Hotel in Blackpool in 1907. In which sport?
*b6*  *In which sport is the Suntory Championship held?*
**a7**  As what did Leopoldo Galtieri become famous?
*b7*  *To listen to which speaker did 180,000 people pack Wembley Stadium in 1954?*
**a8**  Which was the musician Paul Tortelier's instrument?
*b8*  *Which instrument did bebop musician Dizzy Gillespie play?*
**a9**  What name is given to the night in June 1934 when Hitler had many comrades shot and killed because he said they were plotting against him?
*b9*  *What political change involved 'coloured' or 'mixed race' people in South Africa in 1951?*
**a10**  A proposed extension to which London building was described as 'a monstrous carbuncle' by Prince Charles?
*b10*  *Of what were the Dome of Discovery and Skylon both a part?*
**a11**  About what did King Edward VIII say, 'Something must be done'?
*b11*  *Which member of the Royal Family died a few weeks before Elizabeth II's coronation?*
**a12**  Of which country did Daniel arap Moi become president in 1978?
*b12*  *Of which country was Lee Kuan Yew prime minister for 1959 until 1990?*

# No. 168 Answers

**a1** Banking, insurance or finance (Banking, Insurance and Finance Union)
***b1*** *Education (National Association of Schoolmasters Union of Women Teachers)*
**a2** The Gulf War (1991)
***b2*** *Star Wars programme*
**a3** Mickey Mouse
***b3*** *MGM ('Art for art's sake')*
**a4** Adding or re-recording the sound track
***b4*** *Sesame Street or Fraggle Rock*
**a5** Shoe (canvas upper, rope sole)
***b5*** *The art of producing miniature trees*
**a6** Bowls
***b6*** *Golf*
**a7** Argentinean general (during Falklands War)
***b7*** *Billy Graham (the evangelist)*
**a8** Cello
***b8*** *Trumpet*
**a9** 'Night of the Long Knives'
***b9*** *They lost the right to vote*
**a10** National Gallery
***b10*** *The (1951) Festival of Britain (on London's South Bank)*
**a11** Unemployment (in South Wales)
***b11*** *Queen Mary (widow of George V)*
**a12** Kenya
***b12*** *Singapore*

## Tie-breaker

**Q** In which film festival is the 'Golden Bear' awarded to the best film?
**A** *Berlin*

# No. 169

**a1** In the police and aviation alphabet, how is the letter N identified?

**b1** *And how is R identified?*

**a2** What part of the body can suffer from glaucoma?

**b2** *What part of the body can suffer from dermatitis?*

**a3** According to the 1953 popular hit tune, what are 'a girl's best friend'?

**b3** *In the thirties pop song, where were the 'red sails'?*

**a4** What is the IMF?

**b4** *By what name or initials is the British association or organization of employers known?*

**a5** What is measured by ASA or ISO numbers?

**b5** *In physics, for what is UV an abbreviation?*

**a6** Which play opened in London in 1952 – and was still running in 1998?

**b6** *In 1923, who wrote the play St Joan?*

**a7** Which England goalkeeper's son has played professional football at the same club as his father?

**b7** *Specifically, what has been Peter Scudamore's sport?*

**a8** Which English composer (who died in 1934) was associated with the Malvern Hills?

**b8** *Aged 52 in 1930, he was England's oldest ever test cricketer. Who was he?*

**a9** Of which country was Mozambique a colony until 1903?

**b9** *Until 1960, of which country was Madagascar a colony?*

**a10** Which educational toy construction system was invented by Sir Frank Hornby?

**b10** *J Robert Oppenheimer is sometimes called 'the father of the …' what?*

**a11** What is Iwo Jima?

**b11** *What caused an entire island (Eniwetok Atoll) to disappear in 1952?*

**a12** Who has been president of the European Commission since 1984?

**b12** *Of which country has Ruud Lubbers been prime minister?*

# No. 169 Answers

**a1** November
**b1** *Romeo*
**a2** The eye
**b2** *The skin*
**a3** Diamonds
**b3** *In the sunset ('Red Sails in the Sunset')*
**a4** International Monetary Fund
**b4** *CBI (Confederation of British Industry)*
**a5** The 'speed' of films
**b5** *Ultra-violet*
**a6** *The Mousetrap* (by Agatha Christie)
**b6** *George Bernard Shaw*
**a7** Ray Clemence
**b7** *National Hunt racing/steeplechasing*
**a8** Sir Edward Elgar
**b8** *Wilfred Rhodes*
**a9** Portugal
**b9** *France*
**a10** Meccano (he also manufactured Hornby trains and Dinky Toys)
**b10** *The father of the atom bomb*
**a11** Japanese island (captured by USA in 1945; returned to Japan in 1968)
**b11** *America's first hydrogen bomb test*
**a12** Jacques Delors
**b12** *Netherlands (Holland)*

## Tie-breaker

**Q** Which American tennis player won her first Wimbledon title in 1974 and became the first woman player to win a million dollars in prize money?
**A** *Chris(tine) Evert*

338

# No. 170

**a1**  As what did Lee Remick become famous?
*b1*  *How did Stan Mortensen become famous?*
**a2**  Which comic strip wing-helmeted character first appeared in France in 1959?
*b2*  *Which cartoon character shouts 'Yabba dabba do'?*
**a3**  Which group's album was called 'Rumours'?
*b3*  *What kind of singer was Hank Williams?*
**a4**  What do Geoff Cooke and Jack Rowell have in common?
*b4*  *Which cricketer has crossed the Alps in the style of Hannibal?*
**a5**  For what is GCHQ the abbreviation?
*b5*  *And in which town is GCHQ?*
**a6**  Which war was portrayed in the 1915 film *The Birth of a Nation*?
*b6*  *And who directed this landmark film?*
**a7**  In which country do the Tigré people live?
*b7*  *Where do the Tamil people live?*
**a8**  Who was prime minister of Australia from 1983 to 1991?
*b8*  *And of which political party was he a member?*
**a9**  Following the 1986 Chernobyl disaster, which livestock trade was affected in Britain?
*b9*  *What disaster put the north London town of Harrow in the headlines in 1952?*
**a10**  Which famous American aviator's baby was kidnapped and murdered in the thirties?
*b10*  *Which pair of young American gangsters and robbers did the law finally catch up with in 1934?*
**a11**  The monarchs of which two empires met for the first time in 1908?
*b11*  *What happened in 1936 for the first time since the year 1399?*
**a12**  How long did Hitler claim his Reich (or state) would last?
*b12*  *In which year was the Battle of Arras?*

# No. 170 Answers

**a1** Film actress
*b1* *As a soccer player*
**a2** Astérix
*b2* *Fred Flintstone*
**a3** Fleetwood Mac
*b3* *Country and Western*
**a4** England rugby coaches
*b4* *Ian Botham*
**a5** Government Communications Headquarters
*b5* *Cheltenham*
**a6** American Civil War
*b6* *D W Griffiths*
**a7** Ethiopia
*b7* *India (the state of Tamil Nadu); also Sri Lanka, Malaysia, Singapore and South Africa*
**a8** Bob Hawke
*b8* *Labour*
**a9** Lamb (movement of sheep restricted)
*b9* *A train crash (112 dead; the second worst ever at that time)*
**a10** (Charles) Lindberg
*b10* *Bonnie and Clyde (Clyde Barrow; Bonnie Parker)*
**a11** Russian; British (Czar Nicholas II; King Edward VII)
*b11* *An English king abdicated*
**a12** 1,000 years
*b12* *1917*

---

## Tie-breaker

**Q**  Who said this about whom? 'He stands for nothing; he is nothing. He is grey. He has no ideas. I have been totally deceived.'

**A**  *Mrs Thatcher about John Major*

# No. 171: The Second World War

**a1**  What was an 'Axis' power?
*b1*  *What was a 'siren suit'?*
**a2**  In which year did Rommel open his north African campaign?
*b2*  *In the same year, which 'unsinkable' German battleship was sunk?*
**a3**  Who was nicknamed the 'Desert Fox'?
*b3*  *What was the nickname of the Thompson sub-machine gun?*
**a4**  In which country did Vidkun Quisling collaborate with the Nazis?
*b4*  *What name was given to the French government which collaborated with the Germans?*
**a5**  In which country is Tobruk?
*b5*  *In which country is Anzio?*
**a6**  In which year were the Battles of El Alamein?
*b6*  *And in which year was the Battle of Arnhem?*
**a7**  American servicemen were called GIs. For what did GI stand?
*b7*  *On D-Day, what were Omaha and Utah?*
**a8**  In which year was the Russian victory at Stalingrad?
*b8*  *Who said in 1940 that Mr Hitler had 'missed the bus'?*
**a9**  What were 'Mulberries'?
*b9*  *What was Changi?*
**a10**  Whose film parodied Hitler as *The Great Dictator*?
*b10*  *Who was Hitler's deputy who flew secretly to Scotland in 1941?*
**a11**  Whereabouts in Europe did the 'Battle of the Bulge' take place in 1944–5?
*b11*  *Which city was devastated by the Allies in February 1945?*
**a12**  Who succeeded Hitler in 1945?
*b12*  *Which American general was known as 'Blood and Guts'?*

# No. 171 Answers

**a1**    Germany and those countries allied to it

*b1*    *One-piece overall, dungaree-like garment (made popular by Churchill)*

**a2**    1941

*b2*    *Bismarck*

**a3**    (Field Marshal) Rommel

*b3*    *The tommy gun*

**a4**    Norway

*b4*    *Vicky*

**a5**    Libya

*b5*    *Italy*

**a6**    1942

*b6*    *1944*

**a7**    Government issue

*b7*    *(American) landing beaches*

**a8**    1943

*b8*    *Neville Chamberlain*

**a9**    Artificial harbours, used on D-Day

*b9*    *Japanese prison camp*

**a10**    Charlie Chaplin's

*b10*    *Rudolf Hess*

**a11**    The Ardennes; southern Belgium

*b11*    *Dresden*

**a12**    Admiral Dönitz

*b12*    *General Patton*

---

## Tie-breaker

**Q**    How did (a) Hitler, (b) Mussolini and (c) Goering die?

**A**    *(a) Suicide, by gunshot in the mouth; (b) shot by partisans and then hung by his heels; (c) suicide, by cyanide just before execution*

# No. 172

**a1**   Which group released an album called 'Hunting High and Low'?

*b1*   *One of the best-selling albums of all time is 'Brothers in Arms'. Who is it by?*

**a2**   In the police and aviation alphabet, B is Bravo. What is E?

*b2*   *In the same alphabet, what is O?*

**a3**   And what is S?

*b3*   *And what is L?*

**a4**   Which industry is supervised by OFWAT?

*b4*   *And which industry is supervised by OFTEL?*

**a5**   In which position did Rory and Tony Underwood play for England?

*b5*   *Which country did David Campese represent?*

**a6**   Who are the Algonquin people?

*b6*   *From which country do the Gurkhas come?*

**a7**   Which natural disaster hit England in January 1953?

*b7*   *Which new town is near Gatwick Airport?*

**a8**   On salt flats in which American state did Malcolm Campbell set a world speed record in 1935?

*b8*   *By what name is the Harrier jet aircraft popularly known?*

**a9**   Of which country was Franz Josef Emperor until 1916?

*b9*   *Of which country was Victor Emmanuel III King until 1946?*

**a10**   Who was Secretary-General of the United Nations from 1982 to 1991?

*b10*   *And what is his nationality?*

**a11**   The king of which country was assassinated by a Croatian nationalist in France in 1934?

*b11*   *Which Chinese communist headed 'the Long March' in the thirties?*

**a12**   What were Atlantas, Discovery and Endeavour?

*b12*   *Which fictional spaceman fought the Mekon?*

# No. 172 Answers

**a1**    A-Ha
*b1*    *Dire Straits*
**a2**    Echo
*b2*    *Oscar*
**a3**    Sierra
*b3*    *Lima*
**a4**    Water (Office of Water Services)
*b4*    *Telecommunications*
**a5**    Wingers
*b5*    *Australia*
**a6**    North American Indians (formerly living around the Ottawa River)
*b6*    *Nepal*
**a7**    The East Coast floods
*b7*    *Crawley*
**a8**    Utah
*b8*    *The Jump Jet*
**a9**    Austro-Hungary
*b9*    *Italy*
**a10**    (Javier) Pérez de Cuéllar (say: havier pereth de qway-ya)
*b10*    *Peruvian*
**a11**    Yugoslavia
*b11*    *Mao Tse-tung*
**a12**    (United States) Space missions (or spacecraft)
*b12*    *Dan Dare (in the comic* The Eagle*)*

---

## Tie-breaker

**Q**    Of which country did Flavio Cotti become head of state in 1991?
*A*    *Switzerland*

# No. 173

**a1**  Which group teamed up with Lulu to sing 'Relight My Fire'?

***b1**  Which female pop singer starred in the films* Desperately Seeking Susan *and* Dick Tracy*?*

**a2**  What medical term is given to the lack of desire to eat?

***b2**  What medical term is used to describe word-blindness?*

**a3**  Which American jockey was UK champion jockey in 1984, 1985 and 1987?

***b3**  Which English middle-distance runner started a new career in 1990 as a Conservative politician?*

**a4**  What have the following in common: Geneva, Reykjavik and Washington?

***b4**  What have Trawsfynydd (say: traws-fun-uth) and Wylfa (say: wil-va) in common?*

**a5**  With what is UCAS concerned?

***b5**  And for what do the initials PSBR stand?*

**a6**  In which country do the Khmer people live?

***b6**  In which country do the Ibo people mainly live?*

**a7**  What is the RPI?

***b7**  Which ministry is (or has been) known as MAFF?*

**a8**  Who starred in the film The Silence of the Lambs?

***b8**  Which French film maker created the character Monsieur Hulot (say: huw-lo) who appeared in films such as* Mon Oncle*?*

**a9**  In the Rupert cartoon strips, what was the name of the elephant?

***b9**  And what was the name of the pug dog?*

**a10**  In 1934, Harry Beck designed what was to become a famous diagrammatic map. What was it of?

***b10**  What celebration took place in London's streets on May 6, 1935?*

**a11**  For what has Eric Hosking become famous?

***b11**  As what did Isaac Bashevis Singer achieve fame?*

**a12**  What is the French name for Bergen (in Belgium), where a First World War battle took place?

***b12**  Which country did Mussolini invade in 1935?*

# No. 173 Answers

**a1**  Take That
*b1*  *Madonna*
**a2**  Anorexia
*b2*  *Dyslexia*
**a3**  Steve Cauthen
*b3*  *Sebastian Coe*
**a4**  They were all meeting places between the USA and Soviet leaders (Reagan and Gorbachev)
*b4*  *Both are nuclear power stations (in Wales)*
**a5**  University admissions (Universities and Colleges Admissions Service)
*b5*  *Public Sector Borrowing Requirements*
**a6**  Cambodia
*b6*  *Nigeria*
**a7**  Retail price index
*b7*  *Ministry of Agriculture, Fisheries and Food*
**a8**  Anthony Hopkins
*b8*  *Jacques Tati*
**a9**  Edward Trunk
*b9*  *Algy Pug*
**a10**  London's Underground
*b10*  *King George V's silver jubilee*
**a11**  (Wild-life) photography
*b11*  *Writer (of novels and short stories)*
**a12**  Mons
*b12*  *Abyssinia (Ethiopia)*

---

## Tie-breaker

**Q**  1994 was the centenary year of London's Promenade Concerts. Who founded the concerts and in which concert hall were they originally held?

**A**  *Sir Henry Wood; Queen's Hall*

---

# No. 174

**a1**   Which television cartoon featured Ermintrude and Mr Rusty?

***b1***   *Which space-travelling cartoon's female companion was Dale Arden?*

**a2**   Militarily speaking, what is 'R and R'?

***b2***   *In the Gulf War, what was a 'Patriot'?*

**a3**   In which country do members of parliament have the letters TD after their names?

***b3***   *For what is SJ an abbreviation?*

**a4**   Which international sporting team was captained from 1985 by Allan Border?

***b4***   *Which is the home country of tennis player Stefan Edberg?*

**a5**   Which American film actress was married to Mickey Rooney, Artie Shaw and Frank Sinatra?

***b5***   *Which French actress became known as the 'Sex Kitten'?*

**a6**   By what name is the American index or scale for measuring share prices known?

***b6***   *And what is the Japanese equivalent?*

**a7**   From 1934, what did British motorists have to observe when driving?

***b7***   *In 1951, with which other motor manufacturer did Morris amalgamate?*

**a8**   Of which political party has President Mitterand been a founder member?

***b8***   *In which country has Menachem Begin been a right-wing leader?*

**a9**   What medical term describes a shortage of haemoglobin (say: hee-mo-glo-bin), part of the red blood cells?

***b9***   *What is paraplegia?*

**a10**   Hindenburg ceased being president of Germany on his death. Was that in 1929, 1934 or 1939?

***b10***   *In which year did Swiss women first get the vote in federal elections? Was it 1931, 1961 or 1971?*

**a11**   As what did André Gide (say: an-dray jeed) become famous?

***b11***   *In which field did Stan Getz become famous?*

**a12**   Since 1982, King Fahd has been head of state of which country?

***b12***   *Of which island was Queen Salote once the ruler?*

# No. 174 Answers

a1  *The Magic Roundabout*
b1  *Flash Gordon*
a2  'Rest and recuperation'
b2  *(Ground-to-air) missile (used against Iraqi Scud missiles)*
a3  Ireland (Teachta Dála = a member of the Irish parliament)
b3  *Society of Jesus (the Jesuits)*
a4  Australian cricket
b4  *Sweden*
a5  Ava Gardner
b5  *Brigitte Bardot*
a6  Dow Jones
b6  *Nikkei*
a7  Speed limits; also pedestrian crossings
b7  *Austin*
a8  (French) Socialist Party
b8  *Israel*
a9  Anaemia
b9  *Paralysis of the lower limbs*
a10 1934
b10 *1971*
a11 (French) novelist/writer
b11 *Jazz*
a12 Saudi Arabia
b12 *Tonga*

---

## Tie-breaker

Q   In 1944, which was the first major French port to fall to
    the Allies after the Normandy landings?
A   *Cherbourg*

---

# No. 175

**a1**  In which sport might you win the US Triple Crown?
*b1*  *In which sport can you compete in the US Masters?*
**a2**  Which union represents workers in local government and the health service?
*b2*  *Which is the principal shopworkers 'trade union'?*
**a3**  Which environmental group campaigns to conserve the world's resources?
*b3*  *And which group campaigns to persuade governments to protect and improve the environment?*
**a4**  For what has Kenneth Branagh become famous?
*b4*  *In the Christian church, why did Barbara Harris become well known in 1989?*
**a5**  What medical term is used to describe the process which imitates the work of the kidneys?
*b5*  *And what name is given to the treatment of cancer with synthetic chemical drugs?*
**a6**  Which movement did the author Simone de Beauvoir (say: bo-voir) do much to inspire?
*b6*  *In 1934, Dale Carnegie published a book called* How to Win Friends and ... *what?*
**a7**  Which soccer player spent most of his career with Manchester United and is the younger brother of Jack?
*b7*  *Which Belfast sportswoman won the pentathlon gold medal in the Munich Olympics?*
**a8**  Muhammad Jinnah was the first governor general of which country?
*b8*  *Which country was ruled by Erich Honecker?*
**a9**  In religion, what is the WCC?
*b9*  *In sport, what is the WBC?*
**a10**  Where do the Masai people live?
*b10*  *Who are the Navajo (say: na-va-ho)?*
**a11**  On which planet is the Great Red Spot?
*b11*  *Which planet in our solar system was discovered in 1930?*
**a12**  Which Italian wrote the play *Six Characters in Search of an Author*?
*b12*  *Who wrote the play* What the Butler Saw?

# No. 175 Answers

**a1**   (Horse) racing
*b1*   *Golf*
**a2**   UNISON
*b2*   *USDAW (Union of Shop, Distributive and Allied Workers)*
**a3**   Friends of the Earth
*b3*   *Greenpeace*
**a4**   Acting
*b4*   *First woman to become a bishop*
**a5**   Dialysis
*b5*   *Chemotherapy*
**a6**   Feminism, the Women's Movement
*b6*   *... Influence People*
**a7**   Bobbie Charlton
*b7*   *Mary Peters*
**a8**   Pakistan
*b8*   *East Germany*
**a9**   World Council of Churches
*b9*   *World Boxing Championship*
**a10**   East Africa (Tanzania, Kenya)
*b10*   *North American Indians (living in Arizona)*
**a11**   Jupiter
*b11*   *Pluto*
**a12**   (Luigi) Pirandello
*b12*   *Joe Orton*

---

## Tie-breaker

**Q**   Just before the start of the Second World War, MPs (in the House of Commons) shouted, 'Speak for England, Arthur.' Arthur was Arthur Greenwood MP. What was his importance?

**A**   *He was Labour's leader (Neville Chamberlain, the prime minister, appeared reluctant to declare war)*

---

# No. 176

**a1** The Bee Gees song 'Stayin' Alive' featured in which film?

*b1* *Which film family gives their children meat cleavers to play with and plays a graveyard game 'Wake the Dead'?*

**a2** In the police and aviation alphabet, what is P?

*b2* *And in the same alphabet, what is H?*

**a3** For which country did Willie John McBride play rugby union?

*b3* *For which country does Sunil Gavaskar play cricket?*

**a4** Which cartoon character turns into shy college student Peter Parker?

*b4* *Which cartoon character appeared in a number of films involving Inspector Clouseau (played by Peter Sellers)?*

**a5** Did Carl David Anderson become famous for his work in education, modern dance or physics?

*b5* *As what did Edward Gordon Craig become famous?*

**a6** In October 1936, who was famously divorced from her husband Ernest at a court in Ipswich?

*b6* *Which member of the Royal Family was nicknamed 'Bertie'?*

**a7** With what is obstetrics concerned?

*b7* *With what is haematology (say: hee-ma-tol-ogy) concerned?*

**a8** What was Abu Simbel?

*b8* *Which expedition set out to prove that Polynesian islanders must have sailed there from South America?*

**a9** What is a 'blue chip' company?

*b9* *What name is given to the illegal use of private information when dealing on the Stock Exchange?*

**a10** From 1949 to 1963, who was Chancellor of West Germany?

*b10* *Which Burmese diplomat was Secretary-General of the United Nations from 1962 to 1971?*

**a11** Which agency launched the Ariane rockets?

*b11* *Where in America is the Kennedy Space Center (used for space-shuttle launches)?*

**a12** In 1902, which famous novelist published *The Ambassadors*?

*b12* *Which English author (and 'poet of the Empire') won the Nobel literature prize in 1907?*

# No. 176 Answers

**a1**  *Saturday Night Fever*
**b1**  *The Addams Family*
**a2**  Papa
**b2**  *Hotel*
**a3**  Ireland
**b3**  *India*
**a4**  Spiderman
**b4**  *The Pink Panther*
**a5**  Physics (Nobel Physics prizewinner)
**b5**  *Stage designer*
**a6**  Mrs Wallace Simpson
**b6**  *King George VI*
**a7**  Pregnancy, childbirth, postnatal care
**b7**  *Disorders of the blood*
**a8**  Temple (flooded by the Aswan Dam project on the Nile)
**b8**  *The Kon-tiki Expedition*
**a9**  One whose shares are strong and reliable
**b9**  *Insider trading*
**a10**  Dr (Konrad) Adenauer
**b10**  *U Thant*
**a11**  European Space Agency
**b11**  *Cape Canaveral (Florida)*
**a12**  Henry James
**b12**  *Rudyard Kipling*

---

## Tie-breaker

**Q**  Which sporting competitors display a 'barani' and 'pike'?
**A**  *Gymnasts*

---

# No. 177

**a1**    About what does David Bellamy broadcast and campaign?
*b1*    *How did Margaret Lockwood achieve fame?*
**a2**    What are enhancers, emulsifiers and stabilizers?
*b2*    *What international symbol is used to indicate a poisonous or toxic substance?*
**a3**    In which sport do the San Francisco 49ers compete?
*b3*    *In which country is Juventus a soccer club?*
**a4**    Which television police series teamed an American lieutenant (say: loo-ten-ant) with a British (woman) sergeant?
*b4*    *On television, in which city did the detective Taggart operate?*
**a5**    What is meant by AWACS?
*b5*    *In computing, for what does DOS stand?*
**a6**    In which city was the 'no war over Czechoslovakia' deal signed in 1938?
*b6*    *Which Polish port did Hitler have his eye on in the weeks leading up to the Second World War?*
**a7**    Which whale, in particular, is an endangered species?
*b7*    *And which animal has been in danger of being hunted to extinction in East Africa?*
**a8**    What is Farsi?
*b8*    *In India, what is an 'ashram'?*
**a9**    Which is the most popular indoor tourist attraction in London?
*b9*    *Outside London, what is England's most popular tourist attraction?*
**a10**    Who was King of Belgium from 1951 to 1993?
*b10*    *Who became Emperor of Japan in 1989?*
**a11**    Who wrote the novel *Hotel du Lac*?
*b11*    *Who wrote the book* Midnight's Children?
**a12**    In July 1940, which nation sank a large proportion of the French navy?
*b12*    *In 1940 which country eventually defeated Finland?*

# No. 177 Answers

**a1**  The environment; wild life; natural history
*b1*  *As an actress (films and stage)*
**a2**  Food additives
*b2*  *A skull (and crossbones)*
**a3**  American football
*b3*  *Italy*
**a4**  Dempsey and Makepeace
*b4*  *Glasgow*
**a5**  Airborne Warning and Control System (long-range surveillance)
*b5*  *Disc operating system*
**a6**  Munich
*b6*  *Danzig (later Gdansk)*
**a7**  Blue whale
*b7*  *(African) elephant*
**a8**  A Persian language (spoken in Iran, Iraq, Afghanistan and parts of the former Soviet Union)
*b8*  *A place where holy teaching takes place*
**a9**  Madame Tussaud's Waxworks
*b9*  *Alton Towers (1996–7 figures)*
**a10**  King Baudouin
*b10*  *Akihito*
**a11**  Anita Brookner
*b11*  *Salman Rushdie*
**a12**  Britain (to prevent it falling into German control)
*b12*  *Soviet Union (Russia)*

---

## Tie-breaker

**Q**  Which pub game was banned in Glasgow in 1939 as being 'too dangerous'?
**A**  *Darts*

---

# No. 178

**a1**  As what did 'Big Daddie' achieve fame?
***b1***  *For what has Wayne Sleep been famous?*
**a2**  By what name are members of the Unification Church colloquially known?
***b2***  *By what name are members of the Church of Jesus Christ of Latter-Day Saints often known?*
**a3**  What is the capital of Croatia?
***b3***  *Of which European state is the small town or village of Vaduz the capital?*
**a4**  For what did Robert Dougall become a well-known television personality?
***b4***  *Which subject did Patrick Moore broadcast about?*
**a5**  What type of bridge is the famous Forth rail bridge in Scotland?
***b5***  *And what type of bridge is the Humber bridge?*
**a6**  What is Alzheimer's disease?
***b6***  *Rubella is the technical term for which childhood illness?*
**a7**  When is the announcement 'Habemus Papam' (say: hab-ay-mos pa-pam) made?
***b7***  *What has the French phrase 'pied à terre' (say: pya-da-ter) come to mean?*
**a8**  Which war ended in 1939?
***b8***  *On which date in 1939 did Britain declare war on Germany?*
**a9**  Which sport's British Championships are held at Hurlingham?
***b9***  *With which sport do you associate Henry Cecil and Ian Bolding?*
**a10**  Of which country has Edith Cresson been prime minister?
***b10***  *Which European country's prime minister was murdered in 1986?*
**a11**  In which African country did South African troops fight Cuban troops?
***b11***  *In which African country did a war of independence against France begin in 1954?*
**a12**  Who wrote the play *The Corn is Green*?
***b12***  *Who wrote the wartime hit play* Dear Octopus?

# No. 178 Answers

**a1**  As a wrestler (on television)
*b1*  *(Ballet) dancing*
**a2**  Moonies
*b2*  *Mormons*
**a3**  Zagreb
*b3*  *Liechtenstein*
**a4**  Newsreading (BBC)
*b4*  *Astronomy*
**a5**  Cantilever bridge
*b5*  *Suspension bridge*
**a6**  A form of dementia, or memory loss
*b6*  *German measles*
**a7**  When a new pope is elected (Latin: 'We have a pope')
*b7*  *A second home (usually small and in a city)*
**a8**  Spanish Civil War
*b8*  *September 3rd*
**a9**  Croquet
*b9*  *Horse racing*
**a10**  France
*b10*  *Sweden's (Olaf Palme)*
**a11**  Angola
*b11*  *Algeria*
**a12**  Emlyn Williams
*b12*  *Dodie Smith*

## Tie-breaker

**Q**  What were the first four items of food to be rationed in Britain in 1940?
**A**  *Butter, sugar, bacon and ham (cooked and uncooked)*

# No. 179

**a1** Who co-starred with Geoffrey Palmer in television's *As Time Goes By*?

**b1** *In its early days, which children's television programme was introduced by Valerie Singleton and Christopher Trace?*

**a2** Which part of Britain fell to the Nazis in 1940?

**b2** *Which French soldier rallied his nation in a radio message just after Paris fell to the Nazis?*

**a3** Boxer Mike Tyson was disqualified for biting whose ear?

**b3** *Which French footballer faced court action after his kickboxing at Selhurst Park?*

**a4** What did the word 'Blitzkrieg' (say: blitz-kreeg) mean?

**b4** *In 1940, what nickname was given to the Local Defence Volunteers?*

**a5** Which movement was started by the Maharishi Mahesh Yogi?

**b5** *In 1967, which European country declared itself 'the first atheist state in the world'?*

**a6** Which organization (established in 1958) helps Third World development by sending voluntary workers to such countries?

**b6** *For what does the abbreviation BTec (or BTEC) stand?*

**a7** In 1944, which Shakespeare play was made into a patriotic film by Laurence Olivier?

**b7** *In which film did Merle Oberon co-star with Laurence Olivier?*

**a8** As what did Jackson Pollock become famous?

**b8** *Which ballerina starred in the film* The Red Shoes*?*

**a9** Which island became part of Canada in 1949?

**b9** *Until 1949, by what name was the kingdom of Jordan known?*

**a10** In which year was the United States Air Force established, independent of the other services? Was it 1918, 1941 or 1947?

**b10** *What role is performed by America's F-117A Stealth aircraft?*

**a11** Of which country was Major General Zia the ruler?

**b11** *Of which South American country did Carlos Menem become president in 1989?*

**a12** Which famous novel had as its comic hero Jim Dixon?

**b12** *Which international prize did William Golding win in 1983?*

# No. 179 Answers

**a1** Judi Dench
***b1*** *Blue Peter*
**a2** Channel Islands
***b2*** *General de Gaulle*
**a3** Evander Holyfield
***b3*** *Eric Cantona*
**a4** Lightning war
***b4*** *Home Guard (or 'Dad's Army')*
**a5** Transcendental Meditation (TM)
***b5*** *Albania*
**a6** VSO (Voluntary Service Overseas)
***b6*** *Business Technology Education Council*
**a7** *Henry V*
***b7*** *Wuthering Heights*
**a8** Painting (especially 'action painting' or 'Abstract Expressionism')
***b8*** *Moira Shearer*
**a9** Newfoundland
***b9*** *Transjordan*
**a10** 1947 (During the Second World War it was the Army Air Force)
***b10*** *Bomber*
**a11** Bangladesh
***b11*** *Argentina*
**a12** *Lucky Jim* (by Kingsley Amis)
***b12*** *Nobel Prize for Literature*

---

## Tie-breaker

**Q** What name was given to the style of architecture popular in the later thirties, and used in the building of many Odeon cinemas and new railway stations?

**A** *Art deco*

# No. 180

**a1** In which sport do Kayak fours and Canadian pairs compete?
**b1** *In which sport might you either snatch or jerk?*
**a2** In the 1939 popular song, where was the washing to be hung?
**b2** *Where, in a 1948 pop song, would a slow boat take you?*
**a3** For what is the chemical aspartame used?
**b3** *With what is the science of cryogenics concerned?*
**a4** On television, who was the long-time host of *A Question of Sport*?
**b4** *And who was the original host of* Blankety Blank?
**a5** In October 1937, which exhibition or show was held for the first time, at London's Earls Court?
**b5** *From November 1937, what was Scotland Yard's emergency telephone number?*
**a6** In the army, what is a formation of two or more brigades called?
**b6** *Why are minesweepers often built of reinforced plastic?*
**a7** Which commonwealth country moved its seat of government to a new federal capital in 1927?
**b7** *In which city was the Massacre of Tiananmen Square in 1989?*
**a8** In the 1948 film of *Oliver Twist*, who played Fagin?
**b8** *Robert Donat played the lead in a 1939 film about an elderly public schoolmaster. What was the film?*
**a9** Which British aircraft carrier was launched in 1937?
**b9** *Which famous Cunard liner made her maiden transatlantic voyage in May 1936?*
**a10** In which country did 8,000 people 'disappear' between 1976 and 1983, under a repressive military government?
**b10** *In which country did the 1956 'Hundred Flowers' movement encourage criticism of the government?*
**a11** Who wrote the famous (and first) radio play about Jesus Christ, called *The Man Born to be King*?
**b11** *Which physicist wrote the book* A Brief History of Time?
**a12** In which country was Prince Sihanouk a leading political figure?
**b12** *Which country was ruled between 1986 and 1992 by President Najibullah?*

# No. 180 Answers

| | |
|---|---|
| **a1** | Canoeing |
| *b1* | *Weightlifting* |
| **a2** | 'On the Siegfried Line' |
| *b2* | *China ('On a Slow Boat to China')* |
| **a3** | As a sweetener (Nutrasweet) in foods and drinks |
| *b3* | *Very low temperatures; freezing* |
| **a4** | David Coleman |
| *b4* | *Terry Wogan* |
| **a5** | The Motor Show |
| *b5* | *999* |
| **a6** | Division |
| *b6* | *So they are immune to magnetic mines* |
| **a7** | Australia (Canberra) |
| *b7* | *Beijing (Peking)* |
| **a8** | Alec Guinness |
| *b8* | *Goodbye Mr Chips* |
| **a9** | 'Ark Royal' |
| *b9* | *'The Queen Mary'* |
| **a10** | Argentina |
| *b10* | *China* |
| **a11** | Dorothy L Sayers |
| *b11* | *Stephen Hawking* |
| **a12** | Cambodia |
| *b12* | *Afghanistan* |

---

## Tie-breaker

**Q** After association football, what is the next most popular spectator sport in Britain (measured by numbers attending)?

**A** *Greyhound racing*

---

# No. 181: Scoring the Century

**a1**  1999: Which country defends cricket's World Cup as champions?

*b1*  *1998: Which cricket cup competition ended?*

**a2**  1992: Michael Jordan and Magic Johnson were part of the USA's 'dream team'. In which sport?

*b2*  *1991: Who beat England 12–6 in rugby's World Cup final?*

**a3**  1988: Which Brazilian won a record eight Grand Prix?

*b3*  *1988: Name England's youngest rugby captain for 50 years*

**a4**  1979: A 16-year-old won the US Open Tennis Championship. Who was she?

*b4*  *1976: On 4th August England beat Australia at Lord's. What was unique about this?*

**a5**  1957: Which driver became the first Briton for 34 years to win the British Grand Prix in a British car?

*b5*  *1954: Who ran the first '4-minute mile'?*

**a6**  1964: Which Scot became European Footballer of the Year?

*b6*  *1962: Which country won football's World Cup?*

**a7**  1942: Born as Cassius Clay. By what name was he later known?

*b7*  *1938: Which Australian had a batting average of 115.66 for the season?*

**a8**  1933: The Wimbledon men's singles title was won by which British player?

*b8*  *1930: Which game's first World Cup took place in this year?*

**a9**  1926: Gertrude Ederle was the first woman to swim the English channel. Did it take her $14^1/_2$, $16^1/_2$ or 20 hours?

*b9*  *1927–8: Which Everton player scored 60 1st Division goals?*

**a10**  1920: P G H Fender scored the fastest 100 in county cricket, in 35, 40, or 42 minutes?

*b10*  *1919: Which boxer became World Heavyweight Champion?*

**a11**  1914: Which sportsmen might earn £75,000 in their careers at this time?

*b11*  *1913: 1890s crowds averaged 15,000, now they were 10,000. In which sport?*

**a12**  1908: In the London Olympics, which race started under royal windows?

*b12*  *1908: Reginald Walker (South Africa) won the men's 100m in the Olympics. Was his time 12.0, 11.2, or 10.8?*

# No. 181 Answers

**a1** Sri Lanka
*b1* *Benson & Hedges*
**a2** Basketball
*b2* *Australia*
**a3** Ayrton Senna
*b3* *Will Carling*
**a4** Tracy Austin
*b4* *First women's match at Lord's*
**a5** Stirling Moss
*b5* *Roger Bannister*
**a6** Denis Law
*b6* *Brazil*
**a7** Mohammed Ali
*b7* *Don Bradman*
**a8** Fred Perry
*b8* *Soccer*
**a9** 14½
*b9* *Dixie Dean*
**a10** 35
*b10* *Jack Dempsey*
**a11** Jockeys
*b11* *Cricket*
**a12** The Marathon
*b12* *10.8*

---

## Tie-breaker

**Q** What is octopush?
**A** *Underwater hockey*

---

362

# No. 182

**a1**    How did Angela Rippon first become a national figure?

*b1*    *Which chain of shops was founded by Anita Roddick?*

**a2**    In which famous Liverpool club did the Beatles once play?

*b2*    *Who sang about the 'Long Haired Lover from Liverpool'?*

**a3**    In English soccer, the Third Division was formed in 1920. What happened to it a year later?

*b3*    *And what happened to it in 1958?*

**a4**    If you are given a restaurant bill for £37.50 and you want to leave a 10% tip, how much do you leave?

*b4*    *Which is bigger, three hundred thousand or a quarter of a million?*

**a5**    Which envoy of the Archbishop of Canterbury became a hostage in Beirut?

*b5*    *Where did over 1,400 pilgrims die in a stampede in 1990?*

**a6**    What is the purpose of an analgesic?

*b6*    *What is a psychosomatic illness?*

**a7**    In 1907, which sporting stadium became the headquarters of English Rugby Union?

*b7*    *For what kind of sporting activity has Ruislip (say: rye-slip) in west London become especially well known?*

**a8**    Which small historic county in the East Midlands was restored in 1997?

*b8*    *Name one of the three so-called 'new' counties which ceased to exist in 1996?*

**a9**    Which nun won the Nobel Peace Prize in 1979?

*b9*    *In which country was Cardinal Mindszenty a leading religious figure and opponent of Communism?*

**a10**    Who wrote the series of children's novels that includes *Swallows and Amazons*?

*b10*    *Ian Serraillier (say: se-ral-i-ay) wrote a famous children's novel about refugees in the Second World War. What was it called?*

**a11**    In which country is the historical site of the ancient city of Troy?

*b11*    *In which country is the historic site of Luxor?*

**a12**    Of which organization did Oliver Tambo become leader in 1977?

*b12*    *What post did Helmut Schmidt hold from 1974 to 1983?*

# No. 182 Answers

**a1**    As a newsreader
*b1*    *The Body Shop*
**a2**    The Cavern
*b2*    *Little Jimmy Osmond*
**a3**    It divided into Division 3 North and Division 3 South
*b3*    *The two divisions were re-formed into Divisions 3 and 4*
**a4**    £3.75
*b4*    *Three hundred thousand (a quarter of a million = 250,000)*
**a5**    Terry Waite
*b5*    *Mecca (in an underground tunnel)*
**a6**    To relieve pain
*b6*    *One that is thought to arise from emotional or mental causes*
**a7**    Twickenham
*b7*    *Water sports (bathing, water skiing, sailing on Ruislip Lido)*
**a8**    Rutland
*b8*    *Avon, Cleveland or Humberside*
**a9**    Mother Teresa (of Calcutta)
*b9*    *Hungary*
**a10**    Arthur Ransome
*b10*    *The Silver Sword*
**a11**    Turkey
*b11*    *Egypt*
**a12**    ANC (African National Congress)
*b12*    *Chancellor (premier) of West Germany*

---

## Tie-breaker

**Q**    By what name did the case of murderer George Joseph Smith become known, on account of his drowning his new married wives?

**A**    *The Brides in the Bath case*

# No. 183

**a1** For what did John Curry become well-known?
*b1* *How has Anthony Sher become famous?*
**a2** Which popular entertainer sang the lyrics: 'Did you think I would leave you dying when there's room on my horse for two'?
*b2* *From which Christmas hit came the words 'Are you hanging up a stocking on your wall'?*
**a3** For what do the initials HMV stand?
*b3* *And what is a HND?*
**a4** Which fruit became available in Britain in 1946 for the first time for many years?
*b4* *What means of urgent communication was abolished by British Telecom in 1981?*
**a5** To which country are the platypus, wombat and emu unique?
*b5* *What was discovered in caves at Lascaux (say: las-ko) in France in 1940?*
**a6** In which year did Queen Victoria die?
*b6* *In which month and year was Queen Elizabeth II's coronation?*
**a7** In 1997 H D Bird retired from international officialdom in which sport?
*b7* *David Elleray controls Harrow students and professional sportsmen. In which sport?*
**a8** What is the unit of currency in Portugal?
*b8* *And what is it in Spain?*
**a9** Which character did child actor Jack Wild play in the film *Oliver!*?
*b9* *In which film is the ballad 'Some Day My Prince Will Come'?*
**a10** Which holy city came under British control in 1917 after over 700 years under Islamic control?
*b10* *Why is Medina a holy city for Muslims?*
**a11** Who wrote the plays *Roots* and *Chicken Soup With Barley*?
*b11* *Who wrote the score of the musical* The Desert Song*?*
**a12** The sinking of which ship in 1915 infuriated America?
*b12* *And where did the tragedy occur?*

# No. 183 Answers

**a1** Ice-skating
*b1* *As an actor*
**a2** Rolf Harris ('Two Little Boys')
*b2* *'Merry Christmas Everybody' by Slade*
**a3** His Master's Voice
*b3* *Higher National Diploma*
**a4** Bananas
*b4* *Telegrams*
**a5** Australia
*b5* *Prehistoric paintings or carvings*
**a6** 1901
*b6* *June, 1953*
**a7** Cricket
*b7* *Soccer*
**a8** The escudo
*b8* *The peseta*
**a9** The Artful Dodger
*b9* Snow White and the Seven Dwarfs
**a10** Jerusalem
*b10* *It was the home of the prophet of Islam, Muhammad*
**a11** Arnold Wesker
*b11* *Sigmund Romberg*
**a12** Lusitania
*b12* *Off the coast of Ireland (off Kinsale)*

---

## Tie-breaker

**Q** Besides John Major, who challenged Margaret Thatcher for the leadership of the Conservative party in November 1990?

**A** *Michael Heseltine and Douglas Hurd*

---

# No. 184

**a1** What is a junta (say: hunta)?

*b1* *What is a 'mantra'?*

**a2** Besides cricket, in which area has the Australian Kerry Packer become well known?

*b2* *How did Clive Ponting make the headlines in 1985?*

**a3** What do the letters ECB stand for?

*b3* *What do the letters LTA stand for?*

**a4** Which musical features Potiphar's wife and Pharaoh?

*b4* *And which features Aunt Eller, Ado Annie and Curly?*

**a5** Which illness is treated by doses of quinine?

*b5* *And in which common drink can quinine be found?*

**a6** By population, which is the largest metropolitan area in Asia?

*b6* *After London, which is the largest metropolitan area (by population) in Europe?*

**a7** Of which country was Edvard Shevardnadze a leading statesman in the eighties?

*b7* *Of which country was Hans Dietrich (say: dee-trisch) Genscher a long-serving foreign minister?*

**a8** In which radio serial was someone always worried about Jim?

*b8* *Which radio serial, set in north London, replaced* The Dales *in 1969?*

**a9** Near which famous American city are Berkeley, Oakland and Richmond?

*b9* *In which American city are there districts called Arlington and Capitol Heights?*

**a10** 'You're Dancing on my Heart' was the signature tune of which dance band leader – famous for his 'slow, slow, quick-quick, slow'?

*b10* *What was Bing Crosby's signature tune?*

**a11** What has been named after the English logician John Venn (1834–1923)?

*b11* *What are ordinal numbers?*

**a12** Which affair caused the resignations of Bob Haldeman and John D Ehrlichman?

*b12* *The wife of a black South African leader, she has herself been a political and controversial figure. Who is she?*

# No. 184 Answers

**a1**    The military rulers of a country, after seizing power

*b1*    *A word or words repeated during meditation*

**a2**    Television (channel boss) and publisher (of newspapers)

*b2*    *(As a civil servant) he broke the Official Secrets Act (by giving information to MPs about the Falklands War)*

**a3**    English Cricket Board

*b3*    *Lawn Tennis Association*

**a4**    *Joseph and the Amazing Technicolor Dreamcoat*

*b4*    Oklahoma!

**a5**    Malaria (and other fevers)

*b5*    *(Indian) tonic water*

**a6**    Tokyo

*b6*    *Paris*

**a7**    Soviet Union

*b7*    *East Germany (German Federal Republic)*

**a8**    Mrs Dale was worried, in *Mrs Dale's Diary* and (later) *The Dales*

*b8*    Waggoner's Walk

**a9**    San Francisco

*b9*    *Washington*

**a10**    Victor Silvester

*b10*    'Where the Blue of the Night'

**a11**    Venn diagrams (in mathematics: to show the relationship between sets)

*b11*    *First, second, third, fourth, etc. (numbers which indicate order)*

**a12**    Watergate (in the US, 1973)

*b12*    *Winnie Mandela*

## Tie-breaker

**Q**    In space, what are sometimes described as 'dirty snow-balls'?

**A**    *Comets*

# No. 185

**a1** Why has Nigel Kennedy become well known?
*b1* *How did Tony Greig (say: gregg) become well known?*
**a2** As what has Judy Blume become famous?
*b2* *Which Bank of England clerk wrote a children's classic (about animals on a river bank) in 1908?*
**a3** In 1937, where did you have to go for 'a week's holiday for a week's wage'?
*b3* *In advertising, what is the ASA?*
**a4** To which country do the Faeroe Islands belong?
*b4* *To which country do the islands of Lesbos and Rhodes belong?*
**a5** What was Ronan Point?
*b5* *Which controversial 385 foot high office block was built in central London in 1966 and was then not used for some time?*
**a6** In July 1997 Eddie Merekx laid flowers at Jacques Anquetil's grave. Both were winners of which event?
*b6* *Michael Johnson and Butch Reynolds star in which athletics event?*
**a7** In 1966, who had a hit with 'You Don't Have to Say You Love Me'?
*b7* *In 1969, who sang about a 'Boy Named Sue'?*
**a8** Which country was governed as a military dictatorship under Antonio Salazar from 1928 to 1968?
*b8* *Of which country was P W Botha prime minister from 1978?*
**a9** In which film did Judy Garland sing 'The Trolley Song'?
*b9* *Which American film 'sex goddess' starred in* Hell's Angels *and* Riffraff – *and died at the age of 26?*
**a10** The sum of the interior angles of a triangle is 180 degrees. What is the sum of the interior angles of a quadrilateral?
*b10* *And of a pentagon?*
**a11** In which town did the Germans sign the unconditional surrender at the end of the Second World War?
*b11* *And who, on behalf of the Allies, received that surrender?*
**a12** For which element is the chemical symbol Si?
*b12* *And for which is it Ra?*

# No. 185 Answers

**a1**  For his violin playing (and 'punk' style)
*b1*  *As a cricketer*
**a2**  As a writer (of novels for young teenagers, especially girls)
*b2*  *Kenneth Grahame (The Wind in the Willows)*
**a3**  Butlins (holiday camp)
*b3*  *Advertising Standards Authority*
**a4**  Denmark
*b4*  *Greece*
**a5**  A tower block of flats (which collapsed in 1968)
*b5*  *Centrepoint*
**a6**  Tour de France
*b6*  *400 metres*
**a7**  Dusty Springfield
*b7*  *Johnny Cash*
**a8**  Portugal
*b8*  *South Africa*
**a9**  *Meet Me in St Louis*
*b9*  *Jean Harlow*
**a10**  360 degrees
*b10*  *540 degrees*
**a11**  Rheims
*b11*  *General Eisenhower*
**a12**  Silicon
*b12*  *Radium*

## Tie-breaker

**Q**  Besides Liberia, which was the only independent country in Africa in 1911?
**A**  *Ethiopia (Abyssinia)*

# No. 186

**a1** In which television 'soap' did we see Nellie Mangel?
*b1* *And in which soap has Dot Cotton also been something of a 'sour puss'?*
**a2** What is the unit of currency in Greece?
*b2* *And what is it in the Netherlands?*
**a3** In soccer, which Spanish club won the European Cup for the first five years of the competition?
*b3* *In which sport do the Cincinatti Reds compete?*
**a4** Ian Macleod was once Chancellor of the Exchequer. Of which party was he a member?
*b4* *When Yugoslavia became a federal republic in 1945, who became its leader?*
**a5** In 1971, who sang 'Chirpy Chirpy Cheep Cheep'?
*b5* *About which means of transport did the Mixtures have a chart hit?*
**a6** Introduced from 1941 onwards, what were the earliest group of antibiotic drugs?
*b6* *In the field of medicine, what is a placebo (say: pla-see-bo)?*
**a7** Which secular movement in Britain was, for some time, led by a Roman Catholic priest, Bruce Kent?
*b7* *Hope Street runs between an Anglican cathedral and a Roman Catholic cathedral in which English city?*
**a8** Who wrote the novel *Prester John*?
*b8* *Who wrote the satirical novel* Scoop*?*
**a9** In which two continents is the Muslim religion most influential?
*b9* *And in which large country is Hinduism the primary influence?*
**a10** Which two countries fought each other in a Gulf War which began in the early eighties?
*b10* *Which two countries signed a joint 'Pact of Steel' in 1939?*
**a11** Who was William Holman Hunt (who died in 1910)?
*b11* *Who was Marie Tempest?*
**a12** Which European country has a coast line on the Black Sea and includes the Transylvanian Alps?
*b12* *Which Canadian province has a Pacific Ocean coastline?*

# No. 186 Answers

**a1** *Neighbours*
**b1** EastEnders
**a2** The dinar
**b2** *The guilder*
**a3** Real (say: ray-al) Madrid
**b3** *Baseball*
**a4** Conservative
**b4** *Tito*
**a5** Middle of the Road
**b5** *Bicycle ('The Pushbike Song')*
**a6** Penicillin
**b6** *A harmless substance or pill; the person taking it believes it will cure a problem or illness*
**a7** CND (Campaign for Nuclear Disarmament)
**b7** *Liverpool*
**a8** John Buchan
**b8** *Evelyn Waugh*
**a9** Asia, Africa
**b9** *India*
**a10** Iran, Iraq
**b10** *Germany, Italy*
**a11** Artist ('the last of the Pre-Raphaelites')
**b11** *Famous actress*
**a12** Romania
**b12** *British Columbia*

## Tie-breaker

**Q** Which new novel sold a million copies in America in 1936?
**A** Gone With the Wind *(by Margaret Mitchell)*

# No. 187

**a1**  What is probate?
*b1*  *What is parole?*
**a2**  Of which Canadian province is Labrador a part?
*b2*  *On to which lake or sea does the city of Chicago face?*
**a3**  In a film, what was the name of the biggest dog in the world?
*b3*  *In which Walt Disney film do two dogs dine out in an Italian restaurant?*
**a4**  For which sport has Ty Cobb become well known?
*b4*  *For what has Jim (or James) Clark become famous?*
**a5**  In which Palace of Justice were Nazi leaders put on trial in 1945?
*b5*  *What was the name of Hitler's mistress and (for the last day of his life, his wife)?*
**a6**  From which hit came the words 'When the moon is in the seventh house and Jupiter aligns with Mars'?
*b6*  *From which hit came the words 'Well, it's one for the money, two for the show, three to get ready, now go cat go'?*
**a7**  For which area is 0161 the telephone dialling code?
*b7*  *And for which city is 0131 the code?*
**a8**  For which poisonous element is the chemical symbol As?
*b8*  *And for which is it Fe?*
**a9**  In which year was England's first official rugby union tour abroad? Was it 1902, 1947 or 1963?
*b9*  *In the eighties, was Vreni Schneider a golfer, swimmer or skier?*
**a10**  Until its civil war, which Mediterranean country was the financial centre of the Middle East?
*b10*  *Which country borders Norway at its extreme northeastern tip?*
**a11**  Who wrote the play *A Streetcar Named Desire*?
*b11*  *Which Arthur Miller play is about Willy Loman?*
**a12**  Of which country did Jim Bolger become prime minister in 1990?
*b12*  *Of which country was Gro Harlem Brundtland elected prime minister in 1986 and 1990?*

# No. 187 Answers

**a1** The formal proof of a will
*b1* *Conditional release of a prisoner*
**a2** Newfoundland
*b2* *Lake Michigan*
**a3** Digby
*b3* Lady and the Tramp
**a4** Baseball
*b4* *Motor-racing*
**a5** Nuremburg
*b5* *Eva Braun*
**a6** 'Aquarius' (by Fifth Dimension)
*b6* *'Blue Suede Shoes' (by Elvis Presley)*
**a7** (Greater) Manchester
*b7* *Edinburgh*
**a8** Arsenic
*b8* *Iron*
**a9** 1963
*b9* *Skier*
**a10** Lebanon
*b10* *Russia*
**a11** Tennessee Williams
*b11* Death of a Salesman
**a12** New Zealand
*b12* *Norway*

---

## Tie-breaker

**Q** What was remarkable about the result of the 1910 British general election?

**A** *It resulted in a tie (Both Liberals and Conservatives winning 272 seats) (42 Labour MPs and 84 Irish Nationalists agreed to support the Conservatives)*

---

# No. 188

**a1** Which cricket umpire hops when the score is 111?
*b1* *Who keeps score on BBC Radio's Test Match Special?*
**a2** Who belong to Equity?
*b2* *In France, what is Le Figaro?*
**a3** In Scotland, for which industry is Bilston Glen known?
*b3* *And what was Ravenscraig's principal industry?*
**a4** In which country is the holiday resort of Acapulco?
*b4* *Which African country includes the Great Rift Valley, Lake Nakuru and the port of Mombasa?*
**a5** Back in 1956, which female singer sang 'Lay Down Your Arms'?
*b5* *Which American bandleader was particularly associated with the tune 'The Peanut Vendor'?*
**a6** What is the unit of currency in Malta?
*b6* *And in Morocco?*
**a7** In the late forties, which 'special agent' appeared in a daily radio serial?
*b7* *In which BBC comedy radio show did Bebe Daniels appear with the rest of her family?*
**a8** What name did Wilhelm Roëntgen (who died in 1923) give to the short electromagnetic waves he discovered earlier in his life?
*b8* *In 1912, Sir Frederick Gowland Hopkins discovered substances we now know are a vital part of our diet. What are they?*
**a9** Which London underground station was the title of a hit by the New Vaudeville Band?
*b9* *Which London underground station is the name of a surreal game played on radio?*
**a10** Which television reporter, famous for his white suit, became an MP?
*b10* *In which riots in 1968 was Daniel Cohn-Bendit a leader?*
**a11** As what did John Piper achieve fame?
*b11* *Why did Gustav Mahler (died 1911) become famous?*
**a12** Of which country was Turgut Ozal the prime minister from 1983 to 1989?
*b12* *Of which country was Bettino Craxi prime minister from 1983 to 1987?*

# No. 188 Answers

**a1** David Shepherd
***b1*** *Bill Frindall*
**a2** Actors (it's their trade union)
***b2*** *Daily newspaper*
**a3** Mining/coal
***b3*** *Steel*
**a4** Mexico
***b4*** *Kenya*
**a5** Anne Shelton
***b5*** *Stan Kenton*
**a6** The Maltese lira
***b6*** *The dirham*
**a7** Dick Barton
***b7*** *Life with the Lyons*
**a8** X-rays
***b8*** *Vitamins*
**a9** Finchley Central
***b9*** *Mornington Crescent*
**a10** Martin Bell
***b10*** *Paris student riots*
**a11** As a painter/artist
***b11*** *He was a composer*
**a12** Turkey
***b12*** *Italy*

---

## Tie-breaker

**Q** Which English county was the first to plan 'comprehensive schools' (in 1948)?
**A** *Middlesex*

---

# No. 189

**a1** Who was Olive Oyl?

*b1* *Can you complete this pop song title: 'Gilly-Gilly-Ossenfeffer ...'?*

**a2** What did Britain suffer from particularly in February 1947?

*b2* *And in the summer of 1976?*

**a3** In a computer, what is a 'buffer'?

*b3* *In space, what is 'Mir'?*

**a4** Which sport is said to have the most active participants in Britain?

*b4* *Which game (or variation of a game) was invented in Scotland in 1924 – and played in Middlesex two years later?*

**a5** In the film *The Prince and the Showgirl*, Marilyn Monroe played the showgirl. Who played her prince?

*b5* *In the film* Blue Skies, *which two male singers were 'Puttin' on the Ritz'?*

**a6** Which dog is partner to Wallace?

*b6* *Who played Rose in the 1997 film* Titanic?

**a7** By population, which is the largest city in India?

*b7* *By population, which is the largest city (that is, metropolitan area) in China?*

**a8** From which musical come the songs 'Luck Be a Lady' and 'A Bushel and a Peck'?

*b8* *Which musical tells the story of a Scottish village that appears only once each century?*

**a9** In the world of finance, what is a dividend?

*b9* *And what is an ISA?*

**a10** Besides Germany, which country invaded Poland in September 1939?

*b10* *Which German port and industrial city was severely bombed by British bombers in August 1943?*

**a11** As what did Ravi Shankar become well known?

*b11* *Why did the Nawab of Pataudi become famous?*

**a12** Which Labour Chancellor of the Exchequer had to resign in 1947 because he told a journalist what would be in his Budget speech?

*b12* *And who simply said about the incident, 'Pity. Never could keep his mouth shut'?*

# No. 189 Answers

**a1**  Popeye's girlfriend (later his wife)
*b1*  *'... Katzenellen-Bogen-By-the-Sea'*
**a2**  Heavy snowstorms; freezing temperatures
*b2*  *A major drought*
**a3**  Temporary memory (or any electronic protective device)
*b3*  *Soviet space station*
**a4**  Angling
*b4*  *Rugby union sevens (seven-a-side rugby)*
**a5**  Laurence Olivier
*b5*  *Bing Crosby and Fred Astaire*
**a6**  Gromit
*b6*  *Kate Winslett*
**a7**  Calcutta
*b7*  *Shanghai*
**a8**  *Guys and Dolls*
*b8*  Brigadoon
**a9**  The part of the profits of a company paid to shareholders (usually annually)
*b9*  *Individual Savings Account*
**a10**  Soviet Union (Russia)
*b10*  *Hamburg*
**a11**  As an (Indian) musician (sitar player)
*b11*  *He was an international Indian cricketer (in the thirties)*
**a12**  Hugh Dalton
*b12*  *Clement Atlee (prime minister)*

---

## Tie-breaker

**Q**  Sandra (played by Nerys Hughes) and Carol (played by Elizabeth Estensen) were the main characters in which television comedy series?

**A**  The Liver Birds

---

# No. 190

**a1** In which television serial was David Hunter a famously dull character?

*b1 And which television serial included the characters Sister Carole Young, Dr Chris Anderson and Alan Dawson?*

**a2** Who was Edith Cavell?

*b2 Who was Sybil Thorndike?*

**a3** In law, what is a 'decree nisi' (say: nye-sye)?

*b3 What is extradition?*

**a4** In which sport would you compete for the Thomas Cup?

*b4 Where is rugby league's Challenge Cup final played?*

**a5** Who sang about 'The Day We Caught the Train'?

*b5 Which solo artist sang about the 'Love Train'?*

**a6** What is the unit of currency in Chile?

*b6 And what is it in Israel?*

**a7** Who wrote *Keep the Aspidistra Flying*?

*b7 How did the novelist Virginia Woolf die?*

**a8** When did Admiral Sandy Woodward make the headlines?

*b8 Which British Foreign Secretary resigned over Argentina's invasion of the Falklands?*

**a9** Which Australian city is close to Botany Bay?

*b9 And which Australian city is neighbour to Fremantle?*

**a10** Off the coast of which country are the sea areas North and South Utsire?

*b10 Between which two countries is the sea area Malin?*

**a11** In which country could you travel by the 'Blue Train' or by the 'Orange Express'?

*b11 Of which people is Chief Buthelezi (say: boo-ta-lay-zi) a leader?*

**a12** If statics is the branch of physics concerned with objects at rest, which branch is concerned with moving objects?

*b12 What is viscosity?*

# No. 190 Answers

**a1**  *Crossroads*
**b1**  Emergency – Ward Ten
**a2**  British nurse, executed by Germans
**b2**  *Famous actress (played St Joan in G B Shaw's play)*
**a3**  A conditional order of divorce
**b3**  *The surrender of a person by a state or country to another country (where the person is 'wanted', possibly for legal reasons)*
**a4**  Badminton
**b4**  *Wembley*
**a5**  Ocean Colour Scene
**b5**  *Holly Johnson*
**a6**  The peso
**b6**  *The shekel*
**a7**  George Orwell
**b7**  *By drowning (believed to be suicide)*
**a8**  During the Falklands War (1982) (He was the Task Force commander)
**b8**  *Lord Carrington*
**a9**  Sydney
**b9**  *Perth*
**a10**  Norway
**b10**  *Scotland and Northern Ireland*
**a11**  South Africa
**b11**  *Zulu; Kwa Zulu black 'homeland' (in South Africa)*
**a12**  Dynamics
**b12**  *The resistance of a liquid to flow*

---

## Tie-breaker

**Q**  What are tectonic plates?
**A**  *The continental 'plates' which are slowly moving and so cause 'continental drift' (that is, they cause the continents to move very slowly in relation to each other)*

---

# No. 191: Brand Names

The following are all brand names of products on sale during the 20th century. What is each product?

a1  Dansette
*b1*  *Tide*
a2  Tibs
*b2*  *Baby Belling*
a3  Wincarnis
*b3*  *Euthymol*
a4  Lilliput
*b4*  *Mullard*
a5  Cerebos
*b5*  *Bemax*
a6  Procea
*b6*  *Eno's*
a7  Virol
*b7*  *Jelloids*
a8  Abdullah
*b8*  *John Bull*
a9  Lexicon
*b9*  *Parlophone*
a10  Triang
*b10*  *Zubes*
a11  Spirella
*b11*  *Symington*
a12  Vidor
*b12*  *Three Castles*

# No. 191 Answers

**a1** Record-player
*b1* *Washing powder*
**a2** Cat food
*b2* *(Small) cooker*
**a3** Health drink
*b3* *Toothpaste (or powder)*
**a4** Magazine (men's)
*b4* *Wireless (or radio) and television sets and valves*
**a5** Salt
*b5* *Vitamin supplement (wheatgerm)*
**a6** Bread
*b6* *'Fruit Salts' (laxative)*
**a7** 'Nutritious supplementary food' for children (malt extract)
*b7* *Iron pills*
**a8** Cigarettes
*b8* *Weekly magazine*
**a9** Card game (not unlike Scrabble)
*b9* *Gramophone records*
**a10** Toys (especially toy cars and trains)
*b10* *Throat pastilles*
**a11** Corsets
*b11* *Soups*
**a12** Batteries
*b12* *Cigarettes*

---

## Tie-breaker

**Q** What was 'The Nugget'?
*A* *A polish for shoes and other leather goods*

---

# No. 192

**a1**  Which child actress was seen in the films *Pollyanna* and *Whistle Down the Wind*?

*b1*  *In The Wizard of Oz, what was the name of Dorothy's dog?*

**a2**  In London, which distinctive tower building was opened in 1964 – complete with a revolving restaurant at the top?

*b2*  *Which new, modernist building was designed for London Zoo by Lord Snowdon and opened in 1965?*

**a3**  Which Australian state is immediately north of New South Wales?

*b3*  *Marlborough, Nelson and Westland are all provincial (or statistical) areas in which country?*

**a4**  Which year was the Russian revolution?

*b4*  *During the Second World War, in which year was Rome liberated?*

**a5**  Of which novel and play is Bill Fisher the untruthful hero?

*b5*  *Which Irish writer created the character Molly Bloom?*

**a6**  From which hit came the lyrics 'And I miss you, like the deserts miss the rain'?

*b6*  *In which are the lyrics 'You just walked in, I make you smile'?*

**a7**  Arnold Sidebottom played cricket for Yorkshire and football for ...?

*b7*  *Yorkshireman Peter Winterbottom was a star in which sport?*

**a8**  For which metal is the chemical symbol Zn?

*b8*  *And for which is it Pb?*

**a9**  Who wrote the plays *Habeas Corpus* and *Forty Years On*?

*b9*  *Which relative of a prime minister wrote the plays* The Chiltern Hundreds *and* Lloyd George Knew My Father*?*

**a10**  In the world of finance, what is APR?

*b10*  *What is the aim of monetarism?*

**a11**  For what have Michael Clark, Twyla Tharp and Merce Cunningham become famous?

*b11*  *How did Harry Tate and 'Little Tich' become famous?*

**a12**  In which city did the United Nations General Assembly hold its first meeting (in 1946)?

*b12*  *Whose visit to Britain in 1982 was a 'first' for 450 years?*

# No. 192 Answers

**a1** Hayley Mills
*b1* *Toto*
**a2** Post Office Tower (now Telecom Tower)
*b2* *The Aviary*
**a3** Queensland
*b3* *New Zealand*
**a4** 1917
*b4* *1944*
**a5** *Billy Liar*
*b5* *James Joyce*
**a6** 'Missing' by Everything But the Girl
*b6* *'Stop' by the Spice Girls*
**a7** Manchester United
*b7* *Rugby union*
**a8** Zinc
*b8* *Lead*
**a9** Alan Bennett
*b9* *William Douglas Home*
**a10** Annual percentage rate (the rate of interest you pay on borrowed money)
*b10* *Reduction of inflation*
**a11** Dance/choreographers
*b11* *As music hall artists*
**a12** London
*b12* *The Pope's*

---

## Tie-breaker

**Q** In a golf tournament, what is the maximum number of clubs that may be carried in your bag?
**A** *14*

# No. 193

**a1**  In which television soap did Fred Feast play Fred Gee?

**b1**  *Who played Felicity Kendall's 'husband' in the television series* The Good Life?

**a2**  According to the war time slogan, what did 'careless talk' cost?

**b2**  *In post-war austerity Britain, there were a number of slogans. 'Export or die' was one; another was 'Work or...' What?*

**a3**  Which is London's principal opera house?

**b3**  *In England in 1916, which prehistoric monument was sold at auction for £6,000?*

**a4**  Which two countries border Tunisia?

**b4**  *Which two countries lie to the south of Bulgaria?*

**a5**  In what sort of setting did most of Angela Brazil's novels take place?

**b5**  *Which famous fictional schoolboy was invented by Anthony Buckeridge?*

**a6**  Which female vocalist sang 'This Ole House'?

**b6**  *In 1962, who had a hit with 'I Can't Stop Loving You'?*

**a7**  In which sport do the Chicago Bears compete?

**b7**  *In which country is PSV Eindhoven a soccer team?*

**a8**  In which country did General Pinochet (say: pi-no-shay) lead a coup in 1973?

**b8**  *On which island did General Grivas wage a guerrilla war?*

**a9**  For what is thermal imaging used?

**b9**  *And what is a seismic (say: size-mick) wave?*

**a10**  In what was the armistice signed at the end of the First World War?

**b10**  *Which American general commanded American forces at the end of the Second World War in the Far East (and received Japan's surrender)?*

**a11**  As what has A S Byatt become famous?

**b11**  *As what did Paul Klee become famous?*

**a12**  What is the unit of currency in Finland?

**b12**  *And in the Greek part of Cyprus?*

# No. 193 Answers

**a1**  *Coronation Street*
**b1**  *Richard Briers*
**a2**  Lives ('Careless talk costs lives')
**b2**  *Want*
**a3**  Royal Opera House, Covent Garden
**b3**  *Stonehenge*
**a4**  Algeria and Libya
**b4**  *Greece and Turkey*
**a5**  In girls' boarding schools
**b5**  *Jennings*
**a6**  Rosemary Clooney
**b6**  *Ray Charles*
**a7**  American football
**b7**  *Netherlands (Holland)*
**a8**  Chile
**b8**  *Cyprus*
**a9**  To help see or photograph objects in the dark (also used by doctors to locate diseased cells)
**b9**  *A wave of energy or vibrations that spread out from the centre of an earthquake*
**a10**  In a railway carriage (in the forest of Compiègne)
**b10**  *General MacArthur*
**a11**  Novelist
**b11**  *Painter/artist*
**a12**  The markka
**b12**  *The Cyprus pound*

---

## Tie-breaker

**Q**  Which chemical element is common to diamonds, soot and coal?
**A**  *Carbon*

---

# No. 194

**a1** The 1943 film *Lassie Come Home* featured an 11-year-old girl. She is still an actress – called ...?

*b1* *In the film* Fantastic Voyage *(about a miniaturized submarine's trip inside a human body), which actress played the only female member of the submarine's crew?*

**a2** Who was Gorgeous Gussie?

*b2* *What is athlete Florence Griffith-Joyner's usual nickname?*

**a3** For which British city is 0141 the telephone dialling code?

*b3* *And for which area is 0151 the code?*

**a4** Lee Hazlewood sang 'Did You Ever' with whom?

*b4* *Which star sang 'Everyone's Gone to the Moon'?*

**a5** What were once called the Home, Light and Third?

*b5* *What is the difference between freehold and leasehold?*

**a6** In which war was the Tet offensive?

*b6* *In which year did the Common Market officially come into being?*

**a7** In 1911, which British physicist discovered the atomic nucleus?

*b7* *In physics, which theory (that energy is absorbed or radiated discontinuously) was first stated in 1900?*

**a8** Where was the British battleship 'Royal Oak' sunk in the first weeks of the Second World War?

*b8* *Operation Dynamo was the official name of which Second World War nautical operation?*

**a9** Which Asian country includes the Hindu Kush mountain range, part of the Khyber Pass and the Panshir Valley?

*b9* *Which republic comprises 13,677 tropical islands (including Bali, Timor and Moluccas)?*

**a10** With which means of transport has the village of Cardington been especially associated?

*b10* *Which motor-racing circuit is near Towcester (say: toaster) in Northamptonshire?*

**a11** Who wrote the novel *Goodbye to Berlin*?

*b11* *Who wrote the novels* No Highway *and* A Town Like Alice*?*

**a12** For what has Norman Thelwell (or Thelwell, as he simply signs himself) become well known?

*b12* *As what has Thomas Keneally become famous?*

# No. 194 Answers

**a1** Elizabeth Taylor
*b1* *Raquel Welch*
**a2** (American) tennis player – with distinctive panties (Gussie Moran)
*b2* *Flo-Jo*
**a3** Glasgow
*b3* *Merseyside (accept: Liverpool)*
**a4** Nancy Sinatra
*b4* *Jonathan King*
**a5** BBC radio networks (until 1967)
*b5* *Freehold is absolute ownership, leasehold is ownership for a specified period*
**a6** Vietnam
*b6* *1957*
**a7** (Ernest) Rutherford
*b7* *Quantum Theory*
**a8** In her home base (Scapa Flow)
*b8* *Evacuation of Dunkirk*
**a9** Afghanistan
*b9* *Indonesia*
**a10** Airships (R101 was built here)
*b10* *Silverstone*
**a11** Christopher Isherwood
*b11* *Nevil Shute*
**a12** His cartoons (particularly of pony club members)
*b12* *Novelist*

## Tie-breaker

**Q** 'I saw something nasty in the woodshed' is a frequent claim made by a character called Aunt Ada Doom. In which novel does she appear (and make her claim)?

**A** Cold Comfort Farm *(by Stella Gibbons)*

# No. 195

**a1**  On television, who was Catweazle?

*b1*  *In Royal circles, who was 'Crawfie'?*

**a2**  Which popular hit refers to 'Father MacKenzie writing the words of a sermon that no one will hear'?

*b2*  *And which includes the line 'I felt the knife in my hand and she laughed no more'?*

**a3**  Why has Bill Giles become a well-known face on television?

*b3*  *Why did Mike Yarwood become a popular television entertainer?*

**a4**  Where is the Sea of Tranquillity?

*b4*  *And where is the giant volcano, Olympus Mons?*

**a5**  In 1953, what form of possibly dangerous footwear for women became popular?

*b5*  *Which British prime minister first said, 'A week is a long time in politics'?*

**a6**  In which Caribbean island are Spanish Town and Montego Bay?

*b6*  *Which country comprises over 1,000 islands and contains Mount Fuji and Mount Aso?*

**a7**  Which report (in 1942) outlined the idea of the Welfare State?

*b7*  *Which organization was formed in 1945 to promote Arab unity?*

**a8**  Of which American city is Long Beach a part?

*b8*  *Fort Worth is neighbour to which American city?*

**a9**  Basketball was played in the 19th century. True or False?

*b9*  *'Eric Heiden is to ice, what Spitz is to water.' What did Heiden do on ice?*

**a10**  'Depart, I say, and let us have done with you. In the name of God, go!' To whom were those words addressed?

*b10*  *What was 'Lease-Lend'?*

**a11**  What is the unit of currency in Hungary?

*b11*  *And what is it in China?*

**a12**  Who wrote a play called *Way Upstream*, which had a Thames cruiser floating on stage?

*b12*  *A 1981 musical is named after a New York thoroughfare (and theatre). What's it called?*

# No. 195 Answers

**a1**  A wizard in a children's television serial (played by Geoffrey Bayldon)
*b1*  *Nanny to the Princesses Elizabeth and Margaret*
**a2**  'Eleanor Rigby' (by The Beatles)
*b2*  *'Delilah' (by Tom Jones)*
**a3**  He's a weather forecaster
*b3*  *Because of his 'impressions' ('show biz' and political)*
**a4**  On the Moon (near side)
*b4*  *On the planet Mars*
**a5**  Stiletto heels
*b5*  *Harold Wilson*
**a6**  Jamaica
*b6*  *Japan*
**a7**  The Beveridge Report
*b7*  *The Arab League*
**a8**  Los Angeles
*b8*  *Dallas*
**a9**  True
*b9*  *Speed skating*
**a10**  Neville Chamberlain (in the House of Commons)
*b10*  *Free loan of American military equipment to Britain during the Second World War*
**a11**  The forint
*b11*  *The yuan*
**a12**  Alan Ayckbourn
*b12*  *42nd Street*

---

## Tie-breaker

**Q**  A Fahrenheit thermometer shows the temperature of a room to be 68°. What temperature would a Celsius (or centigrade) thermometer show in the same room?
**A**  *20°*

---

# No. 196

**a1**  How does the Alexander Technique aim to improve your health?

*b1*  *Medically speaking, what is IVF?*

**a2**  In Britain, why was 12 May 1937 a significant date?

*b2*  *In February 1939, who or what was the cause of bomb blasts at two of London's underground stations?*

**a3**  In which sport did Geoff Duke win a world championship title four times in five years?

*b3*  *Paul Schockemöhle (say: shock-a-muller) was a champion in which sport?*

**a4**  Which British naval base fell to the Japanese in February 1942?

*b4*  *Half a million were built by the motor industry towards the end of the Second World War – and each had two bedrooms, bathroom and lavatory. What were they?*

**a5**  What is the unit of currency in Austria?

*b5*  *And in Denmark?*

**a6**  Cornwall's cathedral was completed in 1910. Where is it?

*b6*  *Which natural gas has been found to seep into houses in Devon and Cornwall, and is thought to increase the risk of cancer?*

**a7**  For which gas is the chemical symbol He (say: aitch-ee)?

*b7*  *And for which is it Ne?*

**a8**  Who wrote the musical *Lock Up Your Daughters*?

*b8*  *Which was the musician Artur Schnabel's instrument?*

**a9**  The first record on BBC Radio 1 in 1967 was by the group the Move. What was it?

*b9*  *Which song did Pearl Carr and Teddy Johnson sing in the 1959 Eurovision Song Contest?*

**a10**  How was Hitler greeted when he invaded Austria in 1938?

*b10*  *The Sudetenland was once under German control. Of which country was it a part between the World Wars?*

**a11**  For what has David Mamet become well known?

*b11*  *Who was Augustus John?*

**a12**  Jessie Matthews sang 'Dancing on the Ceiling' in which film?

*b12*  *Richard Addinsell wrote a concerto for the film* Dangerous Moonlight – *called ...?*

# No. 196 Answers

**a1**  By correcting bad posture (and breathing and muscular tension)
**b1**  *In vitro fertilization ('test tube' fertilization)*
**a2**  Coronation of King George VI
**b2**  *The IRA*
**a3**  Motor-cycling (500 cc)
**b3**  *Showjumping*
**a4**  Singapore
**b4**  *'Pre-fabs' ('Pre-fabricated' houses)*
**a5**  The schilling
**b5**  *The kroner*
**a6**  Truro
**b6**  *Radon*
**a7**  Helium
**b7**  *Neon*
**a8**  Lionel Bart
**b8**  *Piano*
**a9**  'Flowers in the Rain'
**b9**  *'Sing Little Birdie'*
**a10**  By cheering, enthusiastic crowds (99% voted in favour of his 'Anschluss')
**b10**  *Czechoslovakia*
**a11**  Playwright (American)
**b11**  *Painter (1878–1961)*
**a12**  *Evergreen*
**b12**  *The 'Warsaw' Concerto*

---

## Tie-breaker

**Q**  Which famous dam, completed in 1959, controls the waters of the river Zamezi?
**A**  *Kariba Dam*

---

# No. 197

**a1** For what has Andy Irvine become famous?
*b1* *For what has Roy Lichtenstein become famous?*
**a2** Which television series was based (very loosely) on a Walter Scott novel and starred Roger Moore?
*b2* *In which television comedy series did we meet Joey, Adrian and 'our Aveline'?*
**a3** Who had hits with 'Say What You Want' and 'Black Eyed Boy'?
*b3* *Which pop group advised 'Don't Look Back in Anger'?*
**a4** What was *Reynolds News*?
*b4* *What is the Fosbury Flop?*
**a5** Erich Segal wrote a sentimental romantic novel in 1970, which was equally successful when filmed. What was it?
*b5* *William Peter Blatty wrote a controversial and best-selling novel in 1971 – later filmed. What was it?*
**a6** At which disaster did the liner 'Carpathia' play a vital role?
*b6* *What deadly mission was carried out by an American bomber aircraft called 'Enola Gay'?*
**a7** In which country is Kruger National Park?
*b7* *What is linked by the Bosporus Bridge?*
**a8** By what title has the ruler of Kuwait been generally known?
*b8* *Which post did Boutros Boutros Ghali take up in 1992?*
**a9** Where is the region known as Kurdistan?
*b9* *Ajaccio is the capital of which island?*
**a10** What is the unit of currency in Brazil?
*b10* *And what is it in Albania?*
**a11** In which sport was Sean Kerly famous?
*b11* *Jean-Claude Killy was known for which sport?*
**a12** Which law of physics states that energy can neither be destroyed nor created?
*b12* *The Kelvin is the basic scientific unit for measuring ... what?*

# No. 197 Answers

**a1**   Rugby union player
*b1*   *Pop art/artist*
**a2**   *Ivanhoe*
*b2*   Bread
**a3**   Texas
*b3*   *Oasis*
**a4**   A daily (morning) paper
*b4*   *A style of high jumping (it involves crossing the bar backwards)*
**a5**   *Love Story*
*b5*   The Exorcist
**a6**   The sinking of the *Titanic* (it was the first 'rescue' ship on the scene)
*b6*   *It dropped the atomic bomb on Hiroshima*
**a7**   South Africa
*b7*   *European and Asian Turkey (Europe and Asia)*
**a8**   Emir
*b8*   *Secretary-General of the United Nations*
**a9**   Northern and western Iran (and northern Iraq)
*b9*   *Corsica*
**a10**  The cruzado
*b10*  *The lek*
**a11**  Field hockey
*b11*  *Skiing*
**a12**  (First) law of thermodynamics
*b12*  *Temperature*

---

## Tie-breaker

**Q**   In which move in the game of chess may a player move two pieces at once?
**A**   *Castling (when moving a castle and the king at once)*

# No. 198

**a1**  Which 'eagle' came last in the Calgary Winter Olympics?

*b1*  *Who became known as 'Gazza'?*

**a2**  In which film do some astronauts (led by Charlton Heston) think they are on another planet but actually are still on Earth?

*b2*  *What was the name of the modern, almost silent film made by Mel Brooks?*

**a3**  Which pop group had hits with 'Donna' and 'Rubber Bullets'?

*b3*  *Which male pianist had an early hit with 'You're a Lady'?*

**a4**  What does a cereologist study?

*b4*  *What is computer hacking?*

**a5**  Who was elected president of France in 1945?

*b5*  *In 1991, who said, 'It's time to pay up for Mumsie'?*

**a6**  In 1983, whose diaries (later shown to be fakes) were serialized in a German magazine and a British newspaper?

*b6*  *What nickname did William Joyce acquire?*

**a7**  When India was divided into India and Pakistan in 1947, which northern state was the major disputed area?

*b7*  *In 1979, where in America was there a serious nuclear accident?*

**a8**  Which humorous British writer was denounced for broadcasting from Germany to America in 1941?

*b8*  *Who wrote the crime novel* Death of an Expert Witness*?*

**a9**  As what did Sir Edwin Lutyens achieve fame?

*b9*  *Why did Carl Nielsen become famous?*

**a10**  The Isaac Newton telescope is at the new home of the Royal Greenwich Observatory. In which Sussex village is it situated?

*b10*  *Which English town has theatres called The Swan and The Other Place?*

**a11**  Which Czech composer (who died in 1928) was influenced by folk music and wrote operas including *The Cunning Little Vixen*?

*b11*  *Who was the Russian pianist and composer who died in 1943 and is particularly remembered for his piano concertos?*

**a12**  The formula to find the circumference of a circle is $2\Pi r$. What is the formula to find the surface area of a sphere?

*b12*  *And what is the formula to find the volume of a cylinder?*

# No. 198 Answers

**a1** Eddie 'the Eagle' Edwards
*b1* *The footballer, Paul Gascoigne*
**a2** *Planet of the Apes*
*b2* Silent Movie
**a3** 10cc
*b3* *Peter Skellern*
**a4** Crop circles
*b4* *Unauthorized access to someone else's computer*
**a5** General de Gaulle
*b5* *Mark Thatcher, fundraising on behalf of his mother*
**a6** Hitler's
*b6* *Lord Haw-Haw (he broadcast German propaganda to Britain in the Second World War)*
**a7** Kashmir
*b7* *Three Mile Island (Harrisburg, Pennsylvania)*
**a8** P G Wodehouse
*b8* *P D James*
**a9** Architect
*b9* *He was a composer*
**a10** Herstmonceux (say: hurst-mon-soo)
*b10* *Stratford-upon-Avon*
**a11** (Leos) Janácek (say: yan-a-check)
*b11* *(Sergei) Rachmaninov*
**a12** $4\Pi r^2$ (r = radius) ($\Pi$ = say: pi)
*b12* $\Pi r^2 h$ *(where h = height)*

---

## Tie-breaker

**Q** Who said, 'I am a Bear of Very Little Brain and long words Bother me'?
*A* *Winnie-the-Pooh (in the book of that name, by A A Milne)*

---

# No. 199

**a1** Which song includes the line 'I've been to Georgia and California and I've sipped champagne on a yacht'?

*b1* *Which pop hit includes the line, 'Ground control to Major Tom, take your protein pills and put your helmet on'?*

**a2** Which industry has developed at Fawley, near Southampton?

*b2* *Which suspension bridge, opened in 1966, carries the M4 motorway?*

**a3** In Scotland, legally speaking, what is a provost?

*b3* *What is an Act of Parliament called before it receives the Royal Assent?*

**a4** Which disc jockey became known on television as Captain Kremmen?

*b4* *On which sport has Peter Alliss been a television commentator?*

**a5** Until 1974, Belize was known as British ...?

*b5* *Which is the only Hindu Kingdom in the world?*

**a6** For which element is the chemical symbol Mg?

*b6* *And for which gas is the chemical symbol Kr?*

**a7** What is the everyday name for the non-prescription drug, acetylsalicylic acid?

*b7* *What is the general purpose of 'beta-blocker' drugs?*

**a8** What is Ronald Reagan's middle name?

*b8* *Who was the Soviet leader from 1977 to 1982?*

**a9** Which sporting event did Mrs Helen Wills Moody win eight times (Miss Helen Wills before marriage)?

*b9* *Ann Jones represented England at tennis and which other sport?*

**a10** What is the unit of currency in Saudi Arabia?

*b10* *And what is it in Kenya?*

**a11** As what did Eugène Ionesco become famous?

*b11* *For what did Francis Bacon become well known?*

**a12** 'How beastly the bourgeois is ...' wrote a famous (even notorious) novelist and poet who died in 1930. Who was he?

*b12* *'The minority is sometimes right; the majority is always wrong.' Who was the long-living Irish dramatist (who died in 1950) who wrote this?*

# No. 199 Answers

**a1** 'I've Never Been to Me' by Charlene
*b1* *'Space Oddity' (by David Bowie)*
**a2** Oil refining
*b2* *Severn Bridge*
**a3** Chief magistrate of a Scottish burgh (approximately equivalent to an English mayor)
*b3* *A bill*
**a4** Kenny Everett
*b4* *Golf*
**a5** British Honduras
*b5* *Nepal*
**a6** Magnesium
*b6* *Krypton*
**a7** Aspirin
*b7* *To combat raised blood pressure, to treat angina, etc.*
**a8** Wilson (Ronald Wilson Reagan)
*b8* *(Leonid) Brezhnev*
**a9** Wimbledon ladies singles
*b9* *Table tennis*
**a10** The rial
*b10* *The (Kenyan) shilling*
**a11** Playwright
*b11* *Modern painter*
**a12** D H Lawrence
*b12* *G B Shaw*

---

## Tie-breaker

**Q** Remembered in an anniversary celebrated in 1992, what did the 'Santa Maria', 'Nina' and 'Pinta' have in common?

*A* *They were the three ships that made up the fleet of Christopher Columbus on his voyage to find the Indies*

---

# No. 200: The Third Millennium

Despite all the discoveries of the 20th century, there are still many questions to which we do not know the answers. During the next century, we may well discover these answers. Meanwhile, as the last round of questions in this book, here are 25 questions to which we do not yet know the answers!

You may like to discuss what is the most likely answer to each question.

**a1**  Will we be able to cure baldness?

*b1*  *Will we be able to stop people's hair going grey?*

**a2**  How do homing pigeons find their way home?

*b2*  *How do migrating birds navigate?*

**a3**  Will global warming raise sea levels – and which areas of land will be lost?

*b3*  *Will private motor cars become illegal – and what will replace them?*

**a4**  Will we make contact with alien life forms in space?

*b4*  *Will they visit us?*

**a5**  When will the first hotel open on the Moon?

*b5*  *When will we set foot on the planet Mars?*

**a6**  How can we cure the common cold (or prevent it)?

*b6*  *Why do we dream?*

**a7**  Is time travel possible?

*b7*  *Will humans ever be able to make themselves invisible?*

**a8**  What is the centre of the Earth like?

*b8*  *Are there really unidentified flying objects?*

**a9**  Will we be able to prevent earthquakes?

*b9*  *Will we be able to prevent famine?*

**a10**  Why are more male than female babies born during war time? (There were distinct increases in the proportion of boy babies born during the two World Wars and during the Boer War)

*b10*  *Will humans become more or less intelligent over the next millennium?*

**a11**  Is there such a thing as re-incarnation?

*b11*  *Can some people predict the future?*

**a12** By how much will the human life span be extended in the next 50 years?

**b12** *Will it be possible to create artificial 'humans' (consisting entirely of artificial organs)?*

---

## Tie-breaker

**Q** How will the world end?

---